Endorsements

"This volume is a lively and intensely readable contribution to the debate over the intersection of America's two most radioactive issues: religion and politics. Miller brings balance, thoughtfulness, and a great deal of insight to a discussion often marred by fierce polarization and simplistic generalizations. Already among the foremost voices of his generation on religious freedom, this volume further cements his standing among our leading thinkers and writers."

—James D. Standish, JD, MBA, principal, Standish Strategic Consulting; former executive director of the United States Commission on International Religious Freedom; Public Affairs representative for the Seventh-day Adventist Church to the United States Congress

"Professor Miller provides a consistent 'historical overview, reaching back to the Protestant Reformation itself and moving forward to the founding of America and on into the twenty-first century.' This is an excellent book that provides a clearly written analysis of how Protestantism interacted with the development of religious and civil freedom over the past five centuries.

"At a time when issues of religious liberty assume ever greater importance in our globalized world, Miller reveals to us the intensity and conviction that it took to establish freedom of conscience and religious rights in the West. He makes a persuasive argument for how essential religious liberty, and its vehicle of dissenting Protestantism, were in giving America a meaningfully 'great' run."

—Dr. Rosa Maria Martinez de Codes, professor of American history, Complutense University of Madrid; former Religious Freedom deputy director, the Spanish Ministry of Justice

"In this encompassing collection of essays, Nicholas P. Miller brings erudition, clarity, and cogency to the history, theory, and legal interpretation of religious freedom in the American experience. The subject here and abroad is, at present, highly divisive and as such calls for the kind of careful, informed consideration Miller brings to it. One may not agree with everything that is said, but it is hard to doubt that views like these deserve very serious attention."

—David Little, research fellow, Berkley Center for Religion, Peace, and World Affairs, Georgetown University; retired T. J. Dermot Dunphy Professor of the Practice in Religion, Ethnicity, and International Conflict, Harvard Divinity School.

"With characteristic prudence and profound historical thinking, Miller provides an indispensable tool to help Americans understand the meaning and implications of religious liberty. *Five Hundred Years of Protest and Liberty* considers our first freedom like a multifaceted gemstone—the historical and contemporary issues that tax the level of our consensus and comprehension of what can be argued is our most cherished freedom. Every American, no matter what religious or political persuasion, will benefit as he or she drinks from Miller's deep well of insight."

—Dr. John Wilsey, assistant professor of history, Southern Baptist Theological Seminary; author of One Nation Under God: An Evangelical Critique of Christian America.

"Sweeping in their scope, Miller's 'observations' of the ongoing impact of the Reformation on religious liberty during the past five hundred years display a penetrating grasp of both the historical background and the current debates regarding our first freedom. Laid out in deftly selected vignettes that capture high points in the unfolding story, the book will be an asset both to concerned citizens seeking a deeper understanding of core concepts such as conscience, dignity, and human rights and to those following the most urgent current religious-freedom issues. Miller's comprehensive grasp of theological, historical, and current constitutional issues makes this an enduring contribution to American discourse on freedom of religion."

—W. Cole Durham Jr., founding director, International Center for Law and Religion Studies, Brigham Young University

500 Years of Protest and Liberty

From Martin Luther to Modern Civil Rights

Also by Nicholas P. Miller

The Reformation and the Remnant

The Religious Roots of the First Amendment

500 Years of Protest and Liberty

From Martin Luther to Modern Civil Rights

NICHOLAS P. MILLER

Pacific Press®
Publishing Association

Nampa, Idaho | Oshawa, Ontario, Canada
www.pacificpress.com

Cover design by Gerald Lee Monks
Cover design resources from iStockphoto.com

The author assumes full responsibility for the accuracy of all facts and quotations as cited in this book.

Unless otherwise noted, all Scripture quotations are from the King James Version.

Scripture quotations marked NKJV are taken from the New King James Version®. Copyright © 1982 by Thomas Nelson. Used by permission. All rights reserved.

Additional copies of this book are available by calling toll-free 1-800-765-6955 or by visiting http://www.AdventistBookCenter.com.

A study and discussion guide for *500 Years of Protest and Liberty* can be found at Liberty500.com. This resource can be used to prepare for and lead out in small group discussions of the important issues and principles raised in the book. It is suitable for church, school, and civic groups desiring to engage these issues more deeply.

Library of Congress Cataloging-in-Publication Data
Names: Miller, Nicholas Patrick, author.
Title: 500 years of protest and liberty : from Martin Luther to modern civil rights / Nicholas P. Miller, JD, PhD.
Other titles: Five hundred years of protest and liberty
Description: Nampa : Pacific Press Publishing Association, 2017.
Identifiers: LCCN 2017023273 | ISBN 9780816363025 (pbk.)
Subjects: LCSH: United States—Church history. | Liberty—Religious aspects—Christianity.
  | Freedom of religion—United States. | Christianity and politics—United States.
  | Protestantism—United States.
Classification: LCC BR516 .M5425 2017 | DDC 261.7088/2804—dc23 LC record available at
  https://lccn.loc.gov/2017023273

May 2017

Dedication

I dedicate this book to my remarkable parents, Tom and Vera Miller, British missionaries first to California and then to Africa, who first awakened in me a love for reading of all types, an appreciation for history, and finally, a love of fairness, freedom, and faith.

Table of Contents

Foreword

This book bursts upon the scene almost exactly five hundred years after the great religious Reformation upended Europe. More precisely, that upheaval can be set at the moment a Roman Catholic monk-theologian nailed his Ninety-Five Theses to the many-ringed wooden door of an obscure church in Wittenberg, Germany. Why Martin Luther thought he could get away with challenging the entire established order of church and state is one of those mysteries not quite explained by hindsight.

Nicholas P. Miller has reached back to those heady days of Martin Luther, John Calvin, Jan Hus, and even John Wycliffe; and with an energy seldom seen in historians, he explains the Reformation roots for the civil rights movement of the late twentieth century. Moreover, he makes a dynamic case for reinventing the Reformation today: to counter what appears to be a final decline of civil and religious liberties.

While our world today is seemingly awash in online information and libraries mostly remain intact—at least till Google concludes scanning every printed page—real knowledge of history is clearly fading. After all, how likely is it that a generation which already sees Facebook as stodgy will care about the Reformation? We are well into the fleeting-fame era Andy Warhol predicted. The Vietnam War is unknown to a generation becoming used to perpetual war and not too inclined to object. True, the specter of Islamic jihad may trouble the present generation, who know just enough about history to steer clear of any talk of the Crusades and think of religion as a generally passive term, but no one seems to remember the mortal threat of Europe falling under Islamic conquest as the ominous backdrop to the original Protestant Reformation.

I love to study history and read the work of historians. But long ago I realized that one must bring a certain critical facility to the exercise. As the great Russian writer Tolstoy once reportedly observed, "History would be a wonderful thing—if it were only true." History has facts we can discover, but all too often they are used selectively to rewrite the past. We need historians with vigor and comprehension to recount this Reformation. We can't leave it to school textbooks, which might relegate it to a few trite references. We must even beware of the forces rewriting the Reformation today. The Roman Catholic Church is on a charm offensive today and is willing to claim the Reformers as their own. In 2015, the Evangelical Lutheran Church in America signed the *Declaration on the Way*, which encouraged Catholics and Lutherans to "look for the next steps toward Christian unity." Maybe they have forgotten history.

Some of the most readable historians, such as Josephus, Edward Gibbon, and Winston Churchill, showed their genius by collecting the scraps of history into a meaningful narrative that we can link to our experience today. In that regard, this book is among the greats. I commend Professor Miller's magisterial way of integrating the yearnings for individual freedom that so motivated Luther with the later struggles in England and the New World. The American Civil War was more religious than most suppose today, and it flows directly into the civil rights movement of the 1960s.

Nowhere is Professor Miller more assured in his presentation of history than when he enters into the present. After all, he is an author who is both a university professor and a practicing lawyer with constitutional expertise. He explains the real significance of recent legal issues in a way worthy of *Liberty* magazine, the magazine I edit and for which he has often written. (You knew I would get to it somewhere, Nick!) Partisans of different historians will have to forgive me if Will Durant is not to their liking, but I must mention his goal as accomplished in this case: to unify and humanize knowledge and make it contemporary.

This book goes to its first printing as the United States writhes after a contentious presidential election. Are we leaving or entering the swamp? Forces long hidden are now revealed. Civil liberties, long under threat, are now worried over. Religious freedom, long debated, now enters a pejorative phase. Let me quote from the book you have yet to read: "The true danger lies in a popular loss of esteem for the civil and religious rights of minorities. Our constitutional order is endangered most by the inattention and apathy that allow the spirit of its liberties to fade away from the consciousness of the people, and then, by natural progression, from our civil institutions and courts of justice."

Lincoln E. Steed
Editor, *Liberty* magazine

Preface

This year we celebrate the five hundredth year since Martin Luther published his Ninety-Five Theses in opposition to the indulgences sold by Catholic Church leaders for the forgiveness of sins. Many historians tie the formal beginnings of the Protestant Reformation to this assault on an abusive combination of spiritual, financial, and political power. From this auspicious beginning on behalf of freedom and conscience, how did Protestantism go on to interact with the development of religious and civil freedom over the next five hundred years?

No quick or simple answer can be given, as there are as many different kinds of Protestantism as there are civil and religious freedoms. To generalize on any of this is unsafe. Scores of volumes have been written about the particularities of Protestantism in various times and places and its relation to civil and religious freedoms. While still in college, I began to take an interest in this connection of Protestantism and freedom.

During the last twenty-five years of my professional life, first in law, then in the study and teaching of religious and legal history, I have written more than two dozen articles for *Liberty* magazine exploring these themes. I have also written on the same themes in some other professional outlets. These articles give a historical overview, reaching back to the Protestant Reformation itself and moving forward to the founding of America and on into the twentieth-first century. They also pay attention to particular legal and political issues of church and state in modern America, the West, and even other parts of the world.

To commemorate this special year of Protestant history, *Liberty*, in concert with Pacific Press®, has agreed to gather these observations, with some updated thoughts, into one volume. The articles are united by a common theme of trying to understand how Protestantism, in its various forms, has interacted with civil and religious freedom. The record shows that Protestantism has at times promoted liberty and at other times hindered it. But it has almost always been relevant in some way to the growth and progress of liberty in the West, around the world, and especially in America. These articles stand as a corpus of work by which at least some of the questions about America and its true "greatness" can be measured and examined.

I have grouped them together in a loose chronological sequence by the period under discussion and also by common theme at times. I have written new material for the introductory overview and at the start of each section and the conclusion. These sections focus the larger lessons of the collected works on the issues, challenges, and questions of today.

*   *   *   *   *

Historians know that the past never actually repeats. But a study of it can hold the keys to understanding the best, or at a least better, direction for the future. It can also unmask the pretensions and blandishments of those who would promise a return to golden ages or utopias that never were. All too often these are diversions to disguise the implementation of principles that history actually reveals to have resulted in some of the darkest moments of the human story. Insanity has been described as doing the same thing over and over again and expecting a different result. This definition underscores the truth of a quip attributed to George Santayana: "a country without a memory is a country of madmen."

America is presently faced with the challenge of correctly remembering its past. Some would argue that the arc of Protestantism that began with Martin Luther, his priesthood of believers, and the rise of German national identity is finding its logical conclusion in the populism and nationalism of one Donald J. Trump. His campaign, and now presidency, projects as a guiding aspiration to "make America great again." This of course begs the question about the true identity and substance of America's national greatness. Is that greatness bound up in military domination, financial accomplishment, and cultural imperialism? Or is America's military, financial, and cultural success built upon other, more moral and spiritual, foundations that could actually be threatened by a return to a social and cultural chauvinism and jingoism? I believe that the articles gathered in this volume help answer this question by revealing the core and consistent values that have motivated Americans in their pursuit of religious freedom and civil liberties.

While on a recent trip to New Zealand, I was reminded that it is not just Western thinkers who understand the importance of history in charting our future. On a mountain overlooking the lovely city of Queenstown, there is inscribed an old Maori proverb, which when translated says, "Within our history is our future well-being." I pray that these essays may help to contribute a measure of sanity to today's important discussions about the relation of religion, state, and religious liberty to America's true greatness and well-being.

Acknowledgments

I want to thank the editors of *Liberty*. First, Clifford Goldstein, who gave me my first publication platform, and then Lincoln Steed, who has continued the relationship and shared the vision and provided support for this collection of articles for *Liberty* magazine. I also want to thank the editors and the marketing department at Pacific Press®, especially Scott Cady, Douglas Church, and Wendy Marcum, who helped promote and facilitate this project on short notice. Dean Jiri Moskala, Associate Dean Teresa Reeve, and my department chair John Reeve are all owed thanks for providing research and writing time to complete this project, and for being true colleagues in contributing to the dialogue that enriched my working environment. Thanks to Jonathan Leonardo, who was the graduate assistant that helped with the conception and research for this project, and Janine Carlos and Patricia Young, the administrative assistants who helped with the organization and layout, and Professor Brian Strayer who gave me a thorough review on very short notice. Finally, I want to thank my friends and colleagues connected with the International Religious Liberty Association whose presentations and conversation over the last decade has helped shape much of this work. These include John Graz, Ganoune Diop, Rosa Maria Martinez de Codes, David Little, Jeremy Gunn, Silvio Ferrari, Cole Durham, Jaime Contreras, Andrea Bartoli, Amal Idrissi, Blandine Chelini-Pont, Nelu Burcea, Dwayne Leslie, Todd McFarland, Jaime Rossel, and Ambassador Robert Seiple.

Overview

From Martin Luther to Martin Luther King Jr.—
Five Centuries of Protestant Pursuit of Liberty

When Martin Luther King Jr. marched on Selma, Alabama, wrote a defense of civil disobedience from a jail in Birmingham, Alabama, and proclaimed his dream of racial equality on the steps of the Lincoln Memorial, was he acting in any meaningful way in the tradition of his namesake, the sixteenth-century Protestant Reformer, Martin Luther? Or were their connections to the unfolding stream of Protestant history merely accidents or coincidences? Were their protests tied to each other by more than simply the universal human resolve to stand for conviction and truth?

To ask the question more broadly, did the Protestant Reformation play any positive role in the development of human rights in the West? Or did systems of human rights develop apart from, or perhaps even—as some would argue—in opposition to, the influences of Protestantism? The five hundredth anniversary of the publication of Martin Luther's Ninety-Five Theses in 1517 is an opportune time to reflect on these questions.

Perhaps the clearest modern point to start with to make the comparison between the two men is not the events at Selma, Birmingham, or the National Mall, as important as these events were. Rather, the principled connection between the two men may best be seen in a speech given by Martin Luther King Jr. at Riverside Church in New York City on April 4, 1967. Fittingly, that was the year of the 450th anniversary of Martin Luther's Ninety-Five Theses, and it was then that Martin Luther King Jr. gave his controversial speech against the war in Vietnam. The speech was a turning point in Martin Luther King Jr.'s progression as an activist, as it signaled a shift to applying principles of justice, equality, and brotherhood beyond the black community to the problems faced by other people groups. During the following year, the last one before he was killed, Martin Luther King Jr. moved toward working for economic justice, speaking on behalf of multiracial coalitions of the poor and disenfranchised.

The Riverside Church speech, with its foray into commentary on international politics and its criticism of the Johnson administration, caused Martin Luther King Jr. to lose some support in the white community, the media, and the press. But it revealed that the principles he espoused truly were universal principles, not just tools and justifications for the advancement of his own cause and people. The speech is notable for its reliance on arguments about the universal brotherhood of humankind. In its opening paragraphs, King said that the road that led from Montgomery to this speech could be explained simply: "I must be true to my conviction that I share with all men the calling to be a son of the Living God. Beyond the calling of race or nation or creed is this vocation of sonship and brotherhood, and because I believe that the Father is deeply concerned especially for his suffering and helpless and outcast children, I come tonight to speak for them."[1]

This appeal to the universal brotherhood of humankind was a theme that he returned to throughout the speech, and with special force at the end. He mixed this theme with a negative critique of Western capitalism: when unrestrained, it caused those in the West to value money and things more highly than people. He noted that the wars in Southeast Asia originated from the economic goals of colonialism, and that America was stepping into the shoes of the French, who had originally exploited Vietnam.

America, he argued, was also taking on the colonizers' role of using force to protect overseas investments. He called for a "radical revolution of values," in which "we must rapidly begin the shift from a 'thing-oriented' society to a 'person-oriented' society. When machines and computers, profit motives and property rights are considered more important than people, the giant triplets of racism, materialism, and militarism are incapable of being conquered."[2]

He then brought the speech to a climax by calling again for the recognition of the universal brotherhood of humankind, based on the principle—not sentiment—of love.

This call for a world-wide fellowship that lifts neighborly concern beyond one's tribe, race, class and nation is in reality a call for an all-embracing and unconditional love for all men. . . .

This is the calling of the sons of God, and our brothers wait eagerly for our response.[3]

This dual concern of Martin Luther King Jr.'s—the brotherhood of human-kind and the corrosive effects of materialism on that brotherhood—provides an interesting parallel with Luther's efforts in 1517 and the following years. We most often think about Martin Luther in connection with justification by faith, the authority of Scripture, and the centrality of grace. But we probably would not have heard of these concepts in connection with him if he had not wrapped them up in an attack on what he viewed as the corrosive effects of materialism on the spirituality of his age. Historians agree that all Luther's insights into these theological matters were not original with him, but had been seen and written about by other religious thinkers. But it was Luther's attack on a corrupt system of finance, power, and spirituality that brought these other issues front and center.

The Ninety-Five Theses themselves do not say much about justification, faith, or Scripture. But they do talk a great deal about the corrupting effect of the sale of indulgences on a true understanding of repentance and salvation. "They preach only human doctrines," Luther writes in thesis 27, "[and] . . . say that as soon as the money clinks into the chest, the soul flies out of purgatory." Also "it is certain that when money clinks in the money chest, greed and avarice can be increased," states thesis 28. Importantly, thesis 36 says, "Any truly repentant Christian has a right to full remission of penalty and guilt, even without indulgence letters." As far as those who sell the indulgences and confuse the faithful about the path of salvation, thesis 72 urged, "But let him who guards against the lust and license of the indulgence preachers be blessed."[4]

Martin Luther King Jr. accused the American government of allowing materialism and avarice to interfere with and poison the American soul in its relation to universal love for humanity; just as Luther criticized the power structure of his day for allowing the materialism of the system of indulgences to blind church members to the true pathway to God of repentance and grace.

But it is Martin Luther King Jr.'s call to universal brotherhood where the greatest parallel between the two men might lie. Though only implied in the Ninety-Five Theses, Martin Luther was developing a powerful idea about the equality of persons before God—the priesthood of all believers. Every person, Luther believed, had the right and duty to approach God directly for repentance, justification, and salvation. As these truths were revealed in the Word of God, everybody had the equal right and duty to study that Word for themselves. As both praying and studying became personal duties, there was no need for the mediating role that the priests and the church hierarchy played between the believers and God. The notion of an elite, "spiritual" class and authority was set aside for the idea of the fundamental spiritual equality of all believers, and eventually all humanity.[5]

Martin Luther King Jr.'s views extended the boundaries from all believers to all humans; but they were based on the same fundamental notion that as all are the children of God, then all are responsible to Him and have a dignity that should be respected by all. The foundations of Martin Luther King Jr.'s thought regarding human dignity lie in the universal truth of the image of God in humanity.

As one Martin Luther King Jr. scholar summarized it, King built this idea of human dignity on four related points: (1) All people are children of God and have equal value and dignity. (2) This equal worth becomes the basis for "just and fair treatment." (3) This dignity brings with it a moral capacity that gives people the ability to make socially good choices. And (4) this shared image of God provides the "existential common ground for genuine community-building" across races, cultures, and ethnicities, making the "beloved community . . . a distinct historical possibility."[6]

King used this shared dignity as the children of God as a platform to argue for the rights of not just black people but all people around the world. He challenged social institutions and norms, especially collections of financial interests and power, to treat people with the dignity they deserved. In doing so, he echoed the concerns of Martin Luther's Ninety-Five Theses, the development of the priesthood-of-believers teaching, and his protest at the Diet of Worms a few years later. It is one thing to show historical parallels, but it is entirely another to show actual historical, "genetic" connections. Can one trace the development of Martin Luther's ideas in the West in a way that ultimately connects them with King and the larger movement for international human rights in the twentieth century?

Or does the Protestant half millennium more logically end in the "Make America Great Again" project of one Donald J. Trump? During his campaign, Trump claimed to be a "down-the-middle-of-the-road" Protestant Christian.[7] And though Trump's personal ethos, which seems to reject notions at the core of the Protestant, or really any Christian, belief system—such as forgiveness, humility, purity, and charity, especially for the marginalized—he did garner the support of about 80 percent of the Protestant evangelical world in the last election.[8] Can one distinguish between the Protestant tradition that brought us Martin Luther King Jr. and that which has resulted in the support of Trump?

I believe that one can make such a distinction, both historically and in philosophical and theological principles. Such a project in fullness would require many books. But the broad outlines of such a story can be traced, I believe, in this single volume, which consists of a series of vignettes or snapshots at key points during this five-hundred-year history. We will begin with the backstory to the American experiment with freedom, as no explanation can be adequate that ignores the European roots of American religious and civil freedoms.

---

1. Martin Luther King Jr., "Beyond Vietnam," speech, Riverside Church, New York City, April 4, 1967, transcript, King Center, http://www.thekingcenter.org/archive/document/beyond-vietnam (accessed on 5/15/2017).

2. Ibid.

3. Ibid.

4. Martin Luther, "The 95 Theses," A Mighty Fortress Is Our God: Martin Luther, accessed March 30, 2017, http://www.luther.de/en/95thesen.html.

5. See Nicholas P. Miller, *The Religious Roots of the First Amendment* (New York: Oxford University Press, 2012), 15–30.

6. Richard W. Wills Sr., *Martin Luther King, Jr. and the Image of God* (New York: Oxford University Press, 2009), 113–115.

7. Sean Sullivan, "Donald Trump Seeks a Sharp Contrast With Ben Carson's Seventh-day Adventist Faith," *Washington Post*, October 24, 2015, https://www.washingtonpost.com/news/post-politics/wp/2015/10/24/donald-trump-seeks-a-sharp-a-contrast-with-ben-carsons-seventh-day-adventist-faith/?utm_term=.1ee62390b8bd.

8. Sarah Pulliam Bailey, "White Evangelicals Voted Overwhelmingly for Donald Trump, Exit Polls Show," Acts of Faith, *Washington Post*, November 9, 2016, https://www.washingtonpost.com/news/acts-of-faith/wp/2016/11/09/exit-polls-show-white-evangelicals-voted-overwhelmingly-for-donald-trump/?utm_term=.97b225a5d8f2.

PART I

*European Backgrounds of Protestant Liberty, Rights,
and Democracy*

The following chapters explore the Reformation roots of the idea of the priesthood of all believers and that doctrine's connection with the right of private judgment in matters of religion and the separation of church and state. They explore how these ideas impacted the rise of religious freedom in the United States and played a role in the development of democracies and human rights around the world.

Many people relate these doctrines to the "soul freedom" of the Baptists, who were indeed influential in spreading the idea in England and in America. But the story begins earlier, at the fountainhead of the Reformation, with Martin Luther himself. Many are unaware that Luther, in his early days, expressed strong views on the separation of the civil magistrate from the church. For various practical and political reasons, he moved away from this view, and Lutheranism became associated with state-supported, magisterial Protestantism. The first two chapters in this section, "The Scripturally Informed Conscience: Luther and Religious Liberty, Part 1" and "The Revolutionary: Luther and Religious Liberty, Part 2," detail this early journey of Luther and reveal how his ideas were picked up by other religious dissenters, including the Anabaptists.

The third chapter, "The Backgrounds of America's Founding Protestant Philosophy," discusses how the dissenting Protestant views of church and state differed from those of the medieval church and magisterial Protestantism, as well as the separation of church and state generated by thinkers of the skeptical Enlightenment. Finally, the fourth and fifth chapters, "Luther, Locke, and Competing Notions of Human Dignity" and "Protestant Dignity and the Rise of Worldwide Democracy and Human Rights," discuss how dissenting Protestantism not only influenced the shaping of the American Constitution but also played an important role in the development of democracies and human rights around the world. John Locke used Luther's revived notions of the individual under God to express a dignity based on the stewardship of the self. This view contrasted with a medieval paternalistic dignity where the individual never emerged from the shadow of an overweening church and state. It also differed from a modern conception of self-ownership, which is quickly overcome by the needs and wants of the group. This dignity of stewardship was spread internationally by free-church Protestant missionaries; and this proselytism created the educational and institutional framework that allowed democracy and civil rights to develop and flourish.

One lesson to be gathered from these chapters is the close proximity that religious freedom, including the impulse toward religious disestablishment, had to the central and core doctrines of the Protestant Reformation. Often this close relationship is lost sight of due to intervening events, such as Calvin's rule in Geneva, the holy war of England's Puritans, and the New England quasi theocracy. But right from the start, doctrines such as *sola scriptura* and the priesthood of all believers were closely tied to the right of private judgment in religious matters, which served as a main justification for religious disestablishment.

Once the connection between these ideas is understood, it can be seen that the rise of religious freedom in the West was not the accidental result of Protestantism's proliferation of denominations or sects, nor the triumph of subjectivity and relativity in its DNA. Rather, it emerges as a principled strand from doctrines lying at the center of what it meant to be Protestant from the beginning and from what most evangelicals today would view as core Protestant teachings. A moderate separation of church and state, rather than being the product of Communist constitutions as many Christians currently believe, actually has a heritage going back to essential Protestant doctrines.

Another lesson is the importance of minority groups in the history of religion and freedom. While hunted and persecuted by Continental Protestants, Catholics, and Anglicans alike, the Anabaptists never held sway or predominated in any European country. Yet when it came to founding the American republic, it was largely the Anabaptists' views of church and state that were implemented. It is something of a historical truism to call America a historically Protestant country, at least socially and culturally, though not legally. But it is more accurate to call it a *dissenting* Protestant country, as its founders intentionally rejected the mainstream European magisterial Protestant tradition. (Magisterial Protestants were those that desired their churches to continue to have a preferred legal connection with the civil magistrates.)

The same is true of the impact of Protestantism on the growth of global democracy and human rights. Not all mission groups equally contributed to these phenomena. Missions too closely associated or aligned with the government tended to support the often heavy-handed hegemony of the colonial enterprises. Non-state, free-church Protestants, on the other hand, were more likely to oppose and stand against colonial abuses and mobilize constituents back home to pressure colonial governments to treat native peoples with greater fairness. The contributions of non-state, religious minorities continued in the last century, as Latter-day Saints, Jehovah's Witnesses, and Seventh-day Adventists provided more than their fair share to the American federal case law protecting religious freedom.

Finally, the chapters reveal the confusion created by a conflation of the dissenting Protestant and secularist versions of the separation of church and state. America's founders meant to separate the church from the state institutionally, as well as to prevent churches from enforcing spiritual practices and revealed doctrines as public policy. They did not, however, intend to separate morality and the state, even if that morality overlapped with the teachings of religious groups. They had a robust view of natural-law morality—involving the family, children, and sexuality—that they did not consider to be religious. Rather, they viewed these standards as teachings of natural morality and philosophy that could be defended from the designs and ends of nature. This is a lesson that society, church, and state very much need to relearn today.

Chapter 1

The Scripturally Informed Conscience:
Luther and Religious Liberty, Part 1

T he road from the Protestant Reformation to the religious freedom of the American republic was full of unexpected turns, switchbacks, and delays. The ambiguities, tensions, and paradoxes within church-state thought are seen starkly at the second Diet of Speyer in 1529—the event that birthed the term *Protestant.*

The diet, or gathering of German nobility, was convened by Charles V in an attempt to restore spiritual unity to a religiously divided empire. This second diet ended the "cease-fire" of the first Diet of Speyer three years earlier, which had essentially suspended or recessed the Edict of Worms and allowed Lutheranism to spread. The only sop given to the forces of reform was the allowance that Lutheran services could continue within existing Lutheran states. Catholic services could also be held within Lutheran territories. But no Lutheran services could be held within Catholic states. Here the Edict of Worms' ban on Luther's teachings would be strictly enforced. No further spread of Lutheranism would be allowed.

The princes in the Lutheran minority were unwilling to accept the limited toleration offered by the diet. In language oft-quoted by Protestant historians, the minority princes declared, "Let us reject this decree. . . . In matters of conscience the majority has no power." One influential Protestant historian asserted that "the principles contained in this celebrated protest . . . constitute the very essence of

---

This chapter originally appeared in *Liberty*, May/June 2007.

Protestantism. . . . Protestantism sets the power of conscience above the magistrate and the authority of the Word of God above the visible Church."[1] Indeed, the very term *Protestant* originated from the protest lodged by the Lutheran princes at Speyer. Over the centuries, both the event and the name have become associated with the ideas of the rights of conscience and religious freedom.

But these same Protestant historians often leave unmentioned another, darker side of the Diet of Speyer. The diet, including the Lutheran princes, condemned the Anabaptist movement and decreed that rebaptizers should be punished, even with death, if recalcitrant and persistent in their errors. While nobly championing their own "rights" to conscience and religious freedom, the Lutheran princes were apparently blind to any inconsistency in their attitudes and actions in condemning and persecuting the Anabaptists. Thousands of Anabaptists died in the years following, at the hands of both Catholics and Protestants.[2]

Protestant historians generally ignore this aspect of the diet and make little effort to explain the apparent contradictions it reveals. This incident can provide support for those who view the Protestant Reformation as a continuation of medieval ideas, as well as for those who view it as the beginning of modern ideas. It certainly serves as a warning for anyone wishing to trace a simple, direct, and progressive story from the church-state ideas of the early Reformers to the religious liberty and pluralism of the modern world.

But just because a story is more complex than we had thought does not mean that it is wrong or cannot be told. The fact that key near contemporaries of the events of Speyer viewed them as having such significance for issues of conscience and freedom as to coin the name for a movement and a historical epoch is some indication that the world was actually changing and that the events at Speyer were part of that shift. The Diet of Speyer did seem to represent some actual alteration in direction over previous views of church-state arrangement. At the very least, it introduced the rhetoric of religiously based civil disobedience into public discourse.

But the apparent contradiction seen at Speyer may be better understood if we look closely at the balance and tension in the church-state thought of the theologian who had the greatest influence on the Lutheran nobles at Speyer—Martin Luther.

For good or for bad, much of Reformation thought was engaged in some way, either constructively or in opposition, to what Martin Luther said or wrote on any given topic. The world of church and state is no exception. The events at Speyer and its aftermath can be better understood, if not entirely explained, by looking at what Luther did and said on the topic.

This chapter, in its two parts, will examine the development of Luther's thought on church and state, focusing on the question of religious liberty. It will examine how his thought interacted with, reacted against, shaped, or was shaped by his experiences with Catholics, Anabaptists, Reformed thinkers, and other Lutherans, especially his colleague Phillip Melanchthon. In closing, some observations will be made on the possible long-term influence of Luther's religious-liberty thought on the formation of the American republic.

Church and state in the medieval world

On the eve of the Reformation, while church and state were technically distinct entities, they were viewed as inseparable and organic parts of society as a whole. As one medieval authority has succinctly put it, "The identification of the church with the whole of organized society is the fundamental feature which distinguishes the Middle Ages from earlier and later periods of history."[3] Yet the state was—under the theory of the two swords, civil and spiritual—meant to serve as the servant of the church in enforcing the church's religious rules and standards. Through the mechanism of infant baptism, virtually all citizens of the state were also citizens of the church. Church and state combined to oversee and enforce this contractual relationship, in all its civil and spiritual terms.

It was a system with tensions and conflicts, as the interests of church and state could and often did diverge. The pope and his bishops had enormous influence and persuasive powers, but they were limited by their inability to wield force directly. They were, on the whole, dependent on kings and princes loyal to the church to carry out their decrees and to enforce their edicts. But such cooperation was often ad hoc, intermittent, and inconsistent. Lacking the means of consistent coercion, the church had to resort to political and spiritual pressure to get civil rulers to act on its behalf. Its persuasive powers, however, were significant. The threat of excommunication or interdict persuaded many a civil ruler to often cooperate with the church.[4]

The tensions, limits, and powers of this system are clearly seen in the treatment of Luther at the Diet of Worms. If the church had had its way, there would have been no diet at Worms. A papal bull had already condemned Luther's teachings and excommunicated him. All that was left was for the heretic to be arrested and consigned to the rack or the flames. But the Elector Frederick, Luther's patron, was unwilling to hand over his theologian without a formal hearing. He persuaded Emperor Charles V to hold a public hearing for Luther, and the Diet of Worms was convened in mid-April 1521.

That the diet met at all, then, was something of a defeat for Rome. It undercut the authority of the previous papal bulls against Luther. Still, it was a defeat that could yet end in the condemnation and execution of Luther—hardly a victory from the Reformer's perspective. Indeed, events initially unfolded much as the pope had hoped. Luther was quickly questioned about the authorship of his books, which were assumed to be heretical. There was no room for arguing this point. Rather, the question was whether Luther would recant and reject his teachings. After a short delay, Luther made his memorable defense: "My conscience is captive to the Word of God. Thus I cannot and will not recant, for going against conscience is neither safe nor salutary. I can do no other, here I stand, God help me. Amen."[5]

Luther's statement was not exactly a modern conception of conscience as an individual, independent, and unfettered moral center. His conscience was bound and hemmed—but not by the pope or the church, as the medieval view would have it. Rather, his conscience was bound by the Word of God. But neither the emperor nor the church leaders could conceive of a claim to conscience outside the dual sovereignty and oversight of the church and the state. And the line the church drew around conscience with the spiritual sword, the state would enforce with the civil sword.

Thus, Charles V condemned Luther as an unrepentant heretic in the Edict of Worms and ordered his books and writings destroyed and his person arrested and turned over for appropriate punishment—execution. At last, the papacy had the civil mandate and enforcement it had been seeking, or so it seemed. But Charles had left open a small sliver of daylight—a twenty-day delay on the enforcement of the edict. Luther, aided by Elector Frederick, slipped through this narrow window into a productive hiding at Wartburg Castle.[6]

The story of the diet, with its second-guessing, yet ultimate affirmation of papal condemnations and its responsiveness to papal requests and goals—but with just enough ambivalence and delay in execution of plans to let the condemned heretic slip free—illustrates well the cooperative, conflicted, ambivalent, politically charged relationship between the medieval church and state. The church claimed to be the superior authority. The superior sword of the state, however, often made that claim theoretical.

Cooperation, when it happened, was a mutually agreed upon affair. But one thing that both the medieval church and the medieval state consistently agreed upon was that the conscience of the individual citizen was subject to the oversight of the church and the state acting together. As seen at Worms, Luther's new teachings challenged this allied hegemony over the scripturally informed conscience.

Luther on church and state

Luther's ordeal at Worms took place about four years after the release of his Ninety-Five Theses. In the interim, he had given significant thought to the relationship between the church and civil rulers. He had published one of his most significant works on the subject: the 1520 *Address to the Christian Nobility of the German Nation.* There he set down what he viewed as the proper role of the church in relation to the individual, Scripture, and society.[7]

Luther believed that the church had wrongly erected three walls of privilege that prevented the correction of its continuing abuses. The first wall was the assertion that spiritual authority was superior to that of civil. Thus the church was not subject to secular jurisdiction in many temporal matters. The second wall was that the pope alone had the right to authoritatively interpret Scripture. Therefore, he could not be corrected by other persons. The third wall was that the pope alone could call councils. Thus, the pope could effectively control the church and prevent any appeal from his decisions to the body of the church.

Luther attacked these walls by asserting the priesthood of all believers:

> To call popes, bishops, priests, monks, and nuns the religious class, but princes, lords, artisans, and farm-workers the secular class, is a specious device invented by certain time-servers. . . . For all Christians whatsoever really and truly belong to the religious class, and there is no difference among them except insofar as they do different work. . . . The fact is that our baptism consecrates us all without exception, and makes us all priests. As St. Peter says, "You are a royal priesthood and a realm of priests" [1 Peter 2:9] and Revelation, "Thou hast made us priests and kings by Thy blood" [Revelation 5:9].[8]

Luther believed that all Christians had an equal spiritual status, though they might fulfill different spiritual offices. But those selected for such offices, such as pastor or bishop, act merely on behalf of the congregation, all of whom have the same authority he does. He serves at the command and consent of the community, who can equally dismiss him from his office should they desire. This doctrine and its implications truly undercut all three walls of papal privilege. In the first instance, by putting all Christians on a similar plane, it nullified any appeal that the church hierarchy had to being above secular rulers, who themselves were exercising a Christian office of their own.

Luther turned the dual sword of the medieval world into a single sword and placed it firmly in the hand of the secular ruler. "Hence secular authorities should exercise their office freely and unhindered and without fear, whether it be pope, bishop, or priest with whom they are dealing; if a man is guilty let him pay the penalty. . . . For this is what St. Paul says to all Christians, 'Let every soul [I hold that includes the pope's] be subject to the higher powers, . . . for they bear not the sword in vain.' They serve God alone, punishing the evil and praising the good [Romans 13:1–4]."[9]

Luther did not here fully explicate the duties of the state. He did make clear, though, that while the state had a spiritual office, its function and role were secular. "This government is spiritual in status, although it discharges a secular duty."[10] In other words, in affirming that all people, including popes and priests, were subject to the civil sword, he was not in this argument giving the state authority or jurisdiction in spiritual matters. In his treatise *Secular Authority: To What Extent It Should Be Obeyed*, written just three years later, he discussed this point more fully: "Worldly government has laws which extend no farther than to life and property and what is external upon earth. For over the soul

God can and will let no one rule but Himself. Therefore, where temporal power presumes to prescribe laws for the soul, it encroaches upon God's government and only misleads and destroys the souls."[11]

On this basis, he argued that Christians had no need to obey a civil ruler who commanded belief or the giving up of heretical books. "Heresy," he wrote, "can never be prevented by force. That must be taken hold of in a different way, and must be opposed and dealt with otherwise than with the sword. Here God's Word must strive."[12] While such a ruler should be disobeyed, Luther made clear that resistance or active opposition was not allowed the Christian.

The priesthood concept also toppled the second wall, once spiritual equality was established and the primacy of the papacy in interpreting Scripture was undercut. As Luther put it,

Each and all of us are priests because we all have the one faith, the one gospel, one and the same sacrament; why then should we not be entitled to taste or test, and to judge what is right or wrong in the faith? How otherwise does St. Paul's dictum stand, 1 Corinthians 2:15, "He that is spiritual judges all things and is judged by none." . . . We ought to march boldly forward, and test everything the Romanists do or leave undone. We ought to apply that understanding of the Scriptures which we possess as believers. . . . Since God once spoke through an ass, why should He not come in our day and speak through a man of faith and even contradict the pope?[13]

Finally, of course, the priesthood of all believers overturned the third wall as well; under this concept, the church lay in the body of believers rather than in some supreme head. The body had the right to gather and to correct those who served it, including the pope.

The overall effect of Luther's arguments regarding the priesthood of all believers in the *Address* and his teachings in *Secular Authority* was to turn the doctrine of the two swords into a model of the two kingdoms. According to Luther, all people are divided into two classes: "the first belong to the kingdom of God, the second to the kingdom of the world." Those in God's kingdom "need no secular sword or law," since they have in their "hearts the Holy Spirit, who instructs them and causes them to wrong no one." Non-Christians, on the other hand, are "subjected to the sword, so that, even though they would do so, they cannot practice their wickedness" in peace and prosperity.[14]

Luther saw a clear distinction between these two kingdoms and viewed Christ's kingdom as limited to His followers. "For this reason these two kingdoms must be sharply distinguished, and both be permitted to remain; the one to produce piety, the other to bring about external peace. . . . Christ's rule does not extend over all." Further, Christ's kingdom does not involve using the sword. "Christ did not wield the sword nor give it a place in His kingdom; for He is a King over Christians, and rules by His Holy Spirit alone, without law. . . . It is of no use in His kingdom."[15]

In 1522, Luther showed that the commitments described above were more than mere words. Leaving his Wartburg sanctuary, Luther returned to Wittenberg to confront his colleague Andreas Karlstadt and others who were advocating the forcible removal of images and the overturning of the Mass. Luther agreed that the Mass was wrong, even sinful. But he "would not make it an ordinance for them, nor urge a general law." Such "forcing and commanding results in mere mockery, external show, a fool's play, man-made ordinances, sham-saints, and hypocrites." Rather than force, Luther would "preach it, teach it, write it," and allow God's Word to do the rest.[16]

Events of the mid-1520s, however, caused Luther to begin to find different emphases within his views on church and state. The turmoil surrounding the peasants' revolt and the controversy surrounding the Anabaptists focused Luther's mind on the importance of respect for civil authority, as well as the civil implications of some ostensibly spiritual beliefs. To these events, we will turn in chapter 2.

---

1. J. H. Merle D'Aubigne, *History of the Reformation in the Sixteenth Century*, vol. 3, trans. H. White (Glasgow: Blackie and Son, 1847), 57, 62, 63.

2. Diarmaid MacCulloch, *The Reformation* (New York: Penguin, 2005), xviii; R. W. Southern, *Western Society and the Church in the Middle Ages* (New York: Penguin, 1990), 16.

3. Southern, *Western Society and the Church in the Middle Ages*, 16.

4. Ibid., 18–21.

5. Heiko A. Oberman, *Luther: Man Between God and the Devil* (New York: Image Books, 1992). There is some uncertainty as to whether Luther actually uttered the "here I stand" portion of this phrase or whether it was inserted by a later editor as a sort of summary statement. Ibid., 204.

6. Ibid., 227–229.

7. John Dillenberger, ed., *Martin Luther: Selections From His Writings* (New York: Anchor Books, 1961), 406–417.

8. Ibid., 407, 408.

9. Ibid., 409.

10. Ibid., 411.

11. Ibid., 383.

12. Ibid., 389.

13. Ibid., 414.

14. Ibid., 368.

15. Ibid., 369.

16. Hans J. Hillerbrand, ed., *The Protestant Reformation* (New York: Harper and Row, 1968), 35, 36.

Chapter 2

The Revolutionary: Luther and Religious Liberty, Part 2

S cholars have long argued the extent of Luther's influence on the outbreak of a revolution among the German peasants in 1524–1525. Those who would give him significant blame for it point to his intemperate remarks against the institutional authority of the day, his arguments for spiritual equality, and his elevation of the individual conscience over spiritual and civil authorities. But others point to his 1522 opposition to the Zwickau prophets and Andreas Karlstadt as examples of his early stands against populist movements that opposed or challenged civil authority by force.[1] Indeed, it is hard to read Luther's writings between 1520 and 1525 and take seriously the view that he directly or indirectly promoted civil revolt.

On the contrary, Luther is more fairly accused of elevating the status of the prince at the expense of the church as well as the individual, at least in civil matters. His 1520 *Address* subordinates the church in civil matters. His 1523 discourse on the *Secular Authority* made clear that the civil sword was firmly in the hands of the civil magistrate, who was not to be actively opposed, even when overreaching and tyrannical. Even in religious matters, which he acknowledged were outside the civil ruler's legitimate oversight, he taught that spiritual "outrage is not to be resisted, but endured."[2] Duly constituted civil rulers were not to resist their unjust and ungodly superiors.[3] All this was written more than a year prior to the events directly leading to the Peasants' War. These events began unfolding in the summer of 1524 in southwest Germany.[4]

This chapter originally appeared in *Liberty*, July/August 2007.

As the revolt spread, Luther wrote to clearly distinguish his reforms from the populist uprisings advocated by the peasants. In May of 1525, he released a tract aimed at both the rulers and the peasants, pointing out the excesses and abuses of both sides and calling for restraint by the princes and submission by the peasants.[5] He systematically outlined how the peasants' claims diverged from his gospel teachings. But he also insisted that the civil rulers should not punish the peasants for wrong beliefs but only for sedition. "No ruler," Luther wrote, "ought to prevent anyone from teaching or believing what he pleases, whether gospel or lies. It is enough if he prevents the teaching of sedition and rebellion."[6]

A month later, after the peasants had engaged in greater bloodshed, he wrote a tract whose title betrayed its target and its polemical tone—*Against the Robbing and Murdering Hordes of Peasants.* In this pamphlet, he criticized the religious aspirations and leadership of the peasants, particularly singling out Thomas Müntzer and his brand of apocalyptic, revolutionary mysticism.[7] It is here that he first clearly and forcefully confronts ostensibly spiritual beliefs that are seditious and thus the legitimate target of the civil sword.

Luther is often criticized for the extreme tone of his *Against the Peasants* tract ("Let everyone who can, smite, slay and stab, secretly or openly, remembering that nothing can be more poisonous than a rebel."[8]). Luther's tone was newly harsh. But the revolt did not work a change in the substance of his position toward the authoritative role of the magistrate in civil affairs. Luther had always, to that point, clearly rejected any active, forceful opposition to secular authorities.

That this was widely understood at the time is perhaps most clearly shown by the fact that German princes for the first time began formally adopting his cause in 1525, including some who had been most active in quelling the peasants.[9] If Luther's teachings had been seen as a moving part of the peasants' revolt, men such as Duke Johann and Philip of Hesse would have been very unlikely to formally identify with Luther's movement during the very year of the revolt itself.[10]

What the peasants' revolt did was confirm in Luther's mind the connection between certain types of radical religion, especially of the mystical bent, and seditious, anarchic doctrine. In Luther's view, these mystical, seditious tendencies were also associated with the Anabaptists, whom he came to view as continuing the work and tendencies of Thomas Müntzer and the *Schwärmer,* the demagogic spiritualists.[11] This lumping of the left wing of the Reformation was a tendency that Luther persisted in for the rest of his life. It explains, at least in part, his willingness to persecute the Anabaptists, despite his previous statements on the inappropriateness of using force against heresy.

Luther, Melanchthon, and heretics

Luther wrote his most extended work on Anabaptists in 1528, not long after they had become a movement and while he knew little about them. He was asked to write on the Anabaptists by two of his followers who were dealing with them, and he had a brief description from them of the Anabaptists' beliefs and practices.[12] Luther's main concern in his tract was to deal with the question of infant baptism and to show that the Anabaptists' rejection of it was not scriptural. Issues of tolerance and persecution were secondary, as the letter was being sent to a Catholic territory, and Luther's followers did not have to decide on the appropriate civil fate of the Anabaptists. Still, Luther touched on this topic and raised the charges that Anabaptists left family and home to wander with their co-religionists—a type of anarchy.[13]

Luther did not develop the anarchist point further in his tract, although he did apply the term *Schwärmer* to the Anabaptists, clearly tying them to the earlier spiritual enthusiasts whom he counted as seditious. In a letter written to a contact in Bavaria about the same time as the tract, he explicitly accused the Anabaptists of following Müntzer in believing that Christians should kill the godless, and thus that they were completely seditious.[14]

It is apparent that Luther viewed the Anabaptists as the heirs of the Zwickau prophets, Thomas Müntzer, and the spiritualist leaders of the peasants' revolt— gone underground, perhaps, but poised to resurface—and all the more deadly because of their indirection and deception in preaching pacifism.[15] Shortly afterward, Luther and Melanchthon had their views on Anabaptism put to the practical test.

In 1529 in Gotha, a Lutheran territory, ten Anabaptists had been captured. They all recanted but, upon release, relapsed into their dissent. Six were recaptured and executed. Some leaders at Gotha were disturbed at the severity of the punishment and wrote to Wittenberg for guidance. Melanchthon expressed his view that not only rebels but also blasphemers should be executed.[16] Blasphemy, according to Melanchthon, included any public teaching of a heretical doctrine, including the rejection of infant baptism.

Luther did not go on record as opposing Melanchthon's definitions. But in a separate letter to the leadership at Gotha, he noted that the Anabaptists were not only blasphemers but seditious. Thus, they should be executed.[17] Luther had a different emphasis and approach on the topic from those of Melanchthon. Luther required, in addition to heresy, some element of sedition before civil force was brought to bear. Later, Luther seemed at times to tacitly support Melanchthon's broader approach to punishing open heresy.[18] But whenever Luther himself addressed the question of punishing the Anabaptists, he nearly always raised the charges of their sedition and desire to destroy the civil order.[19] The difference between the two Reformers on this question seems to be more than merely a question of style. While Luther did define sedition with a certain liberal breadth—including communal living and rejection of the magisterial role for Christians—he never seemed to fully embrace Melanchthon's broad willingness to execute unrepentant heretics. Toward the end of his life, he distinguished again between the "heretic" and the "seditious heretic." The former could be banished, but only the latter could be executed.

Here is part of the reason for the Lutheran princes' apparent blindness at the Diet of Speyer toward religious freedom for the Anabaptists. They followed Luther in his view of the Anabaptist beliefs, acts, and tendencies as being genuinely seditious and not merely heretical spiritually.

But even Luther's category of seditious heresy soon became increasingly broad so as to make it virtually indistinguishable from heresy generally. This story involves some of the difference in emphasis and even theology between Luther and Melanchthon and Luther's shift over time toward Melanchthon's view.

Resistance theory

The difference in treatment of heretics between the two Reformers, Luther and Melanchthon, cannot be explained by their manner and style. On the contrary, Luther was known for his intemperate outbursts and aggressive posturing, whereas Melanchthon was the milder and gentler of the two. If one were to choose a persecutor by nature, Luther was a far more likely candidate.

The difference between the two was substantive and seems to relate in part to Melanchthon's embrace of the third use of the law and the ongoing role of the magistrate in enforcing both tables of the law upon the citizenry. The first use of the law was to cause a person to outwardly obey for fear of punishment. The second use was to let the sinner know his need of Christ for salvation. Both of these Luther accepted and taught. The third use of the law was educational, to continue to instruct and guide the righteous even after their conversion.[20] Luther never articulated or expressed an acceptance of this use.

It was the third use that seems to serve as a base for Melanchthon's active role of the magistrate as guardian and enforcer of both tables of the law.[21] He most clearly articulated this position in the final edition of his *Loci Communes*, nearly ten years after Luther died. It set out a role for the magistrate in spiritual matters far beyond anything Luther had ever envisioned or that Melanchthon had articulated while Luther was alive.[22] This divide on the third use of the law and the role of the magistrate also explains some of the differences between Luther and the development of Reformed thought—as well illustrated in the story of Calvin and Geneva.

Something that may have prevented Luther from actively opposing Melanchthon's trend toward accepting a spiritual jurisdiction for the magistrate were political developments that caused him to revisit his opposition to resistance theory. At the Diet of Augsburg, it had become apparent that Lutheranism would not be tolerated within the empire. The only open question was when the emperor would have the time and necessary force to exterminate it.[23] Under these circumstances, the Lutheran princes and theologians refocused on the question of resistance to authority that Luther had earlier rejected.

It was asked whether inferior magistrates might not have the right to resist superior magistrates who went beyond their civil jurisdictions and became tyrannical. Luther became persuaded that duly constituted inferior magistrates were also God-appointed authorities. They thus had the right and responsibility of defending their prerogatives as Christian princes and those of their subjects in obeying the gospel. Thus, in 1531, Luther endorsed the formation of the Schmalkaldic League—a defense alliance of Protestant territories against the emperor and any forced "recatholicization."[24]

Once civil rulers were granted the right of resistance in matters of religion, to resist the tyrannical imposition of spiritual matters from above, they became at some level guardians of the people's religion. They thus had some role in determining what religious belief justified resistance to the emperor. It was a small step from there to deciding what beliefs were acceptable within the princes' own territory. While Luther did not initially take this further step himself, he was sufficiently far down the path of magisterial authority to not protest when Melanchthon and others began to take it.[25]

In the mid to late 1530s, Luther himself began writing of the magistrate's role in promoting and supporting true religion. But even with this change, he still emphasized the alternate roles of the civil magistrate and the bishop. He still thought it was the devil who tried to lure secular rulers into being "Christ's masters and teach[ing] Him how He should run His church and spiritual government."[26] While being compelled by circumstance to support magisterial Protestantism, there still lurked within Luther the ideal of the two separate and distinct kingdoms of his earlier teachings.

Luther, Calvin, and ecclesiology

A further reason that Lutheranism basically followed Melanchthon and Calvin down the road of magisterial religions was that Luther had not constructed a sufficiently detailed and independent ecclesiology to allow it to function well apart from the state. Luther had been extremely aware ecclesiologically but largely in a negative sense. His *Address to the Christian Nobility of the German Nation* in 1520 had trumpeted the blast that he hoped would overturn the three walls protecting the papal hierarchy. But he had not offered much to replace it, except for the community of the faithful ministered to by pastors who were no more or less priests than the baptized congregant.[27]

Luther thus initially taught that the congregation should be able to choose and oversee its own pastors.[28] But given that all members of a community should be baptized at birth, it was unclear how the congregation itself, which consisted in large part, as Luther soon discovered, of unregenerate persons, would have the spiritual wisdom and maturity to choose appropriate pastors or otherwise regulate the affairs of the church. At the very least, there would have to be an interim period of oversight and education until the community matured under the influences of the true gospel. Thus, Luther accepted a role for the magistrate to play in church administration and oversight.[29] In 1527, during a particularly unruly time for the church in Saxony, Luther worked with Elector Johann to undertake a series of religious visitations to assess and to bring greater order to the church.[30]

But he did not view this oversight by the civil rule as ideal or desirable. He viewed the arrangement as irregular and called a prince acting this way an "emergency bishop": doing his "duty not as a ruler but as an ordinary Christian in the absence of competent church authorities."[31] But what Luther viewed as an exception—an irregular act provoked by exigent circumstances—others embraced as the long-term solution to the Lutheran ecclesiological weakness. Indeed, there is evidence in the 1530s that Luther himself had accepted, if not embraced, the reality of the *cuius regio, eius religio* ("the prince's realm, the prince's religion") and all it implied for the civil magistrate in overseeing religion.[32] Certainly, those who followed Melanchthon and Calvin on the third use of the law and the role of the magistrate over the two tables had the theological justification to accept Luther's emergency measure as a permanent rule.

The irony is that Calvin, for other reasons, engineered a far more thorough and independent ecclesiology than did Luther. His consistory of elders and network of congregations created a flexible and resilient church structure that could have functioned, and where necessary did function, independently from the state.[33] For other reasons, including a preference for stressing duty over liberty in the Christian life, a de-emphasis on the priesthood of believers, and an embrace of the third use of the law,[34] he chose ecclesiastical cooperation with the magistrate.

Even for Calvin, the magistrate had no general role in actually making decisions about spiritual matters. Rather, the civil ruler should enforce those decisions pertaining to spiritual standards and matters made by the church.[35] So, though Calvin had a genuine separation between civil and spiritual authorities, he also taught a very robust cooperation between those two authorities. The two entities were basically "conjoined"; with the civil ruler wielding the sword on behalf of the spiritual leaders.[36] While later reformed churches incorporated more democratic elements in their structure, including the direct election of pastors by their congregations, this church-state cooperation continued to be a Reformed hallmark, at least where politically practicable.[37]

A doctrine divided

There is an irony in Luther's support of the persecution of the Anabaptists. It was Anabaptism, rather than later Lutheranism or the Reformed movement, that was much closer to Luther's earliest stated ideals on the relation of the civil magistrate to religious beliefs. Had they been able to set aside their differences, Luther and the Anabaptists could have formed a powerful, complementary alliance of ideas.

But there were two profound differences that neither side could surmount. The first was Luther's deep suspicion of rebaptizing and the Anabaptists' insistence on adult baptism. The further irony here is that it was precisely infant baptism that was probably the foremost factor in preventing Luther's church-state arrangement from working. Under Luther's scheme of church membership, almost the entirety of any Lutheran community, whether converted or unconverted, was part of the church. The Anabaptists, on the other hand, had gathered-out communities that had a far higher percentage of deeply committed, if not converted, persons. Such a community would be far more easy to self-regulate than would Luther's, with its much higher chaff-to-wheat ratio.

The second difference was the Anabaptists' rejection of the legitimate role of the Christian magistrate. The question of whether a Christian could serve as a magistrate was no peripheral issue for Luther. Indeed, his attack on the first wall of papal privilege was almost entirely based on the view that the civil ruler held a spiritual office. As fellow Christians, civil magistrates were equal to the ecclesiastical rulers and could have authority over them in civil and secular matters. It seems that his argument of civil and ecclesiastical equality would not apply in Muslim lands. He stated that rulers should apply the law to ecclesiastical persons "without let or hindrance everywhere in Christian countries."[38] Thus, in Luther's eyes, the rejection of a legitimate role for the Christian magistrate had the twofold effect of undermining his critique of the papacy's legal immunities and undermining respect for authorities, who, by the Anabaptists' definition, could not be truly Christian.

If Luther had been willing to accept adult baptism and the Anabaptists had accepted the possibility of Christian magistrates, the subsequent history of the Reformation might have been very different. As it was, the Anabaptists perpetuated views on religious liberty that were very similar to those of early Luther. The extent of the direct influence of Luther's thought on the Anabaptists would be an area of valuable study, but it is known that their leaders did read and even cite Luther in support of some of their positions.[39] Given the wide circulation of Luther's writings in the early 1520s, Anabaptist leaders must have been familiar with his main works on church and state, including the *Address to the Christian Nobility of the German Nation* and *Secular Authority.*

Due to their small numbers and generally outlawed status, however, the Anabaptists themselves had very little direct influence on European political or social affairs, at least until the time of the Dutch Revolt in the late sixteenth century. In the Netherlands, for the first time in Western Europe, a combination of ideas of conscience and the right of private religious judgment held by the Anabaptists, a political milieu that needed a respite from religious wars, and a business community that desired the prosperity of a peaceful toleration, formed the first national, nearly comprehensive exercise in religious toleration and freedom.[40] The Netherlands were an anomaly for nearly a hundred years, at least until the religious toleration of Britain's Glorious Revolution—although even that was a stingier toleration than that achieved by the Dutch—and the freedom of some of the more radical American colonies, such as Rhode Island, Pennsylvania, and New Jersey.

Heirs of the Radical Reformation, including Baptists and Quakers, were directly involved in these later events, especially those in America. Despite Luther's persecution of them, the Anabaptists and their heirs can be seen at least as part of a link between early Lutheran thought on the priesthood of believers, the separate jurisdiction of the two kingdoms, and modern political thought. The Anabaptists grasped and embodied, as it were, parts two and three of the three-walls-of-privilege argument, placing Scripture as the ultimate authority for every believer, both within society and within the church.

The other half, or third, of Luther's argument—the equality of civil and ecclesiastical rulers, the inherent equality of all Christians and citizens, and the representative role of leaders—eventually found greater expression in the reformed churches. Over time, their polity became increasingly representative, and congregations were involved in choosing their pastors.

The reformed churches had far more political and social impact than the Anabaptists. The increasingly democratic natures of their congregations became a model for their political thought. In Europe, reformed churches were flexible enough to adjust to basically whatever church and/or state arrangement they found themselves under, because outside of Geneva, they were usually in the minority. But it was in America where they had the most influence at the ground level over the structure of civil governments. Here, the Puritan-founded New England colonies were decades, in some cases a century or more, ahead of the other colonies in the representative nature of their assemblies and governmental structures.

It is as though Luther's doctrine of the priesthood of believers and its two kingdoms church-state model was divided in half shortly after the Reformation began. The part relating to the right of individual conscience in relation to Scripture was highlighted and championed by the Anabaptists and their allies. The part relating to the equality of believers and citizens, the complementary roles of church and state, and the essentially representative nature of leadership took root and began developing and evolving with the reformed churches.

Of course, this is to drastically oversimplify things, but merely to highlight rather than mislead. Other influences—humanist, Enlightenment, Catholic, Jewish, and Deist—were, of course, at work. The evolution of Reformed polity was a lengthy and multibranched process, one that included forays into theocratic hierarchies, which is far too complex to examine here. The Anabaptists, even in America, were never significant either in numbers or direct influence. (Although they and/or their ideas did affect those who were of greater influence.)

The thread of the story is not so indistinct and vague, not so speculative and fanciful, to prevent one from saying, with a meaningful basis in history, that when the American Constitution and Bill of Rights were drafted, they represented in some way a reuniting and political flowering of the secular implications of the priesthood of all believers that Luther had expressed in the 1520s. Those ideas, which became divided and submerged, now reemerged modified, even transformed, but still recognizable; and they contributed to the formation of a representative form of republican government and to the rights of conscience protected by the Bill of Rights from infringement by the majority.

To end where we started, these threads allow us to view those princes at Speyer, with all their prejudice and blindness to the Anabaptists, as truly asserting a foundational principle—Protestantism, the idea that in matters of conscience, the majority shall have no say—that, through many tortured pathways, false turns, blind alleys reconsidered, eventually formed part of the basis of our form of limited republican government. This was not a government Luther envisioned, certainly, but one in which he would recognize the principles of religious liberty that he early championed.

1. MacCulloch, *The Reformation*, 151.

2. Dillenberger, *Martin Luther*, 388.

3. Ibid., 398.

4. MacCulloch, *The Reformation*, 155.

5. Martin Luther, "Friendly Admonition to Peace Concerning the Twelve Articles of the Swabian Peasants," in Hillerbrand, *The Protestant Reformation*, 67–87.

6. Ibid., 71.

7. MacCulloch, *The Reformation*, 157.

8. Ibid., 156.

9. Ibid., 159.

10. Ibid.

11. John S. Oyer, *Lutheran Reformers Against Anabaptists* (The Hague: Baptist Standard Bearer, 2000), 116.

12. Ibid.

13. Ibid., 122.

14. Ibid.

15. Ibid., 128.

16. Ibid., 126.

17. Ibid.

18. Ibid.

19. Ibid., 138.

20. Harold J. Berman, *Law and Revolution II: The Impact of the Protestant Reformations on the Western Legal Tradition* (Cambridge, MA: Belknap Press, 2006), 80, 81.

21. Ibid., 82, 83.

22. Francis Oakley, "Christian Obedience and Authority, 1520–1550," in *The Cambridge History of Political Thought, 1450–1700*, ed. J. H. Burns (Cambridge: Cambridge University Press, 1995), 174, 175.

23. Mark Greengrass, *The Longman Companion to the European Reformation, c. 1500–1618* (New York: Longman Publishing, 1998), 61, 62.

24. Ibid., 62.

25. James M. Estes, "The Role of the Godly Magistrates in the Church: Melanchthon as Luther's Interpreter and Collaborator," *Church History* 67, no 3 (September 1998): 463–483.

26. Ibid., 479.

27. Oakley, "Christian Obedience," 170.

28. MacCulloch, *The Reformation*, 160.

29. Ibid.

30. Ibid., 161.

31. Ibid.

32. Estes, "The Role of the Godly Magistrates," 478, 479.

33. Philip Benedict, *Christ's Churches Purely Reformed: A Social History of Calvinism* (New Haven, CT: Yale University Press, 2004), 283–285.

34. Harro Höpfl, *The Christian Polity of John Calvin* (Cambridge: Cambridge University Press, 1985), 35.

35. Ibid., 123, 124, 196, 197.

36. Benedict, *Christ's Churches*, 89.

37. Ibid., 71, 72.

38. Dillenberger, *Martin Luther*, 410.

39. For instance, it is known that Luther was annoyed by Balthasar Hübmaier's citation of Luther's writings in support of Hübmaier's arguments on infant baptism. Oyer, *Lutheran Reformers Against Anabaptists,* 118.

40. Martin van Gelderen, *The Political Thought of the Dutch Revolt, 1555–1590* (Cambridge: Cambridge University Press, 2002), 218–220.

Chapter 3

The Backgrounds of America's Founding Protestant Philosophy

The public discussion of religion and religious freedom is generally dominated by two increasingly polarized viewpoints. The first view, largely promoted by President Obama and the Democrats, values a religion-free, basically secular public square, with a certain amount of lip service paid to freedom for religious persons and groups, but a general denial of that freedom when it comes into conflict with other societal values, such as notions of equality, homosexual rights, or other public values they hold in high importance.

The second outlook, held by much of the Republican leadership, has a high regard for America's religious heritage, believes there is an important role for religious values in politics, and views the separation of church and state as a socialist construct that is a threat to both religious freedom and the cultivation of virtues needed for a functioning democracy.

The trouble is that both sides largely overlook the actual Protestant founding heritage and philosophy upon which America's church-state arrangement was based. The current church-state views of both the Republicans and Democrats were also represented at the founding, although they did not carry the influence they have today. To understand today's arguments, it can be very useful to go back and look at a description of these three competing points of view at the time America was being colonized.

Each of the three positions can be helpfully understood by examining the differing approaches each view takes on the relationships between individual, church,

This chapter originally appeared in *Liberty*, January/February 2014.

state, and God. To understand our possible futures, it will be helpful to revisit the past—specifically, the end of the seventeenth century when the revocation of the Edict of Nantes in 1685, the French legal act that had accorded French Protestants some level of toleration from the Catholic majority, sent legal thinkers to their libraries to prepare defenses of religious toleration. These positions were ably expressed by three of the most brilliant legal and theological minds of that time.

The three were Samuel Pufendorf, a Lutheran natural-rights lawyer and counselor to the king of Sweden; John Locke, a political philosopher who was deeply influential on America's founders; and Pierre Bayle, an influential French Huguenot theologian and philosopher. In their writings one can find the basic outlines of the Puritan, semi-theocratic model that is fast becoming the favorite of some in the Republican Party; the separationist model that reflects America's founding Protestant heritage; and the secular, liberal separationist model, so appealing to many of today's Democratic leaders.

Pufendorf and medieval privileges

Born in 1632 in Saxony, Pufendorf was best known for his works on international law, especially *The Law of Nature and Nations*.[1] Published in 1672, this work was widely influential on the Continent, in Scotland, and in the newly formed American colonies.[2] When the Edict of Nantes was revoked, Pufendorf took the opportunity to write what has been described as an "appendix," which applied his natural-law theory to issues of church and state.[3] Entitled *Of the Nature and Qualification of Religion in Reference to Civil Society* ("Religion and Civil Society"), Pufendorf's work was published in 1687. It set out a principled basis for what was ultimately a pragmatic, anemic toleration. It represented the magisterial Protestant continuation of the medieval view of church and state.

Pufendorf dedicated the book to the elector of Brandenburg-Prussia and used it to recommend himself for a post in the elector's Berlin court, which he indeed received.[4] The intended audience perhaps helped shape the work. He sets out a high view of the state and its power and a rather limited and weak basis for religious toleration. The work begins with apparently strong principles of separation between ecclesiastical and civil spheres, as well as a commitment to individual rights. But the last third of the book returns spiritual powers and oversight to the "Christian" ruler, which are denied to secular rulers in the first portions of the book. To simplify his thinking in a useful way, we can diagram it. The diagram contains four basic elements: Truth/God, the church, the state, and the individual. Pufendorf's arrangement of these elements would look like this:

Here, God (G) and the accessibility of Truth (T) are recognized. A distinction between church (C) and state (s) is also accepted. But that distinction allows for a great deal of cooperation, especially when the ruler is a Christian. The importance of the individual (i) is minimized, because of his or her need to go through the organs of church and state to obtain truth, whether spiritual or civil. This model represents the world of the divine right of kings and popes, where no individual rights exist but only privileges extended by rulers. It is one in which church and state are distinct entities but play a role in cooperating to civilly enforce the majority religious beliefs and practices of society. Under this system, the church in theory has a superior position in society, as kings and rulers are subject to the superior spiritual authority of the church. Bishops and popes at times provided legitimacy to the claims of leaders to civil authority, at times crowning them, as Pope Leo III did for Charlemagne. This relationship is shown by the capital *C* and lowercase *s* in the diagram.

Pufendorf criticized the revocation of the Edict of Nantes but not because the Huguenots had some sort of natural-right claim to religious liberty. Rather, he believed that the crown, once having extended toleration, should keep its word and not withdraw it. It was a question of honoring agreements and contracts and the social stability protected by that practice. Pufendorf had no principled or moral argument for why the edict should have been entered into in the first place. That was a policy calculation that brought political peace against an aggressive and armed minority. In Pufendorf's model, religious liberty became a question of policy, a privilege to be extended or denied at the inclination of the ruler. His philosophical fruit fell not far from the medieval tree.

Locke and Protestant rights

John Locke's church-state principles were most clearly outlined in his *Letter on Toleration*, published in 1689. His views show the shape of the new world that Luther helped to create in proposing that each person should access God through prayer and Bible study. The priesthood of all believers inverted the bottom half of Pufendorf's diagram. The belief vaulted the individual to a position above the church and the state, with direct access to God and Truth. Locke's model of these four elements would look like this:

This model accepted, like the medieval model, that God exists and that certain truths can be ascertained about both the world and spiritual things. But the new Protestant view placed the individual above church and state. Each person now had the duty and right to seek this truth from God, through both the Bible (especially about spiritual things) and through nature (especially political matters and civil morality). The church and the state existed to support and protect the rights of the individual: one as a member of the spiritual world, and the other as a citizen of the temporal world. There was a separation between these two powers, since their jurisdiction is limited to their separate spheres of concern, whether spiritual or civil. It is a separation of equality and mutual respect, with each entity respecting the sovereignty of the other in its own sphere. Hence, both are represented by capitals *C* and *S*.

The individual's rights against the state, in turn, derived from the duties that he or she owed to God. This is essentially the political expression of the Protestant model of the priesthood of all believers. It serves as a robust foundation for individual rights; hence, the individual is shown by a capital *I*. This is the model that we have traced through the early modern West and was an important part of the impulse toward disestablishment in colonial America.

Bayle and skeptical rights

The third writer during this period was Pierre Bayle. While ostensibly a Calvinist theologian, Bayle was actually a strongly skeptical thinker who based his view of toleration on broad epistemological skepticism. Bayle was accused by fellow Calvinist theologians of supporting atheism and was deprived of his professorship at his Protestant university as a result.[5] Rather than an heir of Calvin and an ancestor of the New England Puritans, Bayle was more an heir of the Greek skeptic Pyrrho and ancestor to Hume, Voltaire, Rousseau, and eventually Franklin and Jefferson.[6]

Bayle largely shared Pufendorf's view on the supremacy of the state over the individual. He rejected Locke's notion of a reciprocal contract between ruler and people, denied the right of rebellion, and upheld a strong duty of obedience to the ruler.[7] But unlike Pufendorf, Bayle held a skeptical view of the world. Especially in the area of speculative truths, including religion, he affirmed a strong difference from mathematical or empirical truths. For the former, he believed one could only attain a "reputed" truth, rather than actual truth.[8] This led Bayle to defend the notion of individual conscience.

Other thinkers of the day often spoke of the rights of conscience, but it was generally understood that they were not talking about an erroneous conscience or acts against one's conscience. Bayle was one of the first to propose that rights of conscience should extend to consciences that were believed to be in error—the "erroneous conscience."[9] Even if one could know that someone else was in error, argued Bayle, how could one know that the other person was convinced of that error?[10] This question was a central point of contention in the debate between

Roger Williams and John Cotton over the issue of toleration and persecution.

Bayle's strong defense of conscience, then, was based on a weak view of truth, or at least human ability to know truth. This led him to view individual judgment and conscience as important. Thus, he held a strong view of the duty of the state to tolerate religious differences. Putting Bayle's view into a diagram looks like this:

The lowercase *t*'s represent the individualistic conception of truth, where no universal view of truth exists, but everyone conceives his or her own truth. Church and state are still separate, but it is not a separation of mutual equality and sovereign spheres. Rather, it is a separation based on a suspicion of the truth claims made by religious people. The tolerance in this scheme is dependent on a commitment to skepticism—from the logic that if truth cannot be known, then no one can or should enforce it. The real threats to this system are those who claim knowledge of absolute truths.

Churches and people who believe in special revelation were such a threat. Therefore, religious people and their beliefs are to be kept far away from politics and the public square generally. Separation of church and state, rather than being based on a view of separate sovereignties, is founded on hostility to the truth claims of religious people and their views of special revelation. Religious people and their ideas are kept not only out of government but also on the fringes of the public square generally. Under this view, the attitude of the state toward the church was symbolically expressed by Napoleon when, in contrast to Charlemagne, he crowned himself emperor in the presence of the pope. The marginalization of the church and religion in this system is represented by a lowercase *c*.

Rights in this system are not quite as secure as under the Lockean view. Individual autonomy is a somewhat fragile thing when it is based merely on skepticism, rather than on individual duties to, and rights before, God. The solitary autonomy of the individual becomes fairly quickly outweighed by the interest of the group once accommodation of the individual becomes anything more than a slight inconvenience. This is seen very clearly in skeptical and atheistic communist systems, in which respect for the individual is very quickly submerged to the common good. A similar thing happens in a democracy, we have seen, when terrorism threatens national security. Hence, the *i* for individual is lowercase.

Under this model, there is no real reason why religious claims to truth should obtain greater protection than claims to convictions in other areas. Why should religious claims have special protection beyond that received by a wide range of special interest claims, such as environmentalists or animal-rights supporters or advocates of unions and labor? People feel strongly about all these issues. If it is the individual conviction only that provides the basis for rights, as this model suggests, then all these convictions should be treated equally. But ultimately, if all convictions are equally protected, none can be meaningfully protected, or democracy will ultimately become gridlocked amid a cacophony of clashing rights claims.

Three views in American history

My discussion of the third view has moved beyond what Bayle himself would have suggested into how at least parts of modern liberalism has developed this view. All three of these views—the Pufendorfian, the Lockean, and the Baylean models—have been influential at various times in American history. A side-by-side comparison of these models, a representative advocate, the historical periods they represent, and their time of greatest influence in America, is represented in the diagram below.

Samuel Pufendorf	John Locke	Pierre Bayle
Medieval model	Dissenting Protestant	Skeptical model
Puritan New England	Constitutional period to mid-twentieth century	Mid-twentieth century to 9/11/2001
T/G | / \\ C -- s | i	T/G | I / \\ C | S	tttttttttt | i / \\ c | S

The American Puritans developed a Pufendorfian-like church-state arrangement in early New England, with a civil magistrate involved in enforcing ecclesiastical rules and discipline. Thus, the earliest American colonies were founded on the theory of the medieval model on the left, with the exception of Rhode Island. Some later ones, especially New Jersey, Pennsylvania, Delaware, and North Carolina, were founded basically on the Protestant theory in the center column, which also guided the formation of the national constitution. Despite Pufendorf's enormous influence in both Scotland and the American colonies, the founders of the American republic explicitly rejected his form of church-state arrangement.[11] At the time of the Revolution and the formation of the Constitution, Pufendorf's model of toleration was limited to two or three New England states and within a few years vanished even there.

It was Locke's formulation, mediated by James Madison, John Witherspoon, and other key American thinkers, of dissenting Protestantism that carried the day in the founding of the American republic. Their views of the separate roles of the two powers were the ideological victors on the topic of tolerance and religious freedom in the early Republic.

The religious support for American independence and religious liberty was well understood by those closer to the Revolution, such as Edmund Burke, the British parliamentarian. Burke famously explained the independent character of the American colonists by the fact that "the people are Protestants, and of that kind which is the most adverse to all implicit submission of mind and opinion. . . . All Protestantism, even the most cold and passive, is a sort of dissent. But the religion most prevalent in our northern colonies is a refinement on the principle of resistance: it is the dissidence of dissent, and the Protestantism of the Protestant religion."[12]

But by the late nineteenth century, the rise of uncertainty in theology, science, and philosophy undermined the American Protestant outlook and laid the groundwork for a toleration based on skepticism. John Stuart Mill's view of skeptical individualism increasingly became the prism through which Locke was understood. As a consequence, the twentieth century saw a wholesale move, at least in the elite centers of thought, to toleration based on epistemological uncertainty and moral relativism.

After the Civil War, the rise of Darwinism, and the growth of philosophical uncertainty, many American elite institutions, including colleges and universities, the professions, and the media, began to move toward the much more skeptical view represented by Bayle. This shift did not happen overnight, and much has been written on the involved process of secularization in American history.[13] The Protestant umbrella broadened to include an even more generic and diffused sense of American spiritual identity.

The influence of German higher idealism, with its attendant historicism and philosophy of relativism, in the mid-nineteenth to late nineteenth century and early twentieth century called into question the natural-law foundations of the country. This philosophy also undercut the Protestant model of church and society that was based on these views of natural law and natural rights. New approaches to the law, based on social and pragmatic concerns, accompanied the gradual acceptance of legal positivism. These ideas gained ground in the early twentieth century and especially influenced legal thought in the second half of the twentieth century.[14]

These new ideas made progress to different degrees in various parts of society. They made greater inroads earlier in "elite" institutions, such as colleges and universities, and in the press and media. Old paradigms continued to hold sway at more popular levels. The civil rights movement of the 1950s and 1960s could be described as the last gasp of Protestant-style natural-rights and public-morality arguments at the popular level, which combined with a more modern, liberal rights perspective among its leadership, the media, and the courts.

But the cycle of ideas has continued to roll, and now a vocal segment of the American public, especially after the events of September 11, 2001, is vigorously rejecting the skepticism and relativism that have come to be associated with our current system of rights. Rather than returning to a pre-Mill, Lockean view, however, many appear ready to embrace a model more like that of Pufendorf.[15] In this post–September 11 world, significant segments of American society are simultaneously rejecting moral relativism as well as seeking for the security provided by a stronger government.

This rejection of the modern paradigm moves society from the right side of the tolerance diagram generally leftward. It does not require a conscious repudiation of the importance of the individual to move the Locke column into the Pufendorf column. The difference between Locke and Pufendorf was not over their ostensible commitment to the individual and the freedom to worship. Rather, it was that a strong view of the supremacy of the state generally negated Pufendorf's theoretically positive view of the individual.

But the point of all this for overseas observers is that a "secular" version of government that has a healthy and robust freedom of religion can exist in a highly religious community. France, with its "dereligioned" public square, is not the only, or most attractive, model of a secular government that exists. The traditional American system offers a philosophical framework that is sympathetic toward religion and claims about a Supreme Being, while offering respect and accommodation to all religious claims that respect the well-being of the state and other individuals.

In this system, while the state should not promote your religious view, you and your fellow believers should be free to do so, even within the public square, as long as you respect the rights and freedoms of others to do the same. In this sense, a fair and balanced state secularism can actually lead to a greater and more robust religiosity. And these are the points that are often overlooked in our political debates today. We are taking sides as if our founding were a contest between the New England Puritan theocrats and the French secular, skeptical philosophes. Either of these pathways can just as easily lead to a statist philosophy and a state oversight of religious matters that is equally troubling. This makes it vital that we not forget the dissenting Protestant middle way of the middle colonies of Pennsylvania, New Jersey, Delaware, Maryland, and New York, that served as the actual model for our founding.

1. Samuel von Pufendorf, *Of the Nature and Qualification of Religion, in Reference to Civil Society* (Indianapolis, IN: Liberty Fund, 2002), xii, xiii. A discussion of Pufendorf and his views on toleration can be found in Simone Zurbuchen, "From Denominationalism to Enlightenment: Pufendorf, Le Clerc, and Thomasius on Toleration," in *Religious Toleration: "The Variety of Rites" From Cyrus to Defoe*, ed. John Christian Laursen (New York: St. Martin's Press, 1999), 191–204.

2. J. B. Schneewind, *The Invention of Autonomy* (Cambridge: Cambridge University Press, 1998), 118.

3. Pufendorf, *Of the Nature and Qualification of Religion*, xi.

4. Ibid., xiii.

5. Perez Zagorin, *How the Idea of Religious Toleration Came to the West* (Princeton, NJ: Princeton University Press, 2003), 285. For an extended discussion of the opposition to Bayle within French Protestant circles, see Guy H. Dodge, *The Political Theory of the Huguenots of the Dispersion* (New York: Columbia University Press, 1947).

6. Pierre Bayle, *Political Writings*, ed. Sally L. Jenkinson (Cambridge: Cambridge University Press, 2000), back cover. For a helpful overview of Bayle's thought in relation to toleration, see Sally L. Jenkinson, "Bayle and Leibniz: Two Paradigms of Tolerance and Some Reflections on Goodness Without God," in Laursen, *Religious Toleration*, 173–186.

7. Zagorin, *Idea of Religious Toleration*, 270.

8. Ibid., 282, 283.

9. Ibid., 280, 281; Pierre Bayle, *A Philosophical Commentary* (Carmel, IN: The Liberty Fund, Inc., 2005), 219–233.

10. Bayle, 145–149.

11. Schneewind, *The Invention of Autonomy*, 118.

12. Edmund Burke, *The Portable Edmund Burke*, ed. Isaac Kramnick (New York: Penguin Books, 2013), 263.

13. A good overview is provided by Christian Smith, *The Secular Revolution: Power, Interests, and Conflict in the Secularization of American Public Life* (Berkeley, CA: University of California Press, 2003). Helpful works dealing more generally with secularization in the West include the following: Callum G. Brown and Michael Snape, eds., *Secularization in the Christian World: Essays in Honor of Hugh McLeod* (Burlington, VT: Ashgate, 2010); Hugh McLeod and Werner Urstorf, eds., *The Decline of Christendom in Western Europe, 1750–2000* (Cambridge: Cambridge University Press, 2003); and Steve Bruce, ed., *Religion and Modernization: Sociologists and Historians Debate the Secularization Thesis* (Oxford: Oxford University Press, 1992).

14. Steven Green documents the rise of the substitution of secular theories for natural-law foundations occurring as early as the mid-nineteenth century in a wide range of legal areas, from oaths to probate law to church property disputes and to Sunday-closing laws. Steven Green, *The Second Disestablishment* (New York: Oxford University Press, 2010), 204–247.

15. Scholars who would largely reject the stricter separation between church and state and would be sympathetic to a model of greater church-state cooperation would include Robert N. Bellah, *The Broken Covenant: American Civil Religion in Time of Trial* (Chicago: University of Chicago Press, 1992); Daniel Dreisbach, *Thomas Jefferson and the Wall of Separation Between Church and State* (New York: New York University Press, 2003); Philip Hamburger, *Separation of Church and State* (Cambridge, MA: Harvard University Press, 2002); Richard John Neuhaus, *The Public Square: Religion and Democracy in America* (Grand Rapids, MI: Eerdmans, 1986); Harold J. Berman, *Law and Revolution II: The Impact of the Protestant Reformations on the Western Legal Tradition* (Cambridge, MA: Belknap Press, 2006).

Chapter 4

Luther, Locke, and Competing Notions of Human Dignity

I n the overview to this book, we discussed the connection between Martin Luther's priesthood of all believers and modern civil rights philosophy, especially as seen in the thought and action of Martin Luther King Jr. It is apparent that a belief in a Creator and the dignity that derives from being created in His image might create a stronger sense of dignity and rights than a purely secular conception of human dignity.

But a belief in the transcendent alone is not sufficient to protect the concept of human dignity or the practice of human rights. The long and sordid histories of the Crusades and the inquisitions and jihads of the medieval world—all carried out in the name of God, or gods—well illustrate this point. The wrong kind of metaphysical grounding can provide higher justification and motive for the coercion, abuse, and mistreatment of fellow humans.

In the decades after Luther's formulation of the priesthood of all believers, various theologians and political thinkers explored the implications of that new theory of human equality for both church and state. As the role between church and state became adjusted in various countries, new conceptions and understandings of the individual arose. One thinker who took up the challenge of exploring how the individual should relate to the new church-state landscape, created especially by more radical dissenting Protestants who argued for a meaningful separation between the authority of the church and the state, was John Locke.

This chapter will appear in a forthcoming issue of *Liberty*, 2017.

It has been shown that Locke's contribution to our modern conceptions of religious freedom and rights was influenced by a certain strand of dissenting Protestant thought that itself had roots in Luther's early thought about the priesthood of all believers.[1] The competing ideas of the individual and the state that Locke challenged also posited a transcendent realm, overseen by a Creator, who had created humans in His image. Yet they resulted in a much more cramped and limited conception of rights than Locke's view did. What was the difference between these competing schemes of rights and dignity?

The dignity of paternalism, stewardship, and self-ownership

In short, the answer has to do with the kind of relationship between the individual, the community, and the transcendent. In the late seventeenth century, when Locke was writing, three conceptions of the relationship between these elements resulted in three types, or kinds, of human dignity: the dignity of paternalism, seen especially in ideas of the divine right of kings and sacerdotal privilege; the dignity of stewardship, a concept of self-ownership in relation to others but of God's ownership in relation to the transcendent; and the dignity of self-ownership, where the individual, autonomous self is the highest authority in relation to the self. This latter category was only partially developed in the seventeenth century and awaited fuller expression in the eighteenth and especially nineteenth centuries, particularly in the philosophies of John Stuart Mill.

A. *The dignity of paternalism.* The dignity of paternalism is the outlook that dominated the Middle Ages. It is well expressed in the legal philosophy and writing on human rights by Samuel Pufendorf, the seventeenth-century Lutheran political philosopher. Pufendorf defended a system of human rights and religious liberty, but this was filtered through a conception of the king and religious leaders as being in paternal oversight over their subjects. He understood the metaphysical realm as being mediated through religious and civil elites to the individual subjects.

This view resulted, despite its language of rights and human dignity, in a system that was inherently paternalistic, both civilly and religiously. Civil and religious rulers, at least those that were Christian, were ultimately responsible to God on behalf of the community; citizens and church members were the beneficiaries of these mediations and were expected to play subservient roles to these elites, civilly, intellectually, and spiritually.

The king was expected to oversee a state religion, in cooperation with bishops and priests, and guard and promote it with the civil laws and the force of the state. This view cut across confessional lines and was characteristic not just of Catholic countries but also of magisterial Protestantism, as found in Calvin's Geneva, Luther's Germany, much of Elizabeth's England, and even Puritan New England.

But not all of Protestantism embraced this dignity of paternalism. There was a more individualistic brand of Protestantism, flowing from some of the early writings of Luther and kept alive by the Anabaptists and others in the branch of the Radical Reformation. As it spread beyond those historically termed *radicals*, I call it a strand of dissenting Protestantism, meaning that these believers dissented from the magisterial Protestants who combined church and state over the individual believer.

As indicated previously, John Locke, in his views on religious freedom, was influenced by this dissenting brand of Protestant thought. Locke deals at length with the notion of paternalism in government and religion, decisively rejects it, and substitutes a combination of self-ownership and divine ownership that can best be described as stewardship.[2]

John Locke's most famous political work is arguably his *Second Treatise of Government*, which most college students read at one time or another. But most people don't think to ask about the *First Treatise*, which is a much more obscure tract in our day and age. It is an extended attack, using Scripture and logical argument, on the notion of patriarchy in government, with Robert Filmer's *Patriarcha; or, The Natural Power of Kings* (1680) as a foil. Filmer represents a long line of medieval thought that viewed the king as holding a paternal authority, derived from Adam, over his subjects. This authority gives him the right as king and ruler to the unquestioning obedience of his subjects and oversight of their religious beliefs and practices.

After dismantling Filmer's notions of patriarchy in the *First Treatise*, Locke spends much of the *Second Treatise* replacing Filmer's paternalistic oversight with conceptions of dual ownership, the ownership of the individual as against his or her neighbors and rulers, and the ultimate divine ownership of all persons. This dual-ownership concept has caused some confusion, as scholars wonder which Locke really believed in: self-ownership or divine ownership. The apparent conflict is readily resolved once one understands the biblical notion of stewardship. A steward is one to whom property is entrusted, and the steward has the rights of ownership against all other persons, though he or she is responsible ultimately to the owner for the good management of the property.

B. The dignity of stewardship. The dignity of stewardship is a profound concept that gives significant freedom in relation to others, but also a responsibility in relation to the divine and others that avoids the excesses of paternalism and hyper-individualism. While one is free in body and soul from the intrusions of others, one has responsibilities to God to treat one's body as well as one's neighbor with appropriate respect and dignity. This stewardly relationship goes beyond a mere "right to be left alone" or a duty to merely leave others unmolested. Stewardship of self implies a responsibility to act with care of oneself: living in a manner to flourish as a human, but also creating conditions where the dignity of others can be realized, and all being subject to the same divine oversight and expectation.

The ideal of stewardship means that the political question, which comes to us from near the dawn of history, "Am I my brother's keeper?" is answered with a resounding "yes." But it is a "yes" that recognizes that while I am my brother's keeper, I am not his father or ruler, at least in any manner that would interfere with his own stewardship obligations in this world and beyond. Negative liberties are not enough to fulfill these obligations—particularly leaving persons alone who are struggling with conditions that threaten or impair their human dignity. The steward recognizes the need to help foster conditions where the dignity of all can be realized; though aims to do so in a way that does not undermine the impetus or motivation of others to exercise their roles as stewards of their persons, property, and liberty.

In opposing this paternalism in the *First Treatise*, Locke engages in an extended and close reading of Scripture to refute Filmer's arguments about Adam and his descendants. These theological disputes seem arcane to us today, and thus the book has faded into obscurity. Yet, wherever there is an authoritarian, paternalistic government, the Locke-Filmer debate is still very much relevant. The paternalism can be a right-wing dictatorship, such as we saw in the twentieth century with fascism and Nazism.

But this paternalism can also take the form of the statism of left-wing communism or oppressive socialism. Or it can even be a progressive, social welfare state model that engages in a kind of soft tyranny by cultivating citizens' dependence on the state, which undermines their own sense of stewardship, while imposing its transcendent moral framework upon all. While this soft tyranny may not yet fully characterize the nations of the West today, one can see sufficient elements of it in our governments and culture to make revisiting the Locke-Filmer debates a very relevant exercise.

C. The dignity of self-ownership. This soft tyranny also was implicated in another debate that Locke was part of. This argument was with those who would collapse all ownership into self-ownership and either deny or ignore transcendent relationships, rights, and duties. This debate was perhaps less fully developed in Locke's day, as full-fledged arguments about human autonomy in the absence of the divine did not become widespread until the eighteenth and even nineteenth centuries. Still, men such as Pierre Bayle and Baruch Spinoza developed systems of thinking about humanity and its nature, purpose, and liberties, in the absence of knowledge or belief about the Divine, at least as conventionally understood.

Locke's response to these purely secular systems was blunt and succinct: "The taking away of God, though but even in thought, dissolves all."[3] The element of stewardship in his system that created any sort of objective obligations to oneself and others, an external morality, discoverable through reason and experience, was in essence denied by these systems. If all one had was the autonomous, self-defining individual, then the limits of conduct were defined essentially by subjective human desire, except where that desire bumped up against the physical person or desire of another. While one had a duty not to harm another and thus invade the autonomy of another, there was no clear basis for a duty to help another, unless one desired to.

Further, if there was no objective measure as to the worth or value of a desire, which is essentially the case if one rejects a belief in the transcendent, then society would lose the ability to objectively adjudge between conflicting desires. Perhaps the stronger desire should prevail, but how would that be determined except through how many shared that desire? Thus, all values, including ones that had been viewed as transcendent and having objective elements, are transmuted into subjective desires and become subject to standard, majoritarian political processes.

Belief in rights, including the right of religious freedom, would become just another desire that would need to be balanced and traded off with any other desires that persons in society might have. Notions of individual rights might be paid lip service in light of the strong Western tradition. But, in practice, these systems of right would be subsumed under a regime that attempted to equalize all competing desires. *Equality* would replace *liberty* as the central watchword of the civil rights activist. In implementing this equality, most liberties would be subject to majority rule. This would have the effect of subjecting rights to the same majoritarian, democratic processes that deal with most questions of public and political policy.

In effect, the democratic system would revert to a new paternalism, not one based on the divine right of kings, bishops, and dictators, but one based on the collective subjective desires of the community of autonomous individuals. Prevented from acknowledging a transcendent component, there is no objective element of stewardship to consider and nothing to adjudicate between the conflicting desires of the members of the group, except a rule by the majority or the most popular desire.

Under this system, the language of human dignity is retained, because humanity is all we have. Indeed, the human becomes virtually divine in a sense, because it defines and encompasses its own reality. But it is an extraordinarily limited divinity, as it is hemmed and limited by the subjective desires of its divine neighbor. Ultimately, it is a very thin dignity that does not produce many meaningful, measurable duties toward oneself or others, except perhaps the duty to stay alive and to not physically harm others.

In answering the age-old question "Am I my brother's keeper?" the new dignity answers with a version of the clever evasion that the lawyer offered to Christ: "But who is my brother?" The answer to this question offered by the new dignity is, "Those who are aggrieved like me and who I most identify with." Thus, we have the new regime of identity politics, where one's political view is tightly bound to one's racial, ethnic, social, religious, gender, or class identity. Various competing groups will ally on those questions where the greatest number of desires overlap.

Crucially, the new system provides nothing objective or principled to press back against a majoritarian rule based on a new paternalism over the individual. Any number of issues take on the importance previously given to the most sacred notions of human rights, such as bodily integrity, the right to be free from torture and abuse, and the right and freedom of religious worship and practice.

Thus, our collective desire for safety and security in the age of terror is seen as justifying a policy and practice of "enhanced-interrogation" methods that previously the American government had condemned as torture. Persons are held for years without a trial and fail to receive due process that would have been viewed, for the entirety of the twentieth century, as a gross violation of basic constitutional rights.

People, including American citizens, who can be labeled as terrorists are targeted, far from any active field of battle, for assassination by drone strikes based purely on presidential fiat. These assassinations are, again, acts that in pre–war on terror times would have been viewed as illegal and unconstitutional, as well as unethical and immoral. But our desires for safety and security are seen, in both the popular mind and in parts of the legal and political community, as overcoming our perceived enemies' desires for liberty, bodily integrity, and even life.

Additionally, in America, private sexual preferences and behaviors are given equal, and at times superior, legal pride of place and protection in a manner that impairs the convictions and practices of religious persons. In our new regime of human rights, all desires and preferences are equal; but as in George Orwell's *Animal Farm*, some desires and preferences are "more equal than others."[4]

Those preferences that are more equal would be the ones whose ideological bases are those consistent with the ruling ideology of naturalistic materialism and secularism. Thus, personal sexual preferences, including same-sex behavior and marriage generally, prevail against millennia-old religious and moral convictions regarding sexual behavior and the ordering of the family.

All these results flow logically and consistently, I believe, from this new, thin, and purely self-ownership notion of human dignity. But do we have actual hard evidence that the Protestant concept of dignity has actually contributed to notions of modern democracy and human rights in our world? It is one thing to trace the ideas of Luther and Locke and their impact on the founding of America, but international human rights have a much broader base than that. Can Protestantism truly claim to have impacted the world between Locke and the rise of twentieth-century civil rights, Martin Luther King Jr., and international human rights? The next chapter discusses a startling and persuasive answer to the role played by dissenting, free-church Protestant thought in the rise of worldwide democracy and civil rights.

---

1. Miller, *The Religious Roots of the First Amendment*, 63–90.

2. S. Adam Seagrave, "Self-Ownership vs. Divine Ownership: A Lockean Solution to a Liberal Democratic Dilemma," *American Journal of Political Science* 55, no. 3 (July 2011): 710–723.

3. John Locke, *Two Treatises of Government; and, A Letter Concerning Toleration*, ed. Ian Shapiro (New Haven, CT: Yale University Press, 2003), 246. Because his view that atheism would undermine the validity of both morality and rights, Locke drew the conclusion that atheists should not be tolerated. I believe this was a mistaken conclusion that conflicts with his own premise of the importance of private judgment to religious belief. The reality is that the unbeliever and the atheist should have the same freedom as the theist or the supernaturalist to make his or her own judgments about ultimate reality, including a divine realm.

4. George Orwell, *Animal Farm* (New York: Harcourt, Brace, and Co., 1990), 118.

Chapter 5

Protestant Dignity and the Rise of Worldwide Democracy and Human Rights

Have Protestant ideas of human dignity and the importance of the individual impacted global conceptions of human and civil rights? In the previous chapters, we have seen the connection between Protestant concepts of human dignity and the priesthood of all believers and the development of American and Western ideas of religious freedom. But can this connection be extended to the larger world? Strong connections between certain Protestant mission groups and the rise of global democracy and human freedoms and liberties have been revealed in an unlikely source—the pages of a secular political science journal.

Robert Woodberry's groundbreaking article "The Missionary Roots of Liberal Democracy"—published in the flagship secular political science journal the *American Political Science Review* (APSR)—makes the historical and statistical case for this connection between dissenting Protestantism and global democracy.[1] Woodberry demonstrates a very strong correlation between nonconformist Protestant missions and the implementation of mass education, mass printing, the rule of law, and the rise of social institutions, which are all necessary building blocks of functioning democracies. Protestant workers contributed to these factors, Woodberry shows historically, because of their ideology of the equality and dignity of the individual before God.

This chapter will appear in a forthcoming issue of *Liberty, 2017.*

On the face of it, this seems an ambitious and even an audacious claim. Yet Woodberry's thesis withstood secular and skeptical peer reviewers at APSR and the larger academic community. The strength of his documentation is causing political scientists and historians to rethink and reevaluate the causative role of religion in political and social development. Previously, it had often been dismissed as a "soft" or secondary factor driven largely by "hard" factors, such as economic, political, or social-class interests. Woodberry makes a compelling case that this is not so, and that religion not only matters, but often helps shape these other factors.

The paper is too complex to fully summarize here, but the following points are directly relevant to the issues of human dignity and rights:

First, Woodberry notes that it is not just Christianity or Protestantism in general that is associated with the growth and spread of liberal democracy and civil freedoms. Rather, it is with what he terms "conversionary Protestantism," which overlaps significantly with what I called dissenting Protestantism.[2] He notes that the positive correlation between the widespread education of laity, the spread of printing, and the resistance to abuse by the commercial and political interests of the colonizers is only connected with non-state connected or sponsored missionaries. So missionaries from state-connected churches, whether they be Catholic or magisterial Protestant churches, did not show such correlations.[3]

Thus, those missionaries who advanced democratic structures were from churches that took most seriously the human dignity of stewardship rooted in the Protestant doctrine of the priesthood of all believers. This belief emphasized the importance of individual Bible study, leading to personal belief and faith by all. It also ushered in arguments for the separation of church and state, which were eventually systematized by Locke's political philosophy.

As Woodberry states in his discussion of the rise of mass printing as catalyzed by nonconformist or dissenting Protestant missionaries: They "expected lay people to make their own religious choices. They believed people are saved not through sacraments or group membership but by 'true faith in God'; thus, each individual had to decide which faith to follow." These views "changed people's ideas about whom books were for. According to CPs [conversionary Protestants], *everyone* needed access to 'God's word'—not just elites. Therefore, *everyone* needed to read, including women and the poor."[4]

Second, Woodberry's analysis makes clear that it is not just a generic belief in human worth and dignity that spread democratic institutions, but a commitment to helping people actualize that dignity by providing them with the education, tools, and resources to do so. Along with commitments to human equality, the dissenting Protestants engaged in mass education (not just education of the elites as other groups did), the development and spread of mass printing, the activation of non-state civil organizations, and the promotion of the rule of law (equality before the law). All these elements contributed to the shaping of a culture where liberal democracy could take root and flourish.[5]

Thus, it was not just support of human dignity in the abstract that mattered, nor even an implementation of a legal scheme to protect rights. Rather, such a legal structure could only meaningfully operate when these other conditions were in place: an educated populace who could read and write, who could spread ideas and interests in print, and who could organize societies to share and further their views and interests and, ultimately, shape political and legal patterns.

Third, the programs and assistance of the dissenting missionaries did not make persons dependent on their long-term care, nurture, or support. Rather, these programs gave people the ability to care, nurture, and support themselves and others in an engaged and active civil society. Indeed, after the catalyzing influence of these missionaries, other religious and secular groups also became involved with mass education, printing, and institution building, often to compete with the Protestant efforts in these areas. Many countries that developed the features of a liberal democracy soon did not require Protestant involvement to keep it going, and many forgot that they were involved at all. But Woodberry has statistically documented the strong correlation between Protestant missions and the rise of democracy in no fewer than 142 non-European societies.[6]

Fourth, a significant feature of what made the non-state Protestant missionaries effective was their willingness to oppose abusive colonial practices by commercial or governmental officials. It was not that the missionaries were not "racist" in some sense; they were products of their time in many ways.[7] Yet they did possess a commitment to the equality of human dignity, believing that all persons were made in the image of God. Because CP missionaries were not connected with the state, they were able and willing to fight abuses against natives and locals in a variety of ways. These included writing to supporters and newspapers back home, rallying legislative support for proposals reigning in commercial and government leaders, and in some instances, confronting abuses openly in the field.[8]

In carrying out these efforts to curb colonial abuses, the missionaries made explicit their underlying philosophy of the obligations of stewardship in relation to human dignity. As Woodberry puts it, they "popularized the idea of 'trusteeship' [another term for stewardship]—that the only justification of colonization was the 'social uplift' of the colonized people."[9]

This notion of social uplift may have had a paternalistic air to it, and this was undoubtedly reflected in some of their practices. But the missionaries generally did not forget that the social uplift was to put colonized people into a better position to carry out their own roles as stewards of themselves and their countries. Hence, their emphasis on education, printing, and the creation of structures and systems that would give those locals willing to apply themselves the tools to manage themselves and their countries in a world that was rapidly becoming much more globally connected, industrialized, and commercialized.

This argument does not claim that only free-church Protestantism is supportive of the growth of human dignity and civil rights. Any religion or even ideology that chooses to take human dignity seriously, in terms of stewardship, can support and produce such results. Protestants who were more paternalistic in their outlook and connected with state churches, the so-called magisterial Protestants, did not have such a politically significant impact in the mission field. On the other hand, at various times in history, both Jewish and Muslim groups have taken this type of dignity seriously and have had periods of cultural growth and enlightenment as a result. The relative peace and flourishing of Jewish and Christian "heretical" groups in medieval Muslim Spain is one such example.[10]

In response to Protestant educational and printing efforts, Catholics also made significant contributions to these institutions; in many instances, they eventually outstripped Protestant achievements. After Vatican II, Catholics also formally made human dignity and freedom a central part of their philosophy of social and political engagement.

The reality is that most religious or even political groups that take this thick sense of human dignity seriously, and acknowledge the stewardship role of helping others actualize their own role as stewards, can promote meaningful growth and protection of human rights and liberties. However, during much of the eighteenth and nineteenth centuries, the evidence strongly indicates that dissenting Protestants were the primary vessel for the worldwide spread of these values.

Thus, the lesson that should not be lost on us today is not the alleged superiority of any particular religious tradition, but of the importance of a certain kind of human dignity to the creation and maintenance of a meaningful and robust system of human rights in a society. It must strike the balance between too much, or too mediated, transcendence and the absence of any notion of transcendence—the collapse of all values into the subjective, autonomous self.

Further, it must recognize that a commitment to the importance of human rights in speech or on paper is insufficient in itself to guarantee that these rights will be protected. Rather, there must be a constant safeguarding of the institutions that ensure the implementation of these rights: education for all, a vibrant and free press culture, civic organizations that provide a buffer against state institutions, the checks and balances that provide a meaningful rule of law, and all this sustained in the popular mind by an ethos of the transcendent dignity of the individual.

The potential paradox, or irony, this represents is that the dissenting Protestants did their jobs in part because of their separation from the state. So any attempt to enforce or even promote some kind of minimal civil religion will actually undermine the very spirit and ethos it is seeking to promote. But the state does not necessarily need to become religious or promote religion to recognize that there is a power greater than itself—a transcendent realm that will limit its own power in dealing with its citizens.

It is also a realm that can provide value and guidance to the concept of stewardship. Rightly defined, stewardship will supply direction in creating a minimal set of common values that designate the stronger and richer in society with obligations to the poorer and weaker; but they will be obligations to equip and empower rather than to dominate and dictate, either in a hard or soft paternalistic tyranny. Let all people of faith do what we can to recover and promote the transcendent dignity of stewardship as a check and guide to the rising tide of paternalism and tyranny in our modern world.

---

1. Robert Woodberry, "The Missionary Roots of Liberal Democracy," *American Political Science Review* 106, no. 2 (May 2012): 244–270.

2. Ibid., 244n1. "Conversionary Protestantism" is an unfortunate label, as it implies that only non-state churches were concerned with conversion. This is not true, as many state-church missionaries, including Anglicans, Lutherans, and Calvinists, were concerned with the individual experience of conversion of the believer. Better language would focus on the relation of the church to the state, which often indicates the ability of the church to be an independent actor. Thus, in this chapter, I use the language "dissenting" or "nonconforming" Protestant.

3. Ibid., 246, 247.

4. Ibid., 249; emphasis in the original.

5. Ibid., 247–254.

6. Ibid., 245.

7. Woodberry notes that, ironically, racism was worse among more educated missionaries, who had absorbed ideas about "scientific racism." Still, "missionaries were typically far less racist than other colonial groups." Ibid., 255n28.

8. Ibid., 254, 255.

9. Ibid., 255.

10. María Rosa Menocal, *The Ornament of the World: How Muslims, Jews, and Christians Created a Culture of Tolerance in Medieval Spain* (New York: Back Bay, 2002). While claims of a golden age of toleration may be overstated, Jews, and even certain minority Christian groups, were treated with greater freedom and dignity in medieval Spain, especially during the tenth and eleventh centuries, than in most other places in Europe.

PART II

Early American Experiences of Protestant Liberty

The simplistic view that North America was originally settled by religious refugees to escape religious persecution and create a haven for spiritual freedom dissolves under the reality of historical analysis. America was settled by a variety of people with a variety of motives, including commercial and business interests, nationalistic impulses, as well as religious goals. But even those who were seeking to escape religious persecution and found a country to freely practice their religion often viewed religious freedom as the right to practice the *true* religion. This was largely the view of the founders of New England—the Pilgrims and Puritans who left the intolerance of old England for what they hoped would be a more enlightened New England.

"Enlightened" in this context meant, of course, an acceptance of the "correct," Puritan, understanding of the church, its teachings, and its ordinances. Those foolish enough to pursue the radical terrain of Quakerism, or even the biblicist pathway of the Baptists, would be chastised by civil authorities seeking to protect the public peace. There were very few among the early settlers of English-speaking North America that believed in a meaningful view of religious toleration, much less religious freedom, for those who were viewed as heretics or schismatics. Among these few were men such as Roger Williams, who soon came to found Rhode Island, the first government of the West to truly separate the church from the state.

A few decades after Rhode Island was founded, William Penn established Pennsylvania on principles about as equally liberal and tolerant toward religious differences as those in Rhode Island. For a number of reasons, Pennsylvania soon became a commercial and cultural hub for the colonies. It was in a favored geographical location—connecting the northern and southern colonies—possessed a relatively moderate climate, and had a principled commitment to religious diversity and pluralism from its inception due to its founders' beliefs. This caused the colony to become a popular destination for all kinds of religious minorities from Europe, including Quakers, Huguenots, Anabaptists, English Baptists, Moravians, a variety of other Protestants, and even some Jews and Catholics.

Still, the success of Pennsylvania, while creating a model for the early American nation, was very much a minority experience in a nation that mostly had state-supported churches. The New England region generally established Congregational churches; and in the southern colonies, such as Virginia, the Carolinas, and Georgia, an Anglican establishment existed. How was it that America moved in about a half century from a place where the large majority supported established churches to a circumstance where state establishments were a vanishing breed?

The chapters in this section tackle this important question, beginning with how separation became "a populist religious movement," which cannot be pegged to a few Enlightenment elites. Elements of this change include the theological inconsistencies of the Puritan Halfway Covenant, in which second-tier church members could baptize their children but not participate in church governance, and the growing influence of conversionary Christianity in the First Great Awakening of the 1740s, which helped to swell the ranks of disestablishment churches, such as the Baptists. Other influences involved the growth of liberalism in New England Calvinism after the Revolution and the desire of conservative groups to not pay to support increasingly unorthodox ideas.

The First Amendment was drafted in the middle of this period, but it did not instantly change the relations of church and state around the country. As drafted, the amendment forbade Congress from establishing religion and thus allowed the states to do so if they wished. But because the impulse for separation was a populist one by this time, most states had already done so or followed suit shortly afterwards. The question of "liberty" thought was a contested one, as the issues of slavery and federalism haunted the Constitution for decades. Southerners believed that the Constitution protected their liberty in keeping blacks enslaved, while many Northerners believed that the practice was inconsistent with the Constitution's underlying principles. "What Kind of Liberty?" explores this tension and examines how it was only resolved in the Civil War. But there are those today who desire to resurrect this old argument of localism versus federalism as they seek to allow states to implement and promote local religious practices and traditions.

"After the Civil War" looks at how federal civil rights eventually came to be applied to the states. This was a longer and more tortured process than most people imagine. The rise of Jim Crow segregation in the South with commercial interests from the North kept society in the chains of inequality and segregation for nearly a century after the conclusion of the Civil War. During this same period, religious freedom also languished as a national right. It was only in the 1920s and 1930s that the Supreme Court began selectively applying the Bill of Rights to the states. One important lesson from this history is that rights are connected, and the refusal to grant basic rights of equality and civil justice will usually impinge on other rights, including religious freedom.

Finally, the section concludes with an examination of the claims made about this earlier period of United States (US) history by David Barton, a revisionist historian of the religious Right. While Barton's history is a later twentieth-century phenomenon, the periods he deals with lie in these earlier times, and I have chosen to place my critique of his analysis here. Since I wrote the "WallBuilders v. MythBuilders" piece on Barton in the mid-1990s, other historians have become aware of his sloppy and misleading practices that border on, if not cross over into, deception. Barton is right to bring to light the religious language and the culture of the founders that is often overlooked by the more secularly slanted media and the academy. But he so often ignores the larger context of historical quotes, and at times uses quotes with uncertain and even faulty provenance, that what good he might accomplish is undermined by the unreliability of the package he creates.

His practices in this regard came to national prominence in 2012, when Barton wrote a book about Thomas Jefferson, in which he attempted to cast Jefferson as an evangelical Christian. Scholars pointed out, however, that the book was riddled with errors and misstatements. The errors were so serious that the publisher of the book, the Christian press Thomas Nelson, withdrew it from the market.[1] The book was critiqued and criticized by a number of conservative Christian scholars as misleading and inaccurate. But both Barton and his book, which was almost immediately reprinted by a conservative publisher, continue to enjoy widespread circulation and influence in certain evangelical circles.[2]

It should be a concern to all Christians when evangelicals resort to "alternative facts" in order to maintain historical support for their political agendas. Those committed to the One who is the Truth should care a great deal about how the truth of this world is handled, or we will show ourselves as poor stewards for the world to come.

---

1. Elise Hu, "Publisher Pulls Controversial Thomas Jefferson Book, Citing Loss of Confidence," NPR, August 9, 2012, http://www.npr.org/sections/thetwo-way/2012/08/09/158510648/publisher-pulls-controversial-thomas-jefferson-book-citing-loss-of-confidence.

2. See Thomas Kidd, "The David Barton Controversy," World, August 25, 2012, https://world.wng.org/2012/08/the_david_barton_controversy; Kyle Mantyla, "David Barton on Trump's Cabinet Picks and Agenda: 'I'm Loving What I'm Seeing,' " Right Wing Watch, December 9, 2016, http://www.rightwingwatch.org/post/david-barton-on-trumps-cabinet-picks-and-agenda-im-loving-what-im-seeing/.

Chapter 6

A Populist Religious Movement—
How Did Church and State Separate in America?

S tories of religious disestablishment in America usually revolve around discussion of the origins and meaning of the establishment clause of the Federal Constitution. But the story of disestablishment of state churches, at least in the early Republic, was much more a state-centered event. This is true for the simple fact that the First Amendment did not originally apply to state governments. As law professor Carl Esbeck recently noted, "The American disestablishment occurred over a fifty to sixty year period, from 1774 to the early 1830s" and was "entirely a state-law affair," completely independent of the adoption of the Bill of Rights.[1]

Thus, the blame or the credit for disestablishment cannot be placed on the small, elite group of largely Enlightenment thinkers gathered in Philadelphia to draft a new national constitution. Rather, disestablishment was a populist movement, in which religious rather than Enlightenment influences were predominant. As Esbeck puts it, "At the state level, where the work of disestablishment did take place, the vast number of those pushing for it were not doing so out of rationalism or secularism. Rather, they were religious people who sought disestablishment for (as they saw it) biblical reasons."[2] Once one turns, in an attempt to account for widespread state disestablishment, from the elites to the grassroots, religious thought becomes central.

There were four basic steps in the acceptance of the disestablishment ideal

---

This chapter originally appeared in *Liberty*, March/April 2006.

in the world of American religious thought. First, in the New England Puritan community, the heart of establishment in America, there was a bitter controversy over something called the Halfway Covenant, a standard of church membership, and this led to two main factions that, for different reasons, both became influential for disestablishment. Second, dissenting religions supported disestablishment for both theological and practical reasons, and these religions rapidly grew in size and influence because of their resonance with the ascendant ideologies of democracy and republicanism during and after the Revolution. Third, after the Revolution, New England was affected by the Calvinist struggle with liberalism, and this forced a rethinking of establishment in its former stronghold. Finally, the ascendant idea of disestablishment was reinforced by the revivalism of the Second Great Awakening.

1. Jonathan Edwards, the Halfway Covenant, and the shaking of the Puritan way

The Great Awakening sowed seeds of disestablishment that were not fully reaped until the Second Great Awakening. These seeds were not always intentionally sown. A prime example of this is Jonathan Edwards and his rejection of the Halfway Covenant. The Halfway Covenant was an innovation created to keep alive New England's covenant with God in the face of growing numbers of marginally religious citizens. After the first generation or so of Puritans, it became apparent that not all in the community were capable of being faithful to the covenant of grace promoted by the church. This posed a civic problem, as the Puritan ideal was that society and the church would basically be coextensive, making both part of a united covenant with God.

A disturbingly large population began to emerge who could not make the needed testimony of conversion. Their children would thus be ineligible for baptism and remain outside of the church and outside of the covenant. This meant that the community of believers and larger society would gradually drift farther apart. The solution was the Halfway Covenant. This covenant created two tiers of church membership. It allowed socially upright, but not regenerate, citizens to attend church and allowed their children to be baptized and obtain church membership. Thus, the community at large was linked together and was able to retain its covenant relationship with God.

The leaders and participants in the Great Awakening of the 1740s challenged some of the fundamental assumptions of the Halfway Covenant. Spiritual conversion was posited as a prerequisite for *any* covenant with God. The church was viewed as consisting of *only* those who were renewed. Large numbers of unconverted church members, it was argued, caused spiritual lethargy and compromise within the church. These new emphases caused the "new lights" of the Awakening to challenge the legitimacy of the Halfway Covenant.

The most prominent figure to openly challenge the Halfway Covenant was

Jonathan Edwards. He moved the covenant from being a nexus between person, church, and society to being one that simply connected the converted individual and the church. Those who "were not in his sense visible saints were not saints at all." He rejected the idea of "halfway" church members, who could have the privilege of either Communion or the baptism of their children. Edwards's covenant theology struck directly at the core of the Puritan covenant of the larger community. Edwards's early preaching had focused on God's covenant with New England. But later in his life he questioned whether any covenant existed outside God's covenant of grace with His church.[3]

It would be a mistake to overstate Edwards's influence in his own time. He was fired from his church for preaching against the Halfway Covenant. And the traditional standing order, with its interconnection between church and state, remained largely in place. But his dismissal freed up time for him to write his major theological treatises, which did have an ongoing influence. Edwards's speaking and writing contributed to the division of the New England religious community into at least three factions in regard to the covenant.

The largest group continued to favor the traditional standing order that linked church and state under a single covenant. But this paradigm began to be challenged by a small but energetic and growing group of Separatist and Baptist radicals who followed Edwards's points to what they considered their logical conclusions: that no church or churches should be established. The final group was where Edwards himself stood, rejecting the Halfway Covenant, but accepting a continued role for the state in promoting the church's interest. This last group shrank over time as it became clear that if Edwards's logic was right, then so were the full Separatists, and if he was incorrect, then the standing order was correct.

Edwards stood on dwindling middle ground. But the two groups he helped solidify would both contribute, in their own ways, to disestablishment. We take up the fate of the first group, the established standing order, below. But first we will look at the new and growing group of dissenting religions that shared Edwards's conclusions regarding the covenant and took these conclusions to their logical, or at least radical, disestablishment conclusions.

2. Religions of equality: The success of populist religion

The churches most favorable to disestablishment, the Baptists and Methodists, were also those with the greatest democratic or populist spirit. Their polity was not necessarily democratic—most of the Methodist groups had a hierarchical structure—but the message was one of the equality of believers, individual responsibility, and direct biblical authority. These latter points, the authority of the Bible and the individual believer's responsibility to interpret it for himself or herself, were the most revolutionary in civic terms. If each person had a responsibility to read and interpret the Bible personally, then no one else could do that for him or her. Thus, the government had no role in legislating religious matters, because this immediately undercut the role and authority of the priesthood of all believers.[4]

This was, at least in part, the theoretical, theological impulse to disestablishment harbored by these groups. The practical impulse was likely even greater. These groups, to a certain extent prior to the Revolution, were community outsiders, and the laws of establishment constantly restricted and hemmed them in—or in some measure forced them to go through religious tax exemption procedures that were burdensome and often unfairly applied.

But because the core of these dissenting groups found a resonance in the burgeoning democratic and republican impulses in the larger community, these groups flourished. Between 1770 and 1790, Methodists grew from about 20 churches to a little more than 700, a growth multiple of more than 35. The Baptists went from around 150 to 850, a more modest but still impressive multiple of nearly 6. By contrast, the Presbyterians had a much slower rate of growth, going from 500 to 725, or a growth of less than 50 percent. The Congregationalists went from 625 to 750, about a 20 percent growth rate. The Anglican/Episcopal churches actually lost ground, dropping from about 350 to 170, a decline of 50 percent, although this can be attributed in good part to these churches' connections with the losing side of the war.[5]

By 1790, the populist groups, who for both theological and practical reasons supported disestablishment, had grown to the equivalent size of the established churches. But they had reached that point with tremendous momentum, and that momentum continued into the early to mid-nineteenth century. By 1860, the populist churches—one can no longer call them dissenters, as that implies the existence of a long-vanished center—outnumbered the former establishment churches by three to one.

So, in good part, the theological shift was not so much the change of theology within existing churches but the rapid growth of what had been theologically eccentric churches. Dissenting theology had become mainstream because it had become more successful at marketing itself than the former mainstream community. Christian preachers such as Elias Smith and Alexander Campbell and the Methodist "Crazy" Lorenzo Dow bound up individual revival religion with a radical Jeffersonian political message of the rights of the people. They railed at priestcraft and political tyranny in consecutive breaths.

A citizenry effulgent with a republican sense, having just freed itself from political tyranny, was most open to churches that communicated spiritual things in these same terms. Thus, these populist churches grew explosively, and with them, the commitment to disestablishment spread across the country. Much is often made of the practical impulse to disestablishment of these minority religions. Nobody likes to be persecuted, and those experiencing it often develop a theory of minority rights. But that the impulse was also theological and principled is supported by the fact that these churches retained their disestablishment ideals long after they had become the majority.

3. Puritanism and liberalism: Establishing unorthodoxy

The populist religions swept the new country in the early 1800s, leaving the former establishment religions as a majority only in southern New England. Connecticut and Massachusetts retained their establishments for some decades after the other states had given up theirs. Connecticut did not disestablish until 1818, and Massachusetts hung on until 1833. But the Congregationalists were still dominant in southern New England, even in 1850, and thus the disestablishment of New England cannot be fully explained by the rise of populist religions.

What else led to the demise of the standing order in New England? The rest of the story lies in the sequel to the establishment's rejection of Edwards's critique of the Halfway Covenant. The standing order had continued the two standards of church affiliation. There were the full "communicants" and the socially upright but unregenerate Halfway Covenanters, or mere "members." This latter group grew in size and influence over time. But by their very nature, the members were concerned less with theological orthodoxy than the communicants.

It has been noted that from the early to mid-1800s the theology of the New England clergy became more liberal and "feminized"—more focused on sentiment and feeling than on propositions and systems of truth. This has been explained, at least in part, by the effects of clerical disestablishment. Disestablishment caused clergy (or so the theory goes) to become more responsive and attuned to their congregants, who were largely women. Thus, the liberalization and feminization of New England theology was accomplished.[6]

This story can perhaps be better told with the same facts but with the causes and effects reversed. It is apparent that the feminization and liberalization of influential portions of the New England clergy were well under way between 1820 and 1830. Yet disestablishment did not occur in Massachusetts, where much of this liberalization was centered, until 1833. The so-called cause of liberal theology actually occurred well after that liberalization was under way.

It makes more sense that liberalization, rather than being an effect of disestablishment, was in fact one of its causes. A better explanation for the growth of the liberal, feminized theology is the ultimate effects of the dual church membership scheme, the Halfway Covenant, on the standing order. As the "members" grew in number and influence, they caused the clergy to develop a theology that was softer and more acceptable to "unregenerate" ears. If leaders in government and commerce had to be church members to retain their standing in the community, it was not long before they shaped those churches according to their own interests and tastes. Soon there was an outbreak of "diluted" theologies, including Unitarianism, Universalism, and basic biblical liberalism.[7]

While never having a numerical advantage statewide, these unorthodox groups did gain the upper hand in some important locales, including Boston. As the New England establishment was never a centralized, statewide establishment, but was based on parish level preference, the orthodox could only watch in dismay and chagrin as the standing order system was used to turn over certain tax-built churches to Unitarian and Universalist groups. As unorthodoxy became established, some orthodox Congregationalists suddenly found themselves allied with their old dissenter foes in opposing establishment.

Establishment in New England became a victim of the Halfway Covenant, but not before that covenant had itself victimized the theology of the Congregational churches. The attempt to bring the world nearer to the church through the Halfway Covenant had in actuality brought the church nearer the world and its philosophies, much as Jonathan Edwards had predicted.

4. Conclusion: The Second Great Awakening seals disestablishment

The spread of disestablishment as outlined above was sealed and affirmed by the nation's experiences during the Second Great Awakening of the early to mid-nineteenth century. This religious revival was based on voluntary gatherings at which the individual and his or her experience was made the norm, subject only to the authority of the Bible as understood by the laity. The movement's theology and experience reinforced the existing views that the state should not impose or support religious systems or views. It exalted the notion that religious morality could best be promoted through spiritual revival and influence, rather than through legal coercion.

Events in the city of Rochester, New York, related to Charles Finney's revivals illustrated this point in microcosm.[8] In the mid to late 1820s, the city experienced a growth in commerce and industry. This created the need for a number of laborers too numerous to live with employers' families, as had previously been the practice. This caused the family-based moral restraints to loosen. The city fathers became concerned with the increasing drunkenness, violence, and dissipation found within the city. They had tried a number of legal measures, including temperance laws and Sunday laws, to stiffen the moral fibers of the community. These efforts essentially failed.

Then one of the city fathers, merchant and land owner Josiah Bissell, invited Charles Finney to come to Rochester in the autumn of 1830 for a series of revival meetings. The meetings were attended by a wide range of citizens, including large numbers of Bissell's peers from the wealthy merchant and manufacturing classes. The results were dramatic. A new informal but highly effective moral influence was created in the town. This was not the direct control of law but of the internal restraint of an awakened morality and the positive peer pressure of moral coworkers and employers. Those who did not fit in with the new moral environment moved on to other places.

The moral change was felt not just in Rochester but throughout other areas affected by the revival. As one historian succinctly put it, "In 1825 a northern businessman dominated his wife and children, worked irregular hours, consumed enormous amounts of alcohol, and seldom voted or went to church. Ten years later the same man went to church twice a week, treated his family with gentleness and love, drank nothing but water, worked steady hours and forced his employees to do the same. . . . That transformation bore the stamp of evangelical Protestantism."[9] This kind of vital and spiritual transformation became associated with the voluntary and private efforts of churches and religious leaders unconnected with legal measures or tax support.

This experience of the power of the voluntary church in turn strongly affirmed the theological shifts that had already moved the country to disestablishment. With the confirming experiences of the Second Great Awakening, disestablishment became the American way just as surely and as fully as establishment had been the Puritan way.

1. Carl H. Esbeck, "Dissent and Disestablishment: The Church-State Settlement in the Early American Republic," *Brigham Young University Law Review* 2004, no. 4 (2004): 1590.

2. Ibid.

3. A description of Edwards and the Halfway Covenant conflict can be found in Mark A. Noll, *America's God: From Jonathan Edwards to Abraham Lincoln* (New York: Oxford University Press, 2000), 37–48.

4. As Nathan Hatch put it, "The rise of evangelical Christianity in the early republic is, in some measure, a story of the success of the common people in shaping the culture after their own priorities rather than the priorities outlined by gentlemen such as the framers of the Constitution." Nathan O. Hatch, *The Democratization of American Christianity* (New Haven, CT: Yale University Press, 1989), 9.

5. These and the following figures are taken from Noll, *America's God*, 166, table 9.3.

6. Ann Douglas, *The Feminization of American Culture* (New York: Noonday Press, 1977), 22–28.

7. Christopher Grasso, "The Fall of the Massachusetts Standing Order and the Rise of the Boston Brahmins," *Reviews in American History* 27, no. 4 (December 1999): 541–547.

8. Paul E. Johnson, *A Shopkeeper's Millennium: Society and Revivals in Rochester, New York, 1815–1837* (New York: Hill and Wang, 1978), 3–14, 45, 58–60, 75–88, 116–128.

9. Ibid., 8.

Chapter 7

What Kind of Liberty?
The Civil War American Freedoms

I t was the "momentous question" that "awakened" and terrified Thomas Jefferson, like a "fire bell in the night." Jefferson considered it the "knell of the Union."[1] The "question" at issue was ostensibly that of slavery. Jefferson wrote about his nocturnal fright in 1820 and related it to the conflict around the Tallmadge Amendment, which sought to outlaw slavery in Missouri, and the subsequent Missouri Compromise, which averted, or at least postponed, a civil war. But Jefferson of all people knew that the slavery dispute was only the symptom of the real legal question, that of federalism—the proper role the federal government should play in exercising powers and protecting rights in the states.

The Constitution contained a deep flaw—a flaw that Jefferson, or at least his close allies, had intentionally placed in the founding document. The flaw was the deliberately ambiguous nature of federalism, the relation of federal to state governments and the individual, contained in the Constitution. The ambiguity had been placed there precisely to avoid dealing with the issue of slavery at the founding—thereby passing the buck on this deeply divisive issue to the next generation. Given Jefferson's central role in the formation and leadership of the early Republic, it is conceivable that his "fire bell in the night" was a particularly acute attack of conscience at leaving this great moral issue unresolved.

But we cannot be too hard on Jefferson. Most of his colleagues at the founding

This chapter originally appeared in *Liberty*, March/April 2006.

also believed that a constitution with a clear position on the question of federalism could not have gained passage. The ambiguity of the Constitution on this topic allowed both sides to read in their own views of federalism, creating a constitution whose type of federalism—and hence relation to slavery and other fundamental civil rights, including religious freedom—lay in the eye of the beholder.

These competing visions of the Constitution and the nation—whether it was a sovereign nation of states or a confederacy of sovereign states—evolved over time, becoming most sharply contrasted between North and South. The contrast between these competing views of federalism and liberty grew starker and starker until the friction flared into the conflict of the Civil War. While the powder and bullets of that great conflict are a distant national memory, the same national and legal issues that sparked and stoked that controversy are with us today in current arguments over original intent, strict construction, states' rights, and the battle for civil rights. A walk over the terrain of this historic controversy can shed light on today's debates.

1. Colonial foreshadowings: Religious liberty and property rights

Rather than twins separated at birth, the early American colonies were more like distant cousins thrown together by the accident of geography and ties to a common king who became a common enemy. Most of the colonies from Maryland northward had been founded primarily, at least ostensibly, by a desire to find havens of religious freedom. While that desire was often imperfectly expressed, especially in the governments of Puritan New England, religion was a core motivator for these northern colonies. Virginia and southward, the settlements had been primarily commercial enterprises—hopeful seedbeds of a market revolution.

Jamestown and the Massachusetts Bay Colony are perhaps the two archetypes that illustrate this divide: the former settled by fortune seekers representing commercial speculators, and the latter peopled by Puritans fleeing the turbulent English Reformation. Certainly, the middle and northern colonies had commercial concerns and interests, and the southern colonies had their share of religious devotees and devotions. But it is remarkable how the primary impulse and motivations of the colonies' founders—liberty in the North and commerce in the South—continued to dominate subsequent colonists' views of the role of government.

Outside the South, liberty was understood primarily in terms of personal liberties and the systems that sustained those liberties. Religious liberty was considered the first liberty, but its existence was defended and maintained by other liberties: those of the press, speech, trial by jury, and the ballot, at least for propertied white men. Property was protected as well, but as one right among a system of rights.

In the South, by contrast, liberty was largely identified with pursuing one's own self-interest. Independence was the ability of the local majority to assert its interests, which were usually commercial. Government's first role was to protect the economic interests of society. By the time of the Revolutionary War, this had come to especially mean protecting the institution of slavery, upon which the agrarian South's economy and social stability were largely dependent. In the South, "liberty," ironically, came to mean the freedom to keep other humans in bondage.

2. The Constitutional Convention: Enshrining ambiguity

Thus it was that two contrasting and even contradictory views of liberty and the role of government were well entrenched when it came time to frame the new Republic. This division over the ends of government led to a division over the means of government—the proper role and powers of a federal government. These issues extended beyond the question of slavery and encompassed ranges of possible government actions, from its role in regulating commerce to building public works, such as roads and canals, and how it should define itself in relation to its citizens.

Southern anti-federalists viewed a central state as "extremely pernicious, impolitic, and dangerous because it resulted from . . . an enormous transfer of power from the states to the central government." Such a consolidated, central power would threaten the South's interests in tariff-free trade, equitable taxation, and, most important of all, slavery. Prominent southern leaders, including Patrick Henry and George Mason, believed that the proposed Constitution would allow the North to abolish slavery.[2]

In the end, though the ratification contest was close and severe in some places, the southern federalists carried the day. Men such as James Madison and Charles Pinckney assured their fellow southerners that the Constitution did not destroy state power or rights. They noted that the federal government was one of express and limited powers. Any power not expressly delegated to it was reserved to the states. As for abolishing slavery, Madison asserted, "There is no power to warrant it in the [Constitution]. If there be, I know it not."[3]

But if the South took refuge in ambiguity, so did the North. The Constitution was not entirely silent on the question of slavery. It did allow the slave trade to be abolished after twenty years. Many in the North felt that the implication was that slavery could be abolished then as well. There were also clauses that hinted at broader federal powers, including the ability to regulate commerce and the right to legislate to protect the general welfare.

In the end, there was enough affirmative language to give both views of federalism respectability, enough ambiguity to give both sides hope, and sufficient silence to defeat the anti-federalist critics of both North and South. Subsequent events would only deepen the commitments of both sides to their versions of federalism and the Constitution.

3. Federalism, the courts, and liberty: 1790s to the 1820s

In the federal courts, those favoring a strong federal union began to gain a clear advantage over the states' rights advocates. Thus, while the practice of federalism remained largely inconclusive, the theory began to decisively favor the advocates of a strong central union.

The states' rights advocates did not lack for articulate and prominent champions. Both James Madison and Thomas Jefferson fired some of the opening salvos on the states' behalf in the federalism struggle. The occasion was the passage in 1798 of the constitutionally doubtful Alien and Sedition Acts. In response, Madison drafted for Virginia a statement declaring the acts unconstitutional and calling for their repeal. Jefferson went a step further and on behalf of Kentucky drafted a statement that said a state could nullify a federal act that unconstitutionally oppressed its citizens.

It appeared that the states' rightists were able to hold the strong federalists to at least a stalemate in Congress during this period. But the federalists were gaining a decisive upper hand in the federal courts. Beginning in 1803 with *Marbury v. Madison*, Chief Justice John Marshall placed the federal judiciary in a position to authoritatively define the shape and role of both the Constitution and federalism. Marshall played his hand cautiously for a few years. But soon he issued a series of rulings that placed the federal system in a clearly superior position to that of the states.

Implementing Marshall's view that the Constitution issued from the people, rather than from a confederation of sovereign states, the court declared that it could overrule the decision of a state supreme court on matters of federal law and that it could declare both federal and state legislative acts unconstitutional. And perhaps most important, it authorized a broad construction of federal power under the "necessary and proper" clause. This last power was articulated in *McCulloch v. Maryland* in 1819, the same year that slavery reemerged on the national platform with the conflict over the Tallmadge Amendment and a year before the Missouri Compromise.

So by 1820, it was apparent to the most fervent state rightist that the Supreme Court had tilted the legal balance of federalism strongly toward the Union. It was also clear that Congress was taking a renewed interest in the topic of slavery and was willing to exercise its powers to at least limit and contain the institution. This set the stage for a growing call to Congress by a number of groups, including abolitionists and women's rights advocates, to exercise its growing powers in the arena of citizenship and civil rights. It was a call that would culminate in the Civil War and ultimately in the redefinition of federalism in relation to national citizenship.

4. Citizenship, slavery, and sex: 1830s to 1850s

The growing gap between the legal theory and the practice of federalism was eased somewhat by the success of Andrew Jackson, a southern populist. Jackson did not oppose slavery, but he did support a strong union. After defeating John Quincy

Adams in the election of 1828, Jackson heartened his southern supporters by immediately questioning the legitimacy of the second federal bank. This institution had come to be viewed by many as a symbol of federal overreach—"the original sin against the Constitution."[4]

But southerners were less enthused by Jackson's perceived ambivalence toward the protective tariff. While it was lowered, the tariff continued under his watch. The tariff ignited the South Carolina nullification crisis of 1832, when that state's legislature purported to nullify the federal tariff. Jackson's reaction was prompt and decisive. He publicly declared nullification as treason and branded the nullifiers as traitors. He put the US Army on alert and passed the Force Bill, giving congressional support for the use of force against nullification.

Cooler heads eventually prevailed; a tariff compromise was reached before swords were drawn. But the message had been sent—by a southerner, no less—that the Union would not be trifled with, and that such behavior would be met with force. A national context was being created in which the national government was an independent and sovereign entity whose prerogatives must be taken seriously by the states.[5]

It was in this situation that questions of citizenship became increasingly agitated. The initial catalyst was the widespread social reform movement that arose out of the Second Great Awakening of the 1830s. This outpouring of spiritual commitment has been credited with providing energy for a wide range of reform movements, with the most prominent at the time being that of abolition. The beginnings of the abolitionist movement are associated with the commencement of publication in 1831 of the *Liberator*, William Lloyd Garrison's antislavery paper. By the mid-1830s, slavery was under an unprecedented assault by speech, pen, and petition. The South struck back with almost equal fury: restricting freedom of speech and the press; refusing abolitionist literature in the southern mail system; passing a gag rule forbidding Congress to consider abolitionist petitions; and stirring up mobs to attack abolitionists in the North and the South.

But these southern tactics could not quell the ferment of talk of rights and citizenship. Arguments about blacks being human and deserving natural and constitutional rights inevitably raised these same questions for others denied political and property rights, with the largest and most obvious group being women. The Second Great Awakening had seen women play leadership roles. Some of these women also worked in abolitionist circles and imbibed the ideas of personhood in relation to natural and constitutional rights.

At the first major women's rights conventions, in Seneca Falls, New York, in 1848 and in Worcester, Massachusetts, in 1850, the speakers presented relatively mature and well-formed arguments regarding their natural rights as persons and their constitutional rights as citizens. Their arguments had a coherence and a depth that revealed a growing public sense of what the rights of national citizenship should be, even if the laws did not reflect this standard. This was not a sort of identity politics, a reflection of southern "liberty" concerns, in which interest groups advocated for their narrow interests. Rather, the language of personhood, citizenship, and natural and constitutional rights reflected support for a system of liberty that would benefit those beyond the immediate petitioners.[6]

Thus it was that many of those involved in abolition were also involved in the movement for women's rights, as well as in movements for religious freedom. The arguments for these causes often began with notions of personhood and natural rights. But they usually became framed in terms of citizenship and the Constitution, as these were the concrete legal terms and tools that would or could allow Congress to act on the petitioner's concerns.

While these movements did not talk much about federalism, their petitions and manner of protest clearly indicated that they viewed the problems and the solution as lying with the federal government. Clearly, the South would not throw off the yoke of slavery spontaneously. Neither would each state of its own accord enlarge and protect the prerogatives of national citizenship. The solution to these problems lay with Congress.

Thus the legal question of federalism, so often concerned with the abstract balancing of state and federal rights, became profoundly personalized. In a growing number of minds, it asked whether one was first and primarily a citizen of the state or of the nation. The abolitionists, women's rights activists, and other rights' advocates, insisted that the ties that bound the Union together were, at their base, those of personal liberty and human equality. They argued that the Constitution was not a document standing alone but, rather, that it implemented the promises of the Declaration of Independence and that the Constitution should be interpreted in the spirit of that earlier organic document. They argued, with increasing force and effectiveness, that the national government had an obligation to defend these foundational American rights and commitments to its citizens against all intruders, including the states.

Southerners profoundly disagreed with these arguments. The resulting impasse was resolved only in part by the Civil War.

Conclusion

The Civil War was a decisive event in relation to slavery. And the postwar amendments purported to deal with the broader question of national citizenship. But it would be another generation or more before the federal courts came to terms with these issues in a series of decisions that "incorporated" federal civil rights against the states in the 1920s and 1930s. This little narrative reveals that the war was not about slavery alone, nor about states' rights alone, but about the role of federalism in relation to national citizenship. Seen against this larger backdrop, incorporation was about legally finishing the federalism argument that had been practically decided by the Civil War.

Racial slavery in the US is over and gone. But arguments over federalism, strict construction, and the power of the federal government to define and protect the civil rights and religious liberties of its citizens is as current as today's news headlines. Our cultural divide is no longer one of North and South but of red states (Republican) and blue states (Democrat) and the question of whose moral values will triumph. In this heated contest, will we remember that the federalism the Civil War vindicated was primarily about protecting the liberties of national citizenship, rather than protecting the cultural, property, or religious hegemonies of local majorities? Only time, and the newly configured Supreme Court, will tell us.

---

1. Thomas Jefferson to John Holmes, Monticello, April 22, 1820, *Thomas Jefferson Papers, 1606–1827*, Manuscripts Division, Library of Congress, accessed April 9, 2017, https://www.loc.gov/resource/mtj1.051_1238_1239/?sp=1.

2. William J. Cooper Jr., *Liberty and Slavery: Southern Politics to 1860* (Columbia, SC: University of South Carolina Press, 1983), 15.

3. Ibid., 63.

4. John Tyler, quoted in William J. Cooper Jr., *The South and the Politics of Slavery, 1828–1856* (Baton Rouge, LA: Louisiana State University Press, 1992), 50.

5. Charles Sellers, *The Market Revolution: Jacksonian America, 1815–1846* (New York: Oxford University Press, 1991), 305, 306.

6. Nancy Isenberg, *Sex and Citizenship in Antebellum America* (Chapel Hill, NC: University of North Carolina Press, 1998), 5, 6.

Chapter 8

After the Civil War: Bringing Freedom to the States

Most people know that the First Amendment of the US Constitution has something to do with protecting the freedom of religion and of speech. But most people do not know that the First Amendment does not directly protect citizens from the governments closest to them—state and local governments. The First Amendment begins, "Congress shall make no law . . ." The protections of the First Amendment, and most of the Bill of Rights, applied only against the federal government.

Thus in 1800, nearly ten years after the Bill of Rights was enacted, a state government could, and some did, establish a religion, violate liberty of conscience, and prohibit free speech—and the federal courts could do nothing about it. There were protections for civil liberties in the state constitutions, but these differed in strength from state to state and were usually interpreted in favor of local majorities. State judges were often elected and did not have the life tenure that protected federal judges from the vagaries and pressures of popular opinion.

Today some people argue that we should return to the intent of the founders, especially in regard to religious liberty. They believe that some of the Bill of Rights, especially the establishment clause, which protects the separation of church and state, should never have been applied to the states. Indeed, they believe, as recently argued by Clarence Thomas, a sitting Supreme Court justice, that the clause was meant to protect the ability of states to establish and promote religion.

This chapter is from a previously unpublished blog posting.

Was this really the founders' intent? How did the First Amendment come to apply to the states? These questions are crucial in understanding current debates over religious freedom and the separation of church and state. There are two answers to these questions. One is what the framers of the Constitution intended to happen. The second is what actually happened.

As to the framers' intent, the framers in the 1790s had a strong regard for federalism and states' rights, and they intended to limit the powers of the federal government to federal matters. Thus the Bill of Rights applied only to the federal government out of a desire to limit the federal government's reach. But—and this is very important—the original founders did not limit the Bill of Rights to the federal government in order to allow or enable state governments to violate civil liberties. The original framers desired state governments to protect civil liberties, and for most of them, this included separating the church from the state.

This desire is shown not only by the declarations of leading statesmen, such as Jefferson and Madison, but also by what the framers did when they returned to their states. By the decade after the ratification of the Constitution, all but three states had passed and implemented clauses analogous to the establishment clause.

But one cannot stop in the 1790s when examining the intent of the founders. One must advance nearly seventy-five years and examine the intent of the framers of the Civil War amendments—most importantly, the Fourteenth Amendment. The intent of these framers is an integral part of the meaning of the Constitution. And the intent of the drafters and supporters of the Fourteenth Amendment is without ambiguity on this crucial point—the Fourteenth Amendment was intended to apply the federal Bill of Rights to the state governments.

Such men as Congressman John Bingham, who drafted the amendment; Senator Jacob Howard, a prominent Senate sponsor; and Congressman James Garfield, a future president—all made prominent speeches in which they declared that one of the purposes of the privileges or immunities clause of the Fourteenth Amendment was to apply the Bill of Rights to the states. As Senator Howard put it, "To these privileges and immunities, whatever they may be—for they are not and cannot be fully defined in their entire extent and precise nature—to these should be added the personal rights guarantied and secured by the first eight amendments of the Constitution; such as the freedom of speech and of the press."[1]

But what actually happened? As is often the case, things did not go according to plan. After the failure of Radical Reconstruction in the decade after the Civil War, northern and southern business interests united to pursue common commercial goals. They abandoned, and often reversed, the civil and social gains of the freed blacks, as northern capitalists sought alliances with southern financial and commercial elites. Racism became the cost of doing business in the South—a price all too many northerners were willing to pay.

The Supreme Court itself, abandoning its role as guardian of individual liberties, gave its stamp of approval to this profane mixture of commerce and oppression. In the *Slaughterhouse Cases*, the court interpreted the privileges or immunities clause into nothingness and refused to apply the Bill of Rights to the states. By this time, both Congress and the court were most interested in protecting the rights of business and commercial interests. The civil rights of all Americans, but especially black Americans, languished for nearly fifty years.

Then the First and Second World Wars came along and provided object lessons about the threat of tyranny and the importance of freedom. This prompted the court to revisit the question of the Bill of Rights and the states. With the vivid pictures of European totalitarianism fresh in their minds and with similar forces at work at home, the court decided that it would be wise to apply at least some of the Bill of Rights to the states.

In so doing, the court worked in piecemeal fashion, termed *incorporation*, and relied on due process rather than the privileges or immunities clause. They began with the rights of speech and the press in the mid-1920s; and in the 1940s, they applied both the free exercise and establishment clauses to the states. While the court took a long and slow detour, it finally did implement the Civil War framers' intent to apply the Bill of Rights to the states.

Those who argue that the whole "incorporation" of rights project is judicial activism run amok ignore the intent of the Civil War framers. Those framers intended to protect all the rights of national citizenship from every government—federal, state, and local. Their intent should guide constitutional application as much as the intent of the original founders.

Those who wish, in the name of original intent, to return the guardianship of our civil and religious liberties to the "laboratories" of state majorities must actually ignore original intent. These radical activists—for that is what they are—seek a second American civil war, not of bullets and bombs, but of conservative judicial appointments, enhanced states' rights, and the promotion of strict construction. The goal is nothing less than undoing the liberating results of the first Civil War. These efforts should be opposed and rejected.

---

1. Cong. Globe, 39th Cong., 1st sess., 2765 (1866). Cf. *The Reconstruction Amendments' Debates: The Legislative History and Contemporary Debates in Congress on the 13th, 14th, and 15th Amendments* (Richmond, VA: Virginia Commission on Constitutional Government, 1967), 219.

Chapter 9

WallBuilders v. MythBuilders—
David Barton and the Revising of America's Past

Historical revisionism and the religious Right

With charts, books, graphs, and videos, David Barton is out to remake America. For years, he has been indefatigably crisscrossing the United States, hawking to millions of Americans a simple yet dangerous message, that "separation of church and state is a myth."[1] And unfortunately, people are buying his product.

A careful look at that material, however, shows that "MythBuilders" would describe it more accurately than "WallBuilders,"[2] for the essence of his message rests on eight historical fallacies regarding the Constitution. This chapter examines them all.

1. The myth of the explicit Constitution

In his book *The Myth of Separation*, David Barton repeats the New Right mantra that the phrase "separation of church and state" does not appear in the US Constitution or the Bill of Rights; a fact he uses to try to discredit Supreme Court cases that draw on that metaphor.[3]

Of course, constitutional principles such as the "separation of powers" and "a system of checks and balances" do not appear by name in those documents either; yet all legal scholars would agree that the concepts are part and parcel of the Constitution. In writing that "Congress shall make no law respecting an establishment

This chapter originally appeared in *Liberty*, September/October 1995.

of religion," the founders believed these words contained the idea of separation of church and state. Thomas Jefferson used the "wall of separation" imagery to describe the meaning of the First Amendment religion clauses. He is joined by James Madison, drafter of the Constitution and Bill of Rights, who passed Jefferson's religious-freedom statute in Virginia and whose "Memorial and Remonstrance" explicated the reasons for the wall. Older than the framers but with influence on the nation's ideals of religious freedom, Roger Williams, Baptist preacher and founder of Rhode Island, actually originated the "wall of separation" metaphor.[4]

To claim, as WallBuilders does, that this doctrine is found only in the constitution of the former Soviet Union is like maintaining that baseball originated in Botswana, hot dogs are found in Hungary, and apple pie comes uniquely from Albania.

2. The myth of the hasty metaphor

WallBuilders has written a pamphlet that relegates Thomas Jefferson's views on the First Amendment to legal irrelevancy. The controversy centers on Jefferson's letter of 1802, referenced above, to the Baptists of Danbury, Connecticut, in which he described the First Amendment as "building a wall of separation between Church and State." This metaphor has been referred to over the years by the Supreme Court in its church-state jurisprudence—a use criticized by WallBuilders.

In *The Truth About Thomas Jefferson and the First Amendment*, WallBuilders Press attempts to discredit Jefferson's metaphor by noting his absence from the Constitutional Convention.[5] But ideas are not constrained by geography. Jefferson's absence from the convention doesn't detract from his contributions—through his authorship of both the Declaration of Independence and the Virginia Statute for Religious Freedoms—to the ideas of the Constitution. Madison, who did work on the Constitution and was the initial drafter of the Bill of Rights, had cooperated with Jefferson intimately on the Virginia statute and had ideas on church-state relations nearly identical to Jefferson's.

WallBuilders Press describes the Danbury letter as merely "personal and private" and not "a public policy paper," though Jefferson viewed it as important enough to be reviewed and approved by the US attorney general. Jefferson, in writing, told the attorney general that his Danbury letter condemned an "alliance between church and state" and that it also explained to the Baptists why "I do not proclaim fast and thanksgiving days."[6] These letters are part of Jefferson's public correspondence and certainly express Jefferson's public views on religious matters. To argue otherwise is like saying that Lincoln's Gettysburg Address was for the private consolation of only those in attendance at the burial grounds when he gave it.

Finally, the WallBuilders' pamphlet attempts to marginalize Jefferson's views on religion. It claims that Jefferson's religious views "did not represent the views of the majority of the founders." While Jefferson's deism was somewhat exotic for colonial America, it did not necessarily drive him to unique views on church-state relations. The wall metaphor, as noted above, was coined by Roger Williams, a devout Baptist who organized the government of Rhode Island around the principle of the separation of the civil and ecclesiastical powers. And though Williams had been long dead by the time of the American Revolution, his church-state views were forcefully held by Baptist thought leaders who were contemporaries during the Constitutional Convention. Two notable examples were Baptist ministers Isaac Backus and John Leland, who were involved in the ratification of the Constitution and who conversed with its framers. John Leland had a crucial discussion with James Madison about the need for a bill of rights—a discussion that helped Madison decide to initially draft one.[7] The historical record is abundantly clear that devout Christians played a role in the creation of the separation ideal.

3. The myth of the one-sided wall

Not content in its attempts to show that the wall metaphor is bad history, Wall-Builders also tries to negate its effect by revising its meaning. It claims that the "wall" metaphor was originally understood to be a one-directional wall, meant to protect the church from the government. The wall was to stop government from interfering with religion, the argument goes, not to stop religion from involving itself in government.

A one-sided wall would be a neat feat of engineering, but it is a bad image of the founders' intent. One of Madison's main arguments against a tax in support of all Christian religions in Virginia was that state support of religion endangered the state. He stated this idea in 1785 during the Virginia church-state controversy in his epic "Memorial and Remonstrance," which set forth the principles and reasons behind the wisdom of keeping state and church separate. Madison wrote, "What influence in fact have ecclesiastical establishments had on Civil Society? In some instances they have been seen to erect a spiritual tyranny on the ruins of Civil authority; in many instances they have been seen upholding the thrones of political tyranny: in no instance have they been seen the guardians of the liberties of the people."[8]

Only a two-way wall, one that both keeps government out of religion and religion out of government, can truly protect religion. If some religious groups are allowed to legislate religious morality or use taxes for church activities, ten religious groups too small to influence the legislature will be forced either to live according to the dictates of another religion, and/or to pay money to support activities of other religions. Either way, these minority religious groups will have lost freedoms. As one constitutional scholar put it: "The wall of separation ensures the government's freedom *from* religion and the individual's freedom *of* religion. The second probably cannot flourish without the first."[9]

4. The myth of the national church

Another popular fiction, promoted by WallBuilders, is that the First Amendment was meant merely to prevent the federal government from creating one national church. This position, known as *nonpreferentialism*, allows a government to support religion as long as it does not "prefer" one religion over another. In other words, the Constitution prevents the establishment of one religion but not the establishment of all religions. Apart from the impracticality of establishing all religions (Would most Americans support Zoroastrianism and Jainism, not to mention Satanism?[10]), the major problem with this view is that it's wrong.

The founders viewed government support of *any* religion, or any combinations of religions, as an establishment. As one scholar has commented, "Opponents of a general assessment [nondiscriminatory state aid to all churches] referred to it as an establishment, and at times its proponents did too." Nobody, however, "attempted to show that a general assessment constituted an essentially different kind of establishment or to differentiate it from an exclusive state preference for one religion."[11] The founders considered support of religion, whether of one sect or all, as an establishment of religion.

Madison's "Memorial and Remonstrance" shows that the issue was not merely that of a national church. The proposed Virginia tax that Madison wrote against would be used to fund all churches (in Virginia at the time, there were no mosques or synagogues) on a nondiscriminatory basis. Madison asks, "Who does not see that the same authority which can establish Christianity . . . may establish with the same ease any particular sect of Christians, in exclusion of all other Sects?"[12]

The benefits of the tax in Virginia were designed to go to all "Christian" groups. Madison did not say that the fault of the proposed tax could be cured by extending its benefits to all religions, such as Islam and Judaism. Rather, he argued against the principle of direct government support of religion at all.

5. The myth of founder uniformity

WallBuilders' materials contain an array of quotes from various founders; a number of which genuinely do appear to claim that the US government is based, in some formal sense, on Christ and His gospel. These quotes, however, are part of a debate and represent only one side of that debate—the losing side—a fact that WallBuilders conveniently overlooks.

An example is WallBuilders' use of quotations from one of its favorite founders, Patrick Henry, who is alleged to have said, "It cannot be emphasized too strongly or too often that this great nation was founded, not by religionists, but by Christians; not on religions, but on the gospel of Jesus Christ!"[13] Recently, even Barton has acknowledged that this quote cannot be reliably sourced to Henry, though believes that it is consistent with the spirit of his thought. But apart from the unreliability of the quote is the problem of Barton's failure to discuss the context of Henry's views.

Barton omits to mention the historical debate in which Patrick Henry played a leading role. It was Patrick Henry who submitted the bill to the Virginia legislature for a general tax in support of religion, which caused Madison to respond with his "Memorial and Remonstrance." Henry's views, and those of his Episcopal allies, were the views countered and eventually defeated by the ideas in Madison's document. The issue was controversial and heated, but Madison's side won.

The defeat of Henry's bill was followed shortly by the passage, guided by Madison, of Jefferson's Virginia Statute for Religious Freedom. The Jefferson-Madison side of the debate provided the inspiration and framework, as discussed above, for the creation of the religion clauses in the federal Constitution. To quote Patrick Henry as an authority on how we should order church-state relations is like citing Marx as an authority on the virtues of capitalism.

Another example of WallBuilders' one-sided historical recounting is its description of Benjamin Franklin's suggestion for prayer at the Constitutional Convention. Franklin did indeed make such a proposal, but it was quite soundly defeated. A number of reasons were given, including a lack of funds to hire a pastor and out of deference to Philadelphia's Quakers. Franklin himself noted that at the convention, "except three or four persons, thought prayers unnecessary."[14]

By contrast, here is WallBuilders' recounting of that event: "Franklin's admonition—and the delegates' response to it—had been the turning point not only for the convention, but also for the future of the nation. . . . With their repentance came a desire to begin each morning of official government business with prayer."[15]

6. The myth of the impeccable founders

In fairness to WallBuilders, not all the historical stories of the founders' public involvement with religion are mythical. In his first year as president, George Washington did issue a proclamation designating a day of thanksgiving and prayer to "Almighty God."[16] James Madison issued a similar proclamation when president. Even Thomas Jefferson proclaimed a day of religious thanksgiving when he was governor of Virginia twenty years prior to his presidency.[17] Jefferson, however, refused to issue a prayer and thanksgiving edict during his presidency.

These inconsistencies can be explained. The founders were grappling with principles of universal import and sweep; some of which had never been implemented in the day-to-day workings of a civil government. This was especially true of separating the church from the state, something that had never been attempted at a national level. Thus it should not be surprising that the founders' application of these principles was not always perfect. The truth is that each of the above instances of prayer and thanksgiving proclamations is noteworthy because of the contrast it provides with each founder's general philosophy.

George Washington gave ample evidence of his conviction that religious belief and practice were private matters. In a letter to a Baptist church leader, he wrote,

"In this enlightened age and in this land of equal liberty, it is our boast, that a man's religious tenets will not forfeit the protection of the laws, nor deprive him of the right of attaining and holding the highest offices that are known in the United States."[18]

His most public statement regarding the relation between Christianity and the laws and institutions of the United States is his administration's treaty with Tripoli in 1797. That treaty, in Article XI, stated that "the Government of the United States of America is not, in any sense, founded on the Christian religion; as it has in itself no character of enmity against the laws, religion, or tranquility, of Mussulmen; and . . . that no pretext, arising from religious opinions, shall ever produce an interruption of the harmony existing between the two countries."[19]

To claim that Washington's thanksgiving proclamation was a full, or even a representative, expression of his philosophy of church-state relations, one must ignore these public and emphatic statements of church-state separation.

Writing several years after his presidency, Madison admitted that the existence of congressional chaplains and national days of thanksgiving and prayer were, strictly speaking, violations of the federal Constitution. His solution was to view these excesses as "harmless," as long as they were not used as a basis to argue for further combinations of church and state. Anticipating the arguments WallBuilders makes, Madison wrote, "Rather than let this step beyond the landmarks of power have the effect of a legitimate precedent, it will be better to apply to it the legal aphorism *de minimis non curat lex*."[20] The latter phrase means, in effect, "the law does not concern itself with trifles." WallBuilders treads on dangerous ground when it bases arguments about how society should work on the exceptional and unusual actions or practices of the founders. Many of the founders, Jefferson and Washington included, kept slaves. The founders didn't give voting rights to women. Does WallBuilders believe the founders' practices in these areas show that the Declaration of Independence and the principles of the Constitution should not apply to women and certain minorities? Americans should be guided by the vision of the founders, not by their blind spots.

7. The myth of the unchanging Constitution

It is true, as WallBuilders claims, that the First Amendment to the federal Constitution initially did not apply to state governments. WallBuilders goes a step further, however, and claims that this proves that the founders intended religion to be regulated, and even established by, state governments.[21] This argument overlooks the fact that none of the individual protections found in the Bill of Rights applied to the states. To apply WallBuilders' logic to other parts of the Bill of Rights would require one to believe that the founders did not mind if states infringed on speech rights, freedom of assembly, and the privacy rights of its citizens. The following quote from Madison shows his view on the issue: "Ye States of America, which retain in your Constitutions or Codes, any aberration from the sacred principle of religious liberty, by giving to Caesar what belongs to God, or joining together what God has put asunder, hasten to revise and purify your systems, and make the example of your Country as pure & compleat, in what relates to the freedom of the mind and its allegiance to its maker."[22]

The states heeded Madison's exhortation and rapidly followed the example set by the federal Constitution. Soon all the states had placed clauses strikingly similar to the First Amendment in their own constitutions. The last state to abolish its established church was Massachusetts in 1833.

Furthermore, after the Civil War, Congress passed the Fourteenth Amendment, which eventually was used to apply the Bill of Rights, including the First Amendment, to the states. WallBuilders apparently would prefer that the Fourteenth Amendment did not exist. WallBuilders argues that the amendment was designed exclusively to secure civil rights for the emancipated slaves. "Did the Congress which created the Fourteenth Amendment," it asks, "intend that it should incorporate the First Amendment against the states? The answer . . . is an emphatic and resounding 'No!' "[23]

Once again, WallBuilders misstates its case. Many of the framers of the amendment openly said that the amendment would apply at least the individual liberties to the states. It is true that for many years (until the twentieth century, actually) the US Supreme Court did not carry out this intent, but applied the amendment only to the issues of freed slaves and their rights. Constitutional scholars still debate the intended scope of the Fourteenth Amendment, though some framers expressed their understanding of its intent quite clearly. Congressman Bingham, the primary drafter of the language of section 1 of the Fourteenth Amendment, said years later:

"[The] privileges and immunities of citizens of the United States . . . are chiefly defined in the first eight amendments to the Constitution of the United States. Those eight amendments are as follows. [Bingham then proceeded to read the first eight amendments word for word.]
  . . . These eight articles . . . never were limitations upon the power of the states, until made so by the fourteenth amendment."[24]

Other framers and ratifiers of this amendment shared the understanding that it was meant to apply the Bill of Rights, including the First Amendment, against state governments. Senator Jack Howard, while analyzing the clause, acknowledged that prior to the Fourteenth Amendment the Bill of Rights had not applied to the states, and noted that "the great object of the first section of this [the fourteenth] amendment is, therefore, to restrain the power of the states and compel them at all times to respect these great fundamental guarantees [of the Bill of Rights]."[25]

The application of the Bill of Rights, including the First Amendment, could then be deemed part of the "original intent" of the Constitution, as congressmen of the 1860s became framers in their own right. By ignoring what these men said, WallBuilders is guilty of what it so vociferously accuses others of—that is, ignoring the intent of the framers.

8. The myth of dependent Christianity

WallBuilders' greatest, and most unfortunate, myth has less to do with history than with theology. Its historical arguments imply that Christianity is dependent on civil powers for its strength and effect. Barton claimed that the consequence of the Supreme Court's decision to "remove" prayer from public schools in 1963 has destroyed American society: "Following the judicial rejection of natural law and the embracing of relativism, the United States has become number one in the world in violent crime, divorce, illegal drug use; number one in the western world in teenage pregnancies; and number one in the industrial world in illiteracy. . . . By removing divine law, the Court removed the source of our previous national stability."[26]

Barton asserts that the Supreme Court of the United States can remove divine law through judicial fiat, a jurisdiction beyond all earthly powers. The corollary to this claim is that divine law can be *reinstated* through judicial or legislative enactment—a scary prospect.

Why? Because the basis of all earthly jurisdiction is force. No civil law is really a law unless the state is willing to enforce it. Your house, your car, even your children are physically yours only as long as the government can exercise a greater force than that exercised by thieves, robbers, and anarchists. This simple principle explains the general ineffectiveness of the United Nations (UN) in dealing with belligerent nations. The united disapproval of virtually the entire world will not deter an Iraq or a Serbia; only the barrel of a tank or the muzzle of a rifle will.

Those who advocate the enshrinement of uniquely Christian values in the laws of our land are literally advocating that force be used to coerce people to conform to spiritual ideals. Allowing prayer in public schools seems harmless enough. Those who sue school boards, however, over decisions not to allow prayer at graduations or in the classroom are in effect saying, "Allow prayer at your graduation, or if need be, we will have the sheriff arrest you and throw you in jail and then we will pray."

The biblical prophets warned the kings of Israel against relying on the "arm of flesh" (2 Chronicles 32:8) for their salvation. It was also they who prophesied of God's new covenant, which would be written on the "fleshy tables of the heart" (2 Corinthians 3:3). The New Testament more fully expounds the truth that Christ's kingdom is first, foremost, and (at least while we're here on this earth) exclusively of spiritual authority.

His kingdom, Christ taught, was made up of voluntary adherents who chose to follow Him and have His principles written on their hearts by faith. He said,

"My kingdom is not of this world. If My kingdom were of this world, My servants would fight" (John 18:36, NKJV). He told Peter, a man zealous to wield temporal power on behalf of spiritual truths, "Put your sword in its place, for all who take the sword will perish by the sword" (Matthew 26:52, NKJV). He advocated that the use of teaching and persuasion, combined with the Holy Spirit, would lead people to the truth. This in turn would cause them to have His law, voluntarily and joyfully, written on their hearts in a way that no Supreme Court edict could ever accomplish.

Conclusion

In their zealous advocacy for Christ's kingdom, WallBuilders and its allies cut squarely across the spiritual principles they appear so anxious to uphold. In that sense, then, the name *WallBuilders* is correct: the organization is building unnecessary walls of prejudice in an onlooking world, a world desperately needing to hear about the One who has "broken down the middle wall of separation" (Ephesians 2:14, NKJV) between humanity and God, making possible the building of the divine law in the hearts of human beings. On the other hand, considering the fallacies of its arguments, "MythBuilders" is the one title that really fits.

---

1. David Barton, *The Myth of Separation*, 3rd ed. (Aledo, TX: WallBuilders Press, 1992), back cover. Throughout this chapter, references to Barton's work, except where otherwise indicated, are from *The Myth of Separation*.

2. WallBuilders is David Barton's organization that promotes his version of American history and its heroes.

3. Barton, *The Myth of Separation*, 41–46.

4. Roger Williams wrote in 1644: "First, the faithful labors of many witnesses of Jesus Christ, extant to the world, abundantly proving that the church of the Jews under the Old Testament in the type and the church of the Christians under the New Testament in the antitype were both separate from the world; and that when they have opened a gap in the hedge or wall of *separation* between the garden of the church and the wilderness of the world, God hath ever broke down the wall itself, removed the candlestick, and made His garden a wilderness, as at this day. And that therefore if He will ever please to restore His garden and paradise again, it must of necessity be walled in peculiarly unto Himself from the world; and that all that shall be saved out of the world are to be transplanted out of the wilderness of the world, and added unto His church or garden." Roger Williams, "A Letter of Mr. John Cottons" (1643), quoted in Leonard W. Levy, *The Establishment Clause: Religion and the First Amendment* (New York: Macmillan, 1986), 184.

5. David Barton, *The Truth About Thomas Jefferson and the First Amendment* (Aledo, TX: WallBuilders Press, 1992).

6. Levy, *The Establishment Clause*, 182, 183.

7. William Lee Miller, *The First Liberty: Religion and the American Republic* (St. Paul, MN: Paragon House, 1988), 120–124.

8. James Madison, "Memorial and Remonstrance" (1785), reprinted in Edwin S. Gaustad, *Faith of Our Fathers: Religion and the New Nation* (New York: Harper and Row, 1987), appendix A.

9. Levy, *The Establishment Clause*, 194; emphasis added.

10. WallBuilders avoids this problem by claiming that the founders meant to establish Christi-

anity, rather than religions generally. "When our Fathers enacted the First Amendment, the abuse they intended to avoid was that of having one, and only one, denomination of Christianity selected, protected, or promoted by government. . . . They wanted [however] to establish Christianity as the basis of government and public institutions." Barton, *The Myth of Separation*, 142.

11. Thomas J. Curry, *The First Freedoms: Church and State in America to the Passage of the First Amendment* (New York: Oxford University Press, 1986), 210.

12. Madison, "Memorial and Remonstrance," in Gaustad, *Faith of Our Fathers*, appendix A.

13. Barton, *The Myth of Separation*, 109; see http://www.huffingtonpost.com/thomas-s-kidd /patrick-henry-quotes_b_1247107.html and https://wallbuilders.com/unconfirmed-quotations /#FN32.

14. Levy, *The Establishment Clause*, 64.

15. Barton, *The Myth of Separation*, 110.

16. Ibid., 114, 115.

17. Akhil Reed Amar, "The Bill of Rights as a Constitution," *Yale Law Journal* 100, no. 5 (March 1991): 1131, 1159. It should be noted, however, that Jefferson's proclamation was prior to the passage of the Virginia Statute for Religious Freedom.

18. George Washington to the Members of the New Jerusalem Church of Baltimore, Philadelphia, (ca. January 27, 1793), George Washington Papers, *Letter Book* 30, 110, Manuscript Division, Library of Congress, quoted in William Addison Blakely, ed., *American State Papers on Freedom in Religion*, 3rd. rev. ed. (Washington, DC: Review and Herald® Pub. Assn., 1943), 155.

19. George Washington, quoted in Blakely, *American State Papers*, 130, 131.

20. Robert S. Alley, ed., *James Madison on Religious Liberty* (New York: Prometheus Books, 1985), 92; emphasis added.

21. Barton, *The Myth of Separation*, 167–169; Amar, "The Bill of Rights as a Constitution," 1131, 1157.

22. James Madison, "The Detached Memoranda," quoted in Alley, *James Madison on Religious Liberty*, 90.

23. Barton, *The Myth of Separation*, 169.

24. Cong. Globe, 42nd Cong., 1st sess., 84 app (1871), quoted in Akhil Reed Amar, "The Bill of Rights and the Fourteenth Amendment," *Yale Law Journal* 101, no. 6 (April 1992): 1235.

25. Amar, "The Bill of Rights and the Fourteenth Amendment," 1237.

26. Barton, *The Myth of Separation*, 217.

PART III

Protesting Protestantism:
Twentieth-Century Challenges to Religious Freedom

As the twentieth century opened, new forces were at work in the United States that challenged not only the Protestant view of an institutional separation of church and state but also a practical legal framework of Protestant moral perspectives. That these moral views were largely shared by Catholics, Jews, people of other faiths, and often no faith did not stop critics from contending that many types of morals legislation, whether in relation to the family, sexuality, birth control, or abortion, were unconstitutional enforcements of religious views. This newly invigorated secularist outlook on morality, which had long held sway in Europe, became more widely accepted by the American leadership class, whether in the media, the academy, or Hollywood. Political leaders, while often accepting this new viewpoint personally, had to play a balancing act with constituents, who often stayed more conservative and traditional on these issues.

The new secularist trend in leadership circles and institutions eventually led to a backlash among more conservative religious groups, who became more politically involved after the *Roe v. Wade* abortion decision of the early 1970s. Rather than moving back to the dissenting Protestant positions described in earlier chapters, however, the new evangelical Right began to take their church-state models from the Puritan founding rather than the constitutional founding. Thus, their advocacy moved beyond that of public morality, which could be achieved by arguments from nature and sociology, to endorsing proposals for state involvement with religious (read "Christian") practices and teachings. This included support for prayer and religious practices in schools, as well as the funding of religious schools and mission organizations. The story behind these competing interests in American society and politics is given a historical perspective in "Religious Freedom and Modern American Politics."

This new approach to church and state actually created a conundrum for the evangelical Right. In seeking to compete with a zealous and increasingly absolutist secularism, they argued that religion was just another ideology that should receive equal treatment under the laws and the Constitution. Why should it be kept out of schools, public forums, and even public policy? Was this not just another form of discrimination, much like discrimination based on race or ethnicity?

But what this argument overlooked was the special role that the Constitution carved out for religion. While the establishment clause might appear to penalize it in terms of its role in schools and public life, the free exercise clause gave it protections that other secular ideologies and institutions did not possess. In arguing for "equal treatment," Christians were in danger of undermining the special constitutional status of religion and opening themselves up to a loss of freedoms, especially for minority religions. This story and danger is examined in some detail in "The Religious Right's Assault on the Rights of Religion."

The seriousness of this threat to religious freedom was underscored by the Supreme Court's decision in *Employment Division v. Smith* in 1990. Many defenders of religious freedom have forgotten, or perhaps never knew, that this decision, which radically cut back on the protections for religious minorities under the First Amendment, was authored by devout Catholic Justice Antonin Scalia. His reasoning was that religious freedom should be protected by the legislature, not the Constitution and the courts. He thereby placed the protection of religious minorities in the hands of the majority.

The danger of the fox guarding the henhouse, so to speak, was not lost on the larger religious and civil rights community, and they soon mounted an effort to shore up this breach in American religious freedom. This was done by the passage of the Religious Freedom Restoration Act (RFRA), which was backed by a broad coalition of religious and civil rights groups in 1993. Unfortunately, the Supreme Court again had the final word when in 1997 it declared RFRA unconstitutional, at least as applied to state governments. The religious and civil rights community was back to square one, and they needed to design a new piece of replacement legislation. This story, and its roller coaster ride over several years, is told in "Reconstruction—Rebuilding Religious Freedom."

This chapter was not just an investigative research project for me: during my early years as a lawyer, I was part of the coalition that helped to pursue this religious-freedom project anew. I served as a member of the drafting committee that was responsible for writing the ultimately successful Religious Land Use and Institutionalized Persons Act of 2000. It was a pivotal point in Washington,

DC, that revealed the fracturing fault lines between left-leaning and right-leaning civil rights groups, which were defined largely by attitudes toward the newest civil rights cause in the room, that of the lesbian, gay, bisexual, and transgender (LGBT) community. The new civil rights contest was between LGBT rights and religious freedom.

Thus, as the second millennium came to an end, religious enthusiasts were no longer the most obvious threat to religious freedom. The Clinton presidential years had brought a new vigor and ascendancy to liberal advocacy groups, and the LGBT community was particularly energized. Despite the relative conservatism of the Bush years, the same-sex marriage issue began its forward movement during this time, appearing first in the United States in 2004 in Massachusetts by judicial ruling and in 2008 in California by the same. (It was overturned by the people in the Proposition 8 referendum, which was struck down shortly afterward by a federal court.)

It seemed as though the culture wars of the 1960s had come to a grand new climax, and the secularist, liberal Left had won. Churches and religious institutions were circling the wagons, trying to plan how to carry out worship, education, and mission in a newly zealous secular social and political landscape. These dynamics are also examined in "A Secular Threat to Religious Freedom," as well as in the related chapters about the treatment of marginalized religious movements—often classified as cults—both overseas and in the United States.

Finally, the impact that times of crisis can play on the rollback of liberties is examined in "Freedom Under Fire: The First Amendment in Times of Crisis." The dramatic events of war, terrorism, economic disaster, and similar sudden and abrupt social impacts can have harmful effects on freedoms. Threats from both the Right and the Left are magnified by crisis events, and we need to learn lessons from such times in American history to be better prepared for such crises in the future, as they will undoubtedly come.

One of the heartening lessons from the history of crises is that the damage to civil liberties done during them often serves as a wake-up call and a learning experience, and they can allow a thoughtful people to improve their civil liberties. This usually happens well in the aftermath, however, and cannot always be counted on in the short term. As the founders wisely acknowledged, the price of liberty is constant vigilance, especially during times of civil and political uncertainty.

Chapter 10

Religious Freedom and Modern American Politics

The 2012 presidential election, which installed Barack Obama in a second term as president, showed how complicated the religious-liberty landscape in America has become.

It unfolded a bit like a disorienting game of musical chairs: Catholic bishops defended religious liberty like old-fashioned Protestants; evangelical Protestants supported a Republican presidential ticket that stumped for prayer in schools and government support for religion, sounding like pre–Vatican II Catholics; and President Barack Obama, a self-professed Christian with a Muslim-influenced upbringing, proffered secularist positions on abortion and gay marriage that were contrary to those religious traditions.

President Obama's victory means that secularist values will likely become even more of a concern for religious liberty and institutions during the next four years. This challenge to religious freedom from the Left will ensure that agitation from the evangelical Right and the Roman Catholic Church will also intensify, as they seek to protect religious freedom and to promote a special role for Christianity in our society. The net result will continue to be challenges to genuine religious liberty from both the political Left and the Right.

Going to extremes

Given the political climate, challenges from the Left will be the most immedi-

---

This chapter originally appeared in *Adventist Review,* January 17, 2013.

ately pressing. Adding to the pressure on religious freedom, three more states, Washington, Maryland, and New Hampshire, joined several states that now have legalized gay marriage. Initiatives passed in Colorado and Washington legalizing marijuana use and, in Maryland, vastly expanding casino gambling.

Faith-based schools and colleges, including both Catholic and Protestant, have sued the government over the requirement to provide contraceptive coverage in their private health insurance plans, including paying for drugs that induce abortions.

Where gay marriage is legal, religious institutions, including Seventh-day Adventist ones, have come under pressure to adopt sexual lifestyle policies for employees and students that are contrary to their understandings of Scripture. Commercial institutions have fewer protections than not-for-profits. Already companies such as Hobby Lobby and Chick-fil-A have come under media and legal pressure to conform their practices to the values of the secularist Left.

In another disturbing development—and a portent of things to come—California in October 2012 enacted a law to make illegal any attempt by a licensed counselor, therapist, physician, or health worker to provide counseling to modify or alter same-sex attractions to any person under the age of eighteen, even if that person desires such counseling. This legal development should dash any thought that same-sex marriage regimes will operate in a live-and-let-live manner.

Churches in California can still *teach* and *preach* biblical views of sexuality, but Christian counselors—including pastors with counseling licenses—are forbidden from helping the church's young people to actually *live* and *practice* those beliefs. The law is under legal challenge, so far with mixed results. But whatever the eventual outcome, this is an indicator of the Left's desire to legally suppress those elements of the church's morality and practice that conflict with secularist values.

A very real danger, of course, is that the Left's pressure on religious institutions will provoke a backlash from the Right, one that itself could endanger religious freedoms. Indeed, suppression by majority religions of minority religious rights is what the Adventist prophetic message envisions. We cannot ignore the very present and real danger to religious freedoms because of our concern about a predicted future danger. To do so endangers the church's witness to the present age and our moral authority in future conflicts.

A historical survey
How should Protestant churches respond to these challenges and the potential backlash? History can help us to shape an answer to this question.

In recent years, arguments about religious liberty, and the culture wars in general, seem to have proceeded on a two-sided basis. There are a series of issues—abortion, gay marriage, faith-based funding, gambling casinos—with two apparently possible positions: one for secularists, and the other for faith communities.

But the two-sided nature of this discussion is a recent development. It trended this way in the mid-1970s and 1980s, as Protestants began to make common cause with Catholics, first over the issue of abortion, then on issues of religion and education. The trend has been toward pushing for greater government support for religion and religious viewpoints.

The recent conflict over the Affordable Care Act mandate requiring religious institutions to provide coverage for contraception, including abortifacients, has highlighted the historic Protestant position on keeping matters of religious conscience free from the will of the state. The irony, of course, is that it is primarily Catholics reminding Americans of their Protestant heritage.

That they must do so goes to show that we have lost sight of something important in our recent faith-versus-secularism arguments. For most of American history, from the founding through the 1950s and 1960s, there was a more nuanced dialogue that involved at least three points of view.

On the left were the secular liberals, coming to prominence in the progressive era of the 1910s and 1920s, symbolized by the rise of the American Civil Liberties Union (ACLU). This group has deeper roots, though, going back to Thomas Jefferson and the philosophies of the French Enlightenment.

On the right were the Christian republicans, made up of an uneasy coalition of Catholic groups seeking state funding for parochial schools and evangelical groups supporting Bible reading in public schools (King James Version only, please), Sunday blue laws, and religious tests for political office. These Christian moralists had their roots in the Puritan theocrats of New England and the Anglican establishments of Virginia and the South. They were images of the magisterial Protestantism of Europe, with a church supported by the state, where dissenting groups were regulated and often suppressed.

But there was a third group, whom we can call dissenting, or free-church, Protestants. This group opposed the practice of the state provision of resources to religious groups and also insisted that churches should be free from state oversight or control. This group represents the real ancestors of the Adventist church-state view.

These dissenting Protestants did not reject all state involvement with morality. But they believed that issues of public morality should be legislated in light of the natural moral law, not scriptural injunction. Their colleges taught courses in "moral philosophy," required study for all students to provide a foundation for public moral discourse and debate.

Always a minority in Europe, these dissenting groups were largely unable to guide European political arrangements. But these Baptists, Anabaptists, and Quakers, and eventually Methodists and Scottish-Presbyterians, became politically controlling in a number of American colonies: first in Rhode Island, Pennsylvania, New Jersey, and Delaware, and later in Virginia, New York, and the Carolinas.

These free-church groups grew explosively during the Great Awakening revivals of the 1740s. By the time of the Republic's founding, they were politically ascendant in most colonies outside New England. Thus, when the federal Constitution was framed, its church-state philosophy reflected that of the dissenting Protestants and not that of either Puritan republicanism or French Enlightenment thought.

Much of the modern-day conflict over the Constitution and religious liberty comes from partisans trying to remake the American founding in either the image of a Jeffersonian secularism or a Puritan Christian republicanism. The dissenting Protestant posture, Adventism's true birthright, is increasingly overlooked, even by Adventists.

A prudent position

In our own midst, we have growing numbers who want either to join arms with the religious Right and call for prayer in schools and the Ten Commandments on our public buildings or to ally with the Left and dismiss all morals legislation, such as protection of marriage and family or restrictions on pornography, abortion, or gambling as violations of the separation of church and state. Neither position is consistent with either our dissenting Protestant or Adventist heritages.

We Adventists are nervous when politicians start to talk about morality. Somehow we feel that the political and the moral realms should be entirely disconnected. But this is truly impossible, at least for any government that is to be concerned with justice.

As Socrates, Plato, and Aristotle understood so long ago, every government worth having must be concerned with what is just, and what is just is bound up with what is good, and what is good is inevitably a question of morality. The state should stay out of *spiritual* morality, but notions of public health are directly affected by *civil* morality, which moral philosophy studied.

Nineteenth-century Protestant religious leader and educator Ellen White identified moral philosophy as one of the three most important things that Christian students should study. She wrote, "The plans devised and carried out for the education of our youth are none too broad. They should not have a one-sided education, but all their powers should receive equal attention. *Moral philosophy*, the study of the Scriptures, and physical training should be combined with the studies usually pursued in schools."[1]

It was the judicious use of moral philosophy that allowed nineteenth century free-church Protestants to advocate for social moral issues such as abolition of slavery, temperance reform, and the prohibition of alcohol. They could do this while still upholding the separation of church and state because they distinguished between spiritual and civil morals. To survive the coming religious-liberty challenges, Adventists have to learn to do the same again.

How would a recovery of the dissenting Protestant view help guide Christians and other faith communities in the religious-liberty challenges ahead? It would counsel us to keep out specifically Christian arguments based entirely or primarily on appeals to Scripture. But moral arguments that appealed to common moral experience and human reason would be appropriate.

It would disapprove of direct state funding to overtly religious institutions, something secularists would appreciate. But it would prevent the state from burdening religious entities with regulations contrary to their religious teachings, such as the contraceptive and/or abortifacient insurance coverage requirement found in the Affordable Care Act. The faith-based community would appreciate this.

State-official-led prayer and worship services or rituals would be out of bounds, a position secularists would applaud. But references to a Divine Being, a Creator, even a God, would not be verboten. Notions of the natural moral law revolved around the philosopher's God, which was not considered a product of sectarian religious thought. Even the ardent separationist Thomas Jefferson referred to the "Creator" in the Declaration of Independence. But it was a Creator understood in the light of the "self-evident" truths of nature, of moral philosophy, not those of special revelation.

Issues of abortion and gay rights would require a careful, nuanced approach. The religious Right's moral absolutism would give way to a more fine-grained analysis that would weigh competing moral concerns, which is the hallmark of a reasoned moral philosophy. The state could recognize the moral weight of life at its various stages but also recognize other moral values, such as quality of life, and justice for victims and the oppressed.

Abortion on demand and as a method of birth control could be restricted; but when the life and the health of the mother were at risk, or the pregnancy was due to coercion and rape, these countering moral concerns might be given weight. Such an approach would be consistent with the biblical moral framework, which highly values life but considers it in a matrix of other concerns, including justice, human dignity, even social order, as shown by its allowance of capital punishment for a variety of crimes.

In the area of gay rights, society could recognize the importance of providing close personal relationships with support and protection. Values of privacy and equal treatment would counsel against discrimination of gays in public benefits or the workplace. But the importance of religious freedom would allow religious institutions—both places of worship and educational and health institutions—to preserve their values in relation to sexual conduct.

This approach would also recognize the moral value of protecting the goals and ends of the child-raising unit of a mother and a father and reserve its full approval for such relationships. Such an approach may allow for civil unions for tax and insurance purposes, but it would limit marriage and the right to raise children to heterosexual couples based on moral arguments about the purposes of procreation and the rights of children to benefit from the special care provided by a mother and a father.

Other moral issues, such as gambling, marijuana and drug use, and violence and sex in the media, could be restricted and even outlawed, based, again, not on scriptural injunctions but on studies showing the harmful effects of these things on communities and children. It would be a world that would fully satisfy neither secularists nor Christian advocates. But it would take into account most of their central concerns and provide a common public language of moral discussion.

More than a game

At its best, the recent game of religious-liberty musical chairs may trigger a revival of America's true Protestant heritage, one embraced by our own pioneers, both national and evangelical. If this happens, this odd political parlor game of the recent election may have been very worthwhile indeed.

---

1. Ellen G. White, *Christian Education* (Battle Creek, MI: International Tract Society, 1893), 210; emphasis added.

Chapter 11

The Religious Right's Assault on the Rights of Religion

Lawyers and legal advocacy groups for the religious Right are engaged in a vigorous if not entirely intentional assault on the constitutionally protected status of religion. The rallying cry of the effort is "End religious discrimination now!" and the stated goal is to give religion a level playing field with secular groups. This, it is hoped, will allow religious entities to receive funding and other government benefits allowed to similarly situated nonreligious organizations.

These groups use language and metaphors borrowed from the civil rights movement of the 1960s to paint the picture that religious persons are experiencing the same kind of discrimination today as was experienced by ethnic minorities prior to the 1960s. Ralph Reed, a founder and former head of the Christian Coalition, writes, "The term 'back of the bus' has come into wide use in our language. It refers not only to the system of segregation in the South that attempted to relegate African-Americans to second-class citizenship, but to all efforts to deny citizens basic rights guaranteed under the US Constitution. No one is denying people of faith the right to vote or to live where they choose. But their rights to freedom of speech and religion are under constant attack whenever they enter the public arena."[1]

Taking this claim of discrimination a step further, Keith A. Fournier, executive director of the American Center for Law and Justice, Pat Robertson's legal

This chapter is adapted from an article originally published
in *Journal of Church and State* 42, no. 2 (Spring 2000): 273–295.

advocacy institute, writes that "we are facing growing hostility toward religion and the religious speaker. We are, in fact, witnessing an awful counterpart to ethnic cleansing."[2] In answering the question "what is religious cleansing?" Fournier says, "*Religious Cleansing* is a term I use to describe the current hostility and bigotry toward religion and people of faith that are leading to covert and overt attempts to remove any religious influence from the public arena."[3]

This rhetoric has been translated into legal arguments in a number of court cases, including attempts to get direct state aid for parochial schools. One example is a case that was brought by a small Christian college, Columbia Union College (now Washington Adventist University), against the state of Maryland to gain aid presently given to private secular colleges in that state. Federal district and appeals courts have denied the college's claims of religious discrimination and free speech violations, ruling that the state's refusal to fund a pervasively sectarian school is justified by the compelling interest in preserving the separation of church and state.[4]

The attitude of religious organizations in seeking state aid represents a dramatic shift from the past, when it was thought that government benefits would bring with them a corresponding loss of special privileges and protections. Two leading conservative Christian religious liberty leaders of the 1940s wrote:

> Religious denominations . . . need to take alarm at any attempt to form financial alliances or secure financial funds from the state. Such alliances are costly [and] dangerous. . . . Governmental appropriations of funds of necessity involve government control. . . .
>
> Wherever there is financial responsibility, there also resides administrative authority. The old saying, "It's the one who pays the fiddler that calls the tunes" still has meaning.[5]

Do religious schools that accept state funds today still risk the dangers of loss of autonomy and suppression of religious mission? Or are these concerns the relics of a bygone era, now that religion is prepared to take on a position of "equality" with secular entities? What are the implications of this so-called equality for the health of religious institutions? Have recent Supreme Court decisions sufficiently altered constitutional jurisprudence to allow direct funding of religious schools and institutions?

The constitutional protection of religion

Religion has a special, protected status in the American constitutional scheme and, by extension, so do religious institutions. Historically, this special status is a recognition that the church and state occupy two separate realms, or spheres of concern. The church's realm deals with the spiritual and the heavenly. The state's realm concerns itself with the temporal and earthly. As both entities exist in the present world, there is of necessity some overlap and interchange between the two. But this interchange at the margins should not obscure the fact that neither entity, church or state, has the rightful power to act in the core sphere of the other.

A. Dual and separate realms

The idea that all persons are subjects of two separate realms goes back at least as far as Christ's recognition of the "things that are Caesar's" and the "things that are God's" (Luke 20:25, NKJV). Christ's acknowledgment of the distinct and separate jurisdictions of these two powers was blurred by the medieval church.[6] The concept was revitalized by the Protestant Reformation and had established itself as a presence in American political thought by the time of the framing of the Constitution.

James Madison expressed the consequence of the concept in his famed "Memorial and Remonstrance" of 1785:

> We maintain therefore that in matters of Religion, no mans [sic] right is abridged by the institution of Civil Society, *and that Religion is wholly exempt from its cognizance.* . . .
>   . . . If Religion be exempt from the authority of the Society at large, *still less can it be subject to that of the Legislative Body.*[7]

After the Revolution and prior to the writing of the Constitution, fully eleven of the thirteen states adopted new constitutions, and these generally included religious protection. By the time of the framing in 1789, every state but Connecticut had a constitutional provision protecting religious freedom. A review of these state provisions indicates that "free exercise of religion" was associated with affirmative government protection of both religious belief and action in a manner consistent with the dual-spheres model. In most instances, religious exercise was to have free reign throughout society, up to the limit of the "peace and safety" of that society. These state constitutions displayed the kind of robust and broad vision of religious protection envisioned by the dual-spheres ideal.[8]

Given Madison's philosophy and the colonial backdrop of his day, it is no surprise that when he framed the initial draft of the Constitution, and later the Bill of Rights, he included this fundamental principle of the dual spheres of church and state. These efforts are embodied in three main characteristics of that document: its secular nature (with no mention of God or the supernatural); its prohibition against religious tests for public office, found in Article VI; and in the First Amendment guarantees of religious freedom and autonomy.

The First Amendment to the Constitution contains the most explicit articulation of this separate dual-realms idea. It is set out in the two-part standard that

"Congress shall make no law respecting an establishment of religion, or prohibiting the free exercise thereof."

The first clause prohibited the civil realm from wielding the sword of the state on behalf of religion or peculiarly religious ideas. The second clause saw to it that the state should respect and protect the sphere of religion.

The clauses ideally work in harmony to protect the legitimate spheres and roles of both the church and the state. The "establishment clause, properly viewed, functions as a structural provision regimenting the nature and degree of involvement between government and religious associations. . . . The aim of separation of church and government is for each to give the other sufficient breathing space."[9]

B. Protection of religious functions

The US Supreme Court has held that "the First Amendment rests upon the premise that both religion and government can best work to achieve their lofty aims if each is left from the other *within its respective sphere*."[10] And that the amendment's purpose "was to create a complete and permanent separation of the *spheres of religious activity and civil authority*."[11] An objective of the religion clauses, the court has stated, "is to prevent, as far as possible, the *intrusion of either into the precincts of the other*."[12]

Because of this arrangement, churches have the fundamental right to "decide for themselves, free from state interference, matters of church government as well as those of faith and doctrine."[13] This view of the dual realms of church and state has given courts an influential template upon which to analyze church-state issues and has resulted in important decisions that protect the prerogatives of the church. Under the Constitution, truly religious organizations (known as "pervasively sectarian" entities) have the right to "decide for themselves, free from state interference, matters of church government as well as those of faith and doctrine." Religious organizations have absolute discretion in regard to the employment of ministers, rabbis, priests, and teachers of theology or religion and are shielded from nearly all claims brought under state and federal employment statutes by these employees.[14]

Pervasively sectarian schools are exempted from the jurisdiction of the National Labor Relations Board and can prevent their staff from unionizing. Under the civil rights protection of the federal Title VII, religious entities have the right to hire and fire their employees, from presidents to janitors, on the basis of religious beliefs or criteria.[15]

On the other hand, secular private colleges, even those that are religiously affiliated, are not allowed to hire and fire on the basis of religion. While religiously affiliated colleges may be able to use religious criteria in the hiring of chaplains and religion teachers, the burden is on the college to prove that these positions are religiously related. These types of private colleges cannot regulate student admissions and student behavior based on religious moral standards, as one prominent

Catholic university discovered when it found that it could not refuse to fund or recognize a gay-rights student club.[16]

C. Consequences of the protection of the sphere of religion

To call government nonfunding of church-related affairs a form of viewpoint discrimination is to argue for a selective application of the nonintrusion principle. As discussed above, religious institutions frequently enjoy heightened rights of speech and association in relation to their secular counterparts because of the special deference that the courts extend to the religious realm. While churches applaud this noninterference when it comes to government regulation, some are less happy when the noninterference principle prevents the receipt of state funds.

But can church institutions fairly use the dual-spheres principle of nonintrusion to argue against state regulation if those institutions already violate that nonintrusion principle by accepting state funding? Logic and history would seem to indicate not.

Thus, when the government chooses not to fund a program because of its religious status, that choice should properly be viewed as a recognition of the special status of religion and not as an act of invidious discrimination. When religious groups have complained of a violation of their rights of free speech and association, at times courts have chosen to justify a state decision not to fund religious groups in terms of a "compelling state interest" in avoiding a violation of the establishment clause.

This is perhaps not the best way to put the matter, as it tends to imply a hierarchy of rights, with the free speech and equality rights of believers being trumped by the antiestablishment interests of the state. A better way of stating it would be that the government has a "compelling state interest" in preventing government intrusion and involvement in the realm of religion. This banishes the contest that pits the believer's free speech, associational, and religious rights against the establishment "right" or "concern" of the state. That confrontation is replaced with an inquiry that seeks to preserve the constitutionally recognized "realm" of religion from government intrusion or involvement. The "burden" of nonfunding religious groups can be viewed as a sort of quid pro quo for the special protection and regard religion is given in other areas, such as hiring, self-definition, and structure.

Chief Justice Burger observed that "the highways of church and state relationships are not likely to be one-way streets."[17] Thus, those who aspire to dismantle the wall between church and state in order to receive public assistance will simultaneously be increasing the risk for government control of the church's educational ministry.

Some argue that church schools should accept tax-derived funds until they experience the government's heavy hand on their religious institutions. Such a philosophy assumes that backing out of such an arrangement is as easy, or nearly so, as entering it. Experience teaches, however, that the easy part is letting the camel's nose into the tent or the water out of the dike or the horse out of the barn. The challenge of reversing these processes is what gives the proverbs their bite. Rebuilding a demolished church-state wall would be no easier and may well be impossible as a practical matter.

Conclusion: A prophetic view of the status of church and state

In light of both history and the prophetic claims of the Bible in regard to persecution inspired by religious zeal, the Christian church of today cannot afford to make the mistake of encouraging sectarian political partisanship in America. While choosing to allow religious schools to receive direct state funding seems far removed from the violence of warring religious paramilitaries in Northern Ireland or Lebanon or the former Yugoslavia, the principle involved is the same.

Once the state begins to fund and support certain religious groups, the political arena will tend to fragment along sectarian lines as each denomination and religious group seeks to gain funding and support for its institutions. This will inject the inflexibility of religious dogma into politics and infect religious doctrine with the expediency and compromise of politics. The end result will be that religion will lose its special protected status, and religious institutions will be regulated, treated, and mistreated like any other secular entity.

These are results to be feared and, indeed, were feared by our Founding Fathers. James Madison, in opposing a proposal to allow state tax money to support religious teachers, made the following statement that is equally applicable to similar proposals today: "[This bill] degrades from the equal rank of Citizens all those whose opinions in Religion do not bend to those of the Legislative authority. Distant as it may be in its present form from the Inquisition, it differs from it only in degree. *The one is the first step, the other the last, in the career of intolerance.*"[18]

Christians are not called to play a role in encouraging the state to take this tempting yet fateful first step. Rather, they have a prophetic message of warning to give that such steps go down a pathway toward sectarian division and legislative hypocrisy. They that sow the wind of sectarian controversy will reap the whirlwind of national disunion and disaster. If our nation chooses this pathway, let it be in spite of the Christian church's strong call to respect the God-ordained, separate spheres of church and state and the special place of religion in our Constitution.

---

1. Ralph Reed, *Politically Incorrect: The Emerging Faith Factor in American Politics* (Dallas, TX: Word Publishing, 1994), 41, 42.

2. Keith A. Fournier, *Religious Cleansing in the American Republic* (Washington, DC: Liberty, Life, and Family Publications, 1993), 4.

3. Ibid.

4. Columbia Union College v. Clarke, 1997 US Dist. LEXIS 21131 and 159 F.3d 151 (4th Cir. 1998).

5. Alvin W. Johnson and Frank H. Yost, *Separation of Church and State in the United States*, Minnesota Archive ed. (Minneapolis, MN: Lund Press, 1948), 113.

6. Compare Christ's words in John 18:36, "My kingdom is not of this world. If My kingdom were of this world, My servants would fight" (NKJV) with the declaration of Pope Boniface VIII, "Under the control of the Church are two swords, that is two powers. . . . Both swords are in the power of the Church; the spiritual is wielded in the Church by the hand of the clergy; the secular is to be employed for the Church by the hand of the civil authority, but under the direction of the spiritual power." Boniface VIII, *Unam Sanctam* (The One Holy), November 18, 1302.

7. Madison, "Memorial and Remonstrance," quoted in Gaustad, *Faith of Our Fathers*, appendix A; emphasis added.

8. Michael W. McConnell, "The Origins and Historical Understanding of Free Exercise of Religion," *Harvard Law Review* 103, no. 7 (May 1990): 1409, 1456.

9. Carl H. Esbeck, "Establishment Clause Limits on Governmental Interference With Religious Organizations," *Washington and Lee Law Review* 41, no. 2 (1984): 347, 348.

10. McCollum v. Board of Education, 333 US 203 (1948) at 212; emphasis added.

11. Everson v. Board of Education, 330 US 1 (1947) at 31, 32; emphasis added.

12. Lemon v. Kurtzman, 403 US 602 (1971) at 614; emphasis added.

13. Kedroff v. Saint Nicholas Cathedral, 344 US 94 (1952) at 116.

14. Rayburn v. General Conference of Seventh-day Adventists, 772 F.2d 1164 (4th Cir. 1985), *cert. denied*, 478 US 1020 (1986); McClure v. Salvation Army, 460 F.2d 553, 558, 560 (5th Cir. 1972).

15. NLRB v. Catholic Bishop of Chicago, 440 US 490 (1979) at 502; 42 USC. § 2000e-2(e)(2); Corp. of Presiding Bishop of the Church of Jesus Christ of Latter-Day Saints v. Amos, 483 US 327 (1987).

16. Gay Rights Coalition of Georgetown Univ. Law Center v. Georgetown Univ., 536 A.2d 1, 117 (D.C. Cir. 1987).

17. *Lemon*, 403 US at 623.

18. James Madison, "Memorial and Remonstrance," par. 9 (1785), quoted in Blakely, *American State Papers*, 112–120; emphasis added.

Chapter 12

Reconstruction—
Rebuilding Religious Freedom

What do a Jewish home synagogue, a Baptist minister, and a federal prisoner have in common? All are among the first to be hurt by the demise of the federal Religious Freedom Restoration Act (RFRA). Each of their stories shows why Americans must work to restore free exercise protections, which have been decimated in the wake of the US Supreme Court's *Boerne* decision. Fortunately, attempts are being made, both at federal and state levels, to put some teeth back into free exercise protections. Their success depends, ultimately, upon the value Americans truly place on religious liberty.

Three victims

In the summer of 1997, some Orthodox Jews in Los Angeles attempted to obtain a zoning variance for religious meetings in a rented house along a residential area. That house, or "shul," accommodated ten to fifteen people during the week, fifty to sixty on Sabbath and other Jewish holidays. Orthodox Jews must walk to services on Sabbath because their religion does not permit them to use cars on the seventh day. Thus, neighborhoods without shuls are effectively off limits to Orthodox Jews.

When a neighbor complained, the congregation requested a special use permit from the Los Angeles City Council. Opponents of the permit argued to the

This chapter originally appeared in *Liberty*, July/August 1998.

council that "if you permit this illegal use how do you rationally prevent Muslims from setting up their things, Hindus from having their temples? Once you open up the door, you will ruin a beautiful asset."

The Los Angeles City Council unanimously rejected the request for the special use permit, though a short time later the same council approved the application of a gay sex club for a variance to locate within five hundred feet of another residential area. How could the council knock down the right of thirteen or fourteen people to pray together but allow a sex club to exist near a residential neighborhood?

In one of the more compelling stories to emerge from the post-RFRA world, California Baptist minister Wiley Drake was convicted of housing the homeless in violation of city zoning regulations. His church gives groceries to hundreds of people every month and allows dozens of homeless to sleep in tents and on an enclosed patio at First Southern Baptist Church in Buena Park, California. Pastor Drake was found guilty of four criminal misdemeanor counts, carrying a maximum six-month jail sentence and a thousand-dollar fine each. Pastor Drake said that he would appeal the verdict and continue his ministry.

The demise of RFRA has meant a much more restricted religious environment for prisoners also. Richard Lee Rowold is an inmate at the Plainfield Correctional Facility in Indiana. A Seventh-day Adventist, he abstains from work on Friday evenings and Saturdays. Richard was ordered by the prison authorities to carry out thirty hours of extra duty, some on Sabbath. When Rowold said that he was willing to do the extra work but not on the seventh day, he was disciplined for insubordination. Rowold went to federal court, claiming rights under the First Amendment and the RFRA. The court ruled that the First Amendment did not protect David because the extra work was rationally related to a legitimate interest. The court wrote that if it were "to hold [Rowold's] right to assert his religious beliefs outweighed the rights of the penal system to maintain order and balance it is quite possible other prisoners would convert to Judaism or the Adventist following to avoid Sabbath work duty."[1]

Because RFRA was no longer valid law by the time the court made its decision, it did not have to deal further with Rowold's claim. Had RFRA been in effect, the outcome could have been different. (Other prisoners affected by the demise of RFRA were a Muslim man who protested in vain against being searched by a female prison officer on the grounds that his religion forbade him from being touched by any woman except his wife, and practitioners of Native American religions who were denied access to sweat lodge ceremonies after RFRA was overturned.)

From *Smith* to *Boerne*

What has brought these straits in religious liberty? The immediate cause has been the US Supreme Court's reinterpreting First Amendment free exercise protections. Prior to 1990, the First Amendment was interpreted to give protection to religious belief and conduct in all cases in which such belief or conduct was not outweighed by some compelling government interest in protecting the life, liberty, or property of other citizens.

Then, in the 1990 case *Employment Division v. Smith*, the court decided that the First Amendment should provide protection only if a law or regulation was explicitly aimed at some religious group or practice. Under this reasoning, laws preventing Orthodox Jews from wearing headgear on government property would be unconstitutional, while laws forbidding all people from wearing headgear on government property would, in fact, be constitutional. Under the *Smith* rationale, Orthodox Jews wearing their headgear would have to violate either their consciences or the law if they wanted to walk on government property. The court did say that if a religious claim was brought in combination with some other kind of right, such as speech or parenting rights, that it would give the claim the benefit of the old First Amendment interpretation. This has become known as the "hybrid-rights" exception to the *Smith* standard.

In response to this drastic weakening of protections, a national free exercise coalition of uncommon bedfellows—more than sixty Jewish, Muslim, Christian, and secular civil rights groups—urged the passage of a federal statute restoring the old standard. With unlikely allies such as Beverly LaHaye, Lou Sheldon, the ACLU, and the People for the American Way organization all supporting it, the Religious Freedom Restoration Act, or RFRA, was passed by a virtually unanimous Congress in 1993.

But in June of 1997, the court declared in *Boerne v. Flores* that RFRA was an unconstitutional exercise of congressional power and that Congress had no business protecting the religious liberty of it citizens beyond what was required by the Supreme Court's interpretation. (There is still some possibility that while RFRA is invalid in regard to the fifty states, the federal government may still be bound by it.)

Fighting back

In response to *Boerne*, the free exercise coalition is proceeding on two fronts: in Washington, DC, and in each of the state capitals.

First, it is drafting a replacement for RFRA that takes into account the concerns raised by the Supreme Court in *Boerne*. RFRA II is nearing completion. The drafters have based its protection for religious activities primarily on the commerce clause, whereas the original RFRA was premised on the Fourteenth Amendment to the Constitution. Historically, the Supreme Court has read very broadly Congress's authority to regulate under the commerce clause. Because of this, Congress used this portion of the Constitution as the basis of the civil rights acts of the 1960s, which have generally been upheld as constitutional.

RFRA II would also codify the sparse remaining protection left under the *Smith* decision, including the hybrid-rights exception. It would create a presumption of five thousand dollars in damages whenever a person could prove a violation of his or her religious rights. And it explicitly leaves untouched the protections and requirements of the establishment clause of the First Amendment. This latter point was critical to keeping the free exercise coalition intact.

RFRA II faces definite challenges. It is less comprehensive in its protections than the original RFRA. This is primarily because it can protect only religious acts or services that arguably impact or affect interstate commerce. The act presumes that religious groups with a budget of more than one hundred thousand dollars or who use property worth in excess of one hundred thousand dollars affect interstate commerce. It also attempts to extend its protections to religious activities that use either property or services of a kind regularly bought or sold in interstate commerce.

Under this standard, a large church built from out-of-state lumber and that uses books and papers printed out-of-state would qualify; but the small home church with photocopied song sheets may not. It all depends on whether their activities or purchases have a "substantial effect" on interstate commerce, not likely for a small church or religious group. It's hard to see how individual or small-group religious conduct, such as voluntary school prayer groups or workplace lunch Bible study groups, would be protected. Often it is this form of individual expression that needs the most protection.

Others may find it disturbing to define religious activities as "interstate commerce." Is religion really commerce? While drafters of the bill explicitly state that the act's definitions of interstate commerce are for purposes of "this act only," how can that limitation be ensured? Once religion can be "protected" as interstate commerce, could it also be "regulated" as interstate commerce? At this point, nobody knows.

Will the benefits to religious activity provided by RFRA II outweigh the risks? Because of these concerns, and because of the limitations of the proposed RFRA II, the coalition is also turning to the states as the new defenders of religious freedom.

State RFRAs

One reason the court gave for its ruling in *Boerne* was that RFRA infringed on the "traditional prerogative and general authority" of the states.[2] The free exercise coalition took the court at its word and is seeking to bring the "traditional prerogative and general authority" of the states to bear on the problem of protecting religious freedom.

There are two ways in which this can happen. The simplest is for a state supreme court to interpret its state constitution as providing the higher level of protection that the federal Constitution used to provide. Some states, seven at last count, have done this; fourteen others seem to be headed in this direction. The problem, of course, is that a state supreme court can also interpret its constitution to provide the protection only provided by the federal Constitution as now interpreted—or even less. This lower level of protection has been granted by two states and the District of Columbia, with another four moving this way. The majority of the states have not decided what level of protection to provide.

In those states not providing suitable protection, or in those where the level of protection is undecided, the other approach is to pass a state equivalent of the RFRA. Known as state RFRAs, these bills have been introduced in fourteen state legislatures. The free exercise coalition is actively involved in shepherding these bills through the legislative process and is trying to prevent any debilitating amendment or exemptions from being added.

In evaluating state RFRAs, the coalition is concerned with three basic issues. The first is that it be understood, and codified, that religious freedom is for all. Efforts are made in many states to exclude or exempt prisoners from the coverage of the protective acts, even though such exemptions both dehumanize prisoners, who most need spiritual attention, and turn religious freedom from a human right into a state policy. If prisoners are exempted today, who will be tomorrow? (See "Rethinking Prisoner RFRA Exemptions.")

The second concern is that a state RFRA carefully codify the compelling state interest test abandoned by the Supreme Court. This test should require that before the government can place a "substantial burden" on religion, even unintentionally, the state must prove that it has a compelling reason—such as public health or safety—to do so. Further, the state should prove that it has used the least restrictive method reasonably possible to achieve its compelling end.

Because some state courts have evaded the protections of this standard by narrowly defining religion, the act should define religion as including conduct that is "motivated by religious beliefs or convictions." Thus, while renting an apartment is not a typically "religious" act, a landlord's decision not to rent to an unmarried couple because of the landlord's religious convictions should be viewed as religiously motivated conduct.

Finally, the coalition has agreed that these state RFRAs should contain no extraneous legislative initiative to fix other "problems" in church-state law. These would include changes to the establishment clause, public funding of parochial schools, or the introduction of prayer services into public schools. The coalition is divided on these issues, and any attempt to marry these to the RFRA efforts would result in a splintering, making it much less likely that the bill would pass.

Reconstruction

Unless something is done to reconstruct free exercise protection, stories like those of the Orthodox Jews in Los Angeles, Baptist minister Wiley Drake, and Adventist prisoner Richard Lee Rowold will multiply. America can do better than this. Even if most states pass RFRAs, however, religious liberty will be reduced to a patchwork quilt of varying levels of protection. On a positive note, the need for state and local involvement in protecting religious liberty is awakening citizens across the country to the importance of this precious legacy.

There is an irony in the movement from the state level to protect religious liberty, because it was with the states, such as Rhode Island and Virginia, where it all began. The first state struggle for religious liberty produced some of the most elevated and best articulated expressions of religious freedom: Madison's "Memorial and Remonstrance" and Jefferson's Virginia Statute for Religious Freedom. One can only hope that the second state struggle for religious freedom will produce not just similar expressions but the positive rights embodied in those expressions as well.

---

1. Rowold v. McBride, 973 F. Supp. 829 (N.D. Ind. 1997).
2. City of Boerne v. Flores, 521 US 507 (1997).

Chapter 13

Rethinking Prisoner RFRA Exemptions

Prisoners are not a popular group. They don't have much political clout. Many people view them as having given up, by their conduct, the rights and privileges of society. Prisoners also tend to be a litigious lot. With time being one of their few assets, they spend a good deal of it thinking up creative and often time-consuming lawsuits. It is not surprising, then, that many state RFRAs are targeted by amendments to exempt prisoners from their coverage. Such exemptions are profoundly misguided. First, religious liberty is a human right. The Declaration of Independence envisions the rights of humanity as a gift from God and as preceding the existence of government. Thus the Bill of Rights should be understood, not as a civil grant of rights, but as a civil recognition of rights that existed prior to and apart from the state. While some rights do require community involvement and existence to be realized ("freedom of association" or the exercise of the "freedom of speech" are examples), religious freedom has a peculiarly private, individual aspect. It can be, and often is, exercised solely between a person and God.

Indeed, most religions and enlightened philosophies recognize the responsibility each person has before God for his or her own conscience. This duty to conscience exists by virtue of one's being a human being before God. Prisoners are still human beings before God. They thus continue to have duties before their Creator and must have the corresponding right to exercise those duties. To hold

---

This chapter originally appeared in *Liberty*, July/August 1998.

otherwise is either to deny the humanity of prisoners or to deny the universality of God and conscience. Neither approach is a safe proposition. In exempting prisoners, the government treats religious freedom as a state-created and state-fostered policy that can be withdrawn at the whim of bureaucrats.

Second, prison RFRA cases did not clog the federal court system. Despite widespread claims that prisoners abused RFRA's protections by bringing a flood of federal lawsuits, the Justice Fellowship reports that prison RFRA claims accounted for less than 1 percent of cases in the US courts in 1996. About 269,000 civil cases were filed in federal courts in 1996. Of these, about 41,000, or about 15 percent, were filed by prisoners. Roughly 2,000 of these cases, or less than 1 percent of the total, were RFRA prison suits.

Further, prisoners rarely brought a case under a single cause of action. They would usually throw in at least three different amendments that they claimed had been violated and would toss in the prison kitchen sink for good measure. It is unlikely that withdrawing RFRA's protections from prisoners will reduce the number of suits. New and more creative causes of action will be stated. If prisoners are exempted from RFRA because they abuse it, are they to be exempt them from the Fourth, Fifth, Sixth, Eighth, and Fourteenth Amendments to the US Constitution because they abuse those as well?

Though a number of prisoner suits are frivolous, many aren't. And the frivolous suits are diminishing because of the recently enacted federal Prison Litigation Reform Act. This act requires prisoners to pay filing fees from their institutional accounts, has a three-strikes-and-you're-out rule regarding frivolous suits, and requires that a court clerk screen pro se prisoner suits before any litigation actually commences. Perhaps it would be far more convenient and efficient to do away with prisoner access to our court system entirely. But as one federal judge quipped, if the courts are only about efficiency and not justice, we may as well all go home.

Finally, RFRA did not interfere with legitimate prison operations. Under RFRA, prisons had the right to limit prisoner religious activities that posed a threat to the security or operations of the prison facility, much as the state had the right to curtail the religious activities of free citizens that threatened or endangered the lives, safety, or rights of fellow citizens. But in prison it is a given that the state, because of its security and safety concerns, has an even greater right to intrude into the lives of inmates. This means that prisoners cannot exercise their religious rights with the same expansiveness and breadth as nonprisoners.

But even prisoners have a duty to worship God. A properly crafted RFRA will protect this right and yet still allow prison administrators to maintain good order, security, and discipline. It will prevent, however, prison regulation of religious conduct that is grounded on mere speculation, exaggerated fears, or post hoc rationalizations. Often, because of the scarcity of personnel and resources, prison administrators run only those programs that they have to run. If religious visitation and programming is not a mandated right, administrators unsympathetic to religion may well severely limit such activity or even cut it out entirely—an alarming fate for the "first freedom" in America's constitutional constellation of rights. If this right is not inviolable, then one must say, with James Madison, "that the will of the Legislature is the only measure of their authority; and that in the plenitude of this authority, they may sweep away all our fundamental rights."[1]

For these reasons, prison exemptions to state RFRAs are a bad idea, violating one of humanity's (which includes even prisoners') most basic rights.

---

1. James Madison, *Religious Freedom: A Memorial and Remonstrance* (Boston: Lincoln and Edmands, 1819), 12.

Chapter 14

A Secular Threat to Religious Freedom

Recent events in America have shown that a strong secularism can lead to clashes with religious freedom. This, however, is not a new occurrence in the West. It is at least as old as the French Revolution, where the rallying cry "liberty, fraternity, and equality" was based on a dark philosophy that was antipriest, antichurch, and anti-God. The French experiment soon lost its crude, atheistic edge and morphed into a quasi-tolerant but religion-marginalizing public philosophy.

While this revised French secularism did not deny the existence of God, it essentially denied the ability of religious people to express their religious beliefs anywhere outside the privacy of their homes, churches, synagogues, or mosques. This religion-marginalizing, privatizing philosophy has characterized the role of religion in the societies of most of the nations of western Europe. This has been true even of those nations that have state-supported churches, such as Germany, England, and the Scandinavian countries.

What is quite new in the relationship between secularism and religion is the new potency that this European form of secularism has recently gained in America. Historically, America has been foremost in promoting a certain kind of secular government: one that does not endorse or promote a national church, creed, or even religion generally. It has been more "secular" in this formal sense than most of the nations of Europe.

This chapter originally appeared in *Liberty*, September/October 2012.

Yet the paradox has been that while formally and legally secular, America has allowed for and protected a vibrant religious community. Further, those communities of faith have not expressed that faith in a purely private fashion but have launched enterprises that have impacted public policy and even politics in dramatic and society-altering ways. A few of the movements that have been largely driven and at times led by religious people and churches include antislavery, temperance reform, child-labor laws, and, most recently, the American civil rights movement.

But this healthy respect for religious freedom and the role of religion in shaping society and politics has recently come under open attack in American society. For most of the history of the Christian West, homosexual activity was considered a crime against nature. It was universally condemned by virtually all religions, cultures, and societies, Christian and otherwise. It was only in 1961 that Illinois became the first state to remove criminatory sanctions from the act of sodomy. Even in the modern secular West, homosexual orientation was considered to be a mental defect or illness until 1973. As recently as 1986, the US Supreme Court affirmed that state criminal laws against homosexuality were acceptable under the Constitution.

These facts make all the more stunning the reversal that has happened over the past two decades. A growing secular rights movement has made gay rights the centerpiece of its agenda. In 2003, the US Supreme Court reversed its earlier decision and ruled in the case of *Lawrence v. Texas* that states could not criminalize homosexual behavior between consenting adults. This invalidated sodomy laws in thirteen states and strengthened the cause of a growing same-sex marriage movement.

Just a little over a decade since the Supreme Court decriminalized homosexual acts, the Court declared that gay marriage is a constitutional right. In 2015, in the case of *Obergefell v. Hodges,* the Court ruled that the desire to protect marriage as a union between a man and a woman is merely religious bigotry that deserves no place or consideration in the law. This is a stunning and dramatic reversal that squarely pits the competing claims of a secular, relativistic, even nihilistic morality with the natural-law morality shared by nearly all the great religions and cultures of recorded civilization.

The decision in *Obergefell* puts us today in much the same place as the French Revolution. Something very basic is at stake in our society's moral ordering and framework, and the ability of not just historic Christianity but almost any form of traditional religion to survive is being threatened by a zealous movement to overturn the basic, natural moral order of society. This kind of extreme secularism cannot exist with religion but must displace religion, at least traditional versions of it.

While we might presume that churches, temples, and synagogues will probably never be required to hire or marry homosexuals, the same cannot be said for church-affiliated institutions, such as colleges, hospitals, and social-welfare charities. Already a number of religious charities have had to close in states where gay marriage has been adopted because they refused to provide adoptions or other services to gay couples. The public role of the church's mission is at stake in this very well-known battle over sexual "freedom" and family welfare. Thus it becomes vital for us to be able to distinguish between traditional American secularism and the European version that is hostile to individual religious freedoms.

A recent American Supreme Court case was heralded as a strong victory for religious freedom. But the decision, in the case of *Hosanna-Tabor Evangelical Lutheran Church v. EEOC*, which upheld the ministerial exemption from federal antidiscrimination laws, is, in my view, a mixed bag. That the decision attracted the unanimous support of both very liberal and extremely conservative justices should indicate that there are some deeper things going on than just the protection of religious freedom.

The case involved an elementary-school teacher for a Lutheran church school. The teacher taught a wide variety of subjects, such as math, English, and science, and also taught one religion course a day. The church viewed her as a commissioned minister of religion. The teacher began experiencing some health problems, a sleeping disorder, and needed to take time off from work. After a four- or five-month absence, she desired to return, but was essentially told that she had been replaced, as the board thought that her health issues would prevent her from functioning successfully. She indicated she intended to enforce her legal rights in court under the Americans With Disabilities Act. After receiving the legal threat, the school board voted to rescind the teacher's religious call, as lawsuits within the church are considered a breach of moral duty.

The question the Supreme Court had to decide was whether the teacher really qualified as a pastor and would thus be prevented from bringing any kind of discrimination suit under the ministerial exemption. (Just a word about the ministerial exemption: This is a legal doctrine, based on the Constitution and carved out by federal courts, that says that churches have the right to hire, fire, and otherwise manage ministerial employees without oversight or interference from the state. This is because, courts have reasoned, ministers are so important to the shaping and teaching of doctrine and worship practices, which are the essential, core functions of what churches are about. A church needs to have a free hand to change, replace, or discipline pastors if they start straying from the theological and ritual beliefs of the church.)

A number of federal courts had affirmed this exemption, though it had never been considered by the Supreme Court. So the Supreme Court had to decide two things: (1) Is there actually a ministerial exemption to civil discrimination laws? If so, (2) was this exemption broad enough to cover elementary-school teachers in church schools who have as part of their duties the teaching of Bible classes? The court unanimously answered Yes to both questions. The ministerial exemption is a constitutionally founded doctrine; thus, ministers cannot sue churches under antidiscrimination laws, and schoolteachers who have some religious roles are considered ministers.

Now this seems like a good victory for religious freedom. But what kind of religious freedom is it? Is it individual religious freedom? Or is it more about institutional autonomy—the right of institutions to be free from government oversight? Indeed, if you ask about the individual rights perspective in this case, you might say that individual freedom or rights lost out to institutional interests. It should be of some caution that such strong conservatives as Justices Scalia and Thomas voted for this outcome, along with such liberals as Justices Kagan and Ginsburg. There is a paradox in that Justice Scalia was the author of the opinion in *Oregon v. Smith*, which *denied* religious freedom rights to individuals, but in *Hosanna-Tabor* he *granted* religious-freedom rights to institutions.

What is going on here? Well, for the liberals on the Supreme Court, the notion of group rights, even religious-groups' rights, is of high value. An important aspect of French secularity, even in the early days, was the treatment of religion as a group function. Contrary to popular impressions, French secularism tended not to be entirely atheistic. Voltaire and Rousseau, far from being the atheists that some imagine, were at least deists who saw an important social role for religious belief. Indeed, Rousseau believed religion was sufficiently important that a very basic set of religious beliefs should be officially promoted by the government, and anyone who rejected them should be exiled or even executed. For the French philosophes, religion was not to be entirely abandoned, but a minimalist version needed to be created and then enforced by the state.

This secular Enlightenment model was not so different from what we might call a medieval model, which also valued religion but at the expense of the individual. The medieval church had a sense of the separate spheres of church and state, but it viewed these two as collaborating to oversee and monitor the individual, who had no meaningful rights at all. Religious institutions, on the other hand, had rights to be free from state intrusion or oversight, even in many criminal matters. In the Middle Ages, there was a separate system of church courts that handled many matters relating to the church, including oversight of cases and even criminal claims involving clergy and other church employees.

This parallel system of courts meant that the institutional church was insulated from state oversight, and individual church employees and members would not have recourse in civil courts against abuses, even criminal ones, by the church or its employees. This medieval model was one that Martin Luther sharply criticized. He said that the church should be subject to the laws and magistrates of the land. The issue well illustrates how the protection of so-called group or institutional rights can conflict and even suppress individual religious rights.

Now, I do not want to overstate this point. I think that the *Hosanna-Tabor* case probably came out correctly. I am certainly happy that the Supreme Court upheld the ministerial exemption. I do think that ministers play a special role in defining and propagating the mission and beliefs of a church. But this exception needs to be applied carefully, as not all employees of religious institutions play this special role. Nor do they all have the prestige and respect usually held by ministers, which gives them greater protection and authority in their communities.

This case may mean, depending on how lower courts interpret it, that almost all teaching employees of any church institution will be deemed ministers and thus may well be stripped of civil rights and antidiscrimination protection. Do we really want to accept that once you join a religious employer you trade in most of your civil rights? Do we really believe that the state has an important interest in protecting only the religious rights and autonomy of the institution and not the civil rights and freedoms of the individual? I hope not.

The concern and protection for community institutions—governmental and religious—at the expense of individuals and their rights is found in the skeptical Enlightenment secularism of Rousseau and Hobbes and the medieval absolutism of Aquinas and Innocent III. It is a commitment to the rule of the majority in both the political and religious realms that the Protestant Reformation confronted, slowly unraveled, and ultimately opposed by creating an order of rights based on the individual in the founding of the American republic.

The irony is that the last and greatest attack of secularism on religion and religious freedom may ally itself with the overtly religious model of medieval Europe that also discounted the religious and civil freedoms of individuals and minorities.

It is at this time that we must promote more broadly the dissenting Protestant view of the importance of the individual conscience. The individual's standing before God is of highest import; this standing must be respected by both the state and the church, and our system of rights is first and foremost meant to defend individual, personal rights. Institutional rights, while also meaningful and important and in their own way an expression of individual rights, still must be kept in their proper place and not be allowed to suppress or abuse the individual inappropriately.

We must beware of political candidates, or any other civic or religious leaders, who insist that the threat to religious freedom comes only, or even primarily, from an antireligious secularism. Religious people and forces have shown themselves well capable of doing just as effective a job at trampling on the religious rights of the individual.

Chapter 15

Cults in the Crossfire

Arcane ceremonies, mysterious creeds, and the smell, however faint, of ritual violence—all reasons that religious cults are often criticized and suppressed by both the state and mainstream religious groups. From Japan to China to Russia to the Western democracies of Germany and France, cults and sects are being targeted for investigation, interrogation, and even suppression. This crossfire of criticism and scrutiny is viewed by many people as deserved, because they believe that cultic groups pose a threat to a well-ordered society. But this conclusion begs the question, what is a cult?

Most people believe they know a cult when they see one. Do you? Can you pick the cult out of the description of the following three religious groups?

1. A young man with physical strength and musical talent found himself ostracized from his religious community. Taking a few malcontents with him, he began a new commune in the wilderness, where an arsenal of weapons and survival gear was rapidly collected. Other drifters swelled the ranks of the commune, and the group was united by the music and scriptural teaching of the charismatic leader. Known for his skill in crafting song lyrics and poetry, he often blended references to himself and a Messiah figure. Early on, he began a practice of taking multiple wives. He had a sense of personal prophetic destiny and encouraged a squad of "mighty men" to train militarily for a

---

This chapter originally appeared in *Liberty*, March/April 2001.

future, decisive showdown with government forces that would propel him to a position of authority.

2. A mature man, after years of administrative and legal conflict, felt that his people could not carry out their worship activities in their home country in peace. Emigrating to another land en masse, the religious community soon set up what amounted to a civil state in their new land. Outsiders were not allowed access to the encampment, except on very restrictive terms. Those in violation of the strict codes of the camp were severely punished, usually corporally—and, rumor had it, occasionally killed. Even children were subject to these harsh measures. Official representatives of the home country, sent after the illegally departing group, died under highly mysterious circumstances. Soon afterward, word came that thousands in the group were killed by fellow members after a frenzied ceremony around a cultic object.

3. A dead man was, ostensibly, still the leader of the new religious movement that worshiped him as divine. His followers "spoke" to him in both private and group ritual services and celebrated the act of his death as their central theme—going so far as to mimic the eating of his corpse in secret ceremonies. The adherents shared property on a communal basis and would cut ties with family, friends, and livelihood to follow their dead Messiah. They had a practice of "shunning" those among their group who flouted his moral standards. They refused to pledge the required honor to the ruler of the state and, indeed, broke certain laws of the state, explaining that their religion required them to do so.

Which is the cultic group? All of them—and none of them. The answer depends on when the question is asked and to whom. Most readers probably saw that the third scenario was a description of early Christianity and avoided calling it a cult. But the average first-century Roman citizen, at least one who had heard of Christianity, would view it as one of the more bizarre Eastern cults. The first scenario is not David Koresh at Waco, but rather the early days of King David, the founder of the royal house of David and an ancestor of Christ.[1] And the second scenario? Not Jim Jones going to Guyana, but Moses leading the Hebrews out of Egypt into the Promised Land.[2] All three of these groups were viewed by their mainstream contemporaries as the type of unconventional, nonconformist, charismatic-led religious entities to which we attach the term *cult*. Today, however, each of these sagas is a respected, even hallowed, story in the pantheon of America's respected Christian tradition.

These examples highlight the problem with the term *cult*. While it has a technical, nonpejorative meaning that refers to any organized religious group or practice, the popular meaning of *cult* is inherently negative. When most people identify a group as a cult, they almost always intend to identify what *Webster's* calls "a religion or sect considered to be false, unorthodox, or extremist, with members often living outside of conventional society under the direction of a charismatic leader."[3] Thus, a cult becomes any religion that deviates from what the majority in society view as normal behavior and belief in spiritual matters. We use *cult* as a handy, thoughtless shorthand to describe religious movements with which we are unfamiliar and that we therefore view with suspicion.[4] We forget that virtually *all* of us are cultists *somewhere*—it's just that most of us, by definition, live where *our* religious views are the mainstream.

Battling the "cults" in Maryland

But being human, and inherently parochial, we tend to overlook this fact. Still, it came as some surprise when my own home state at the time, Maryland, the original US colony of tolerance, launched an anticult initiative in May of 1998. Promoted by legislators with backgrounds in the "anticult" movement, the effort came in the form of a task force to study cult activities on Maryland state university campuses.[5] The initiative was unexpected, as there had been no recent incidents of significance on Maryland campuses involving minority religious groups. Indeed, the

Maryland legislation cited no problems with cults in Maryland, but rather referred to events outside the state—including cult-related violence in Mississippi, California, and even Japan. The effort was justified on the grounds that cult-recruitment activities are frequently "directed to students on college campuses."

The resolution identified the task force members, which included politicians, educators, students, and significantly, two parents of cult members. This last addition showed that the government already viewed certain groups as being cults prior to the first meeting of the task force. To form the task force, it had to choose parents with children belonging to cults. The inherent bias of the job given the task force was further revealed by the list of groups from which the task force was directed to seek information. The list included cult-awareness organizations (anticult groups), former cult members, campus ministers, and families of cult members. Significantly, there were no instructions to speak with current members of any groups suspected to be "cults" or with any leaders or representatives of the groups themselves. The goals of the task force were vague and involved filing a report with the governor and the assembly by September 1999 on the type and extent of cult activities on Maryland campuses.

Armed with this ill-defined mandate, the task force embarked on a fishing expedition to find misconduct on the part of minority religious groups. The task force called a series of "anticult" hearings and presented experts who accused a number of groups, including the Unification Church, the International Church of Christ, and the Church of Scientology, of misleading and harming students. They gave very few examples, however, of this occurring in Maryland, and their testimony was primarily hearsay and speculation, inadmissible in any court of law. A different view was presented by one invited speaker, William Stuart, a professor of anthropology at the University of Maryland, who cautioned the panel that defining a cult was inherently problematic and prejudicial and was usually a cover for crude religious bias.

Indeed, the task force soon realized that it could arrive at no working definition of *cult* and thus rewrote its mission statement, omitting the word altogether. The task force was now concerned with destructive and harmful "groups." But this did not change the focus of the task force's inquiry. The speakers at the task force's meetings continued to testify about new religious movements of one sort or another. Recruitment by these groups was termed *proselytizing*. And no witnesses were called to discuss the "harmful" activities of campus fraternities, sororities, or clubs—whose widely reported binge drinking and hazing scandals would seem a logical target of inquiry for any committee genuinely concerned with all groups that pose harm to students.

The final portion of each task force session was open to any speaker who wished to address the committee. It was during this time that the minority religious groups received a chance to speak, but on very limited terms, as these addresses were limited to five minutes. Those who spoke during this period received nothing of the respect or deference from the committee that the formally invited speakers received. Indeed, speakers during this period were frequently interrupted by defensive comments or questions by the task force members or chairperson.

The frustration of the minority religious groups grew at each meeting, until the inevitable occurred, and a lawsuit was filed.[6] The plaintiff requested that the task force be enjoined from releasing its report and that the court declare its activities in violation of the US Constitution. The task force responded by announcing it would hasten the release of the report in order to beat the court action. The chair's haste to avoid constitutional strictures was unnecessary, however, as the federal court refused to prevent the release of the report and later dismissed the suit as moot.

Vague and cryptic, the task force report itself did not reflect the extensive testimony about specific minority religions.[7] In fact, no "harmful" groups were named in the report. Instead, it listed the names of witnesses at the various meetings and indicated that their testimony could be viewed at University System of Maryland (USM) headquarters. In some instances, it gave brief overviews of the testimony, with the deletion of names of criticized groups. This approach adds an aura of mystery to the document, as though the witnesses and questioners were speaking in code about topics to which only they were privy.

The report writers were no doubt trying to avoid constitutional problems. But the opaqueness of the report only makes apparent the inherent legal flaw in the exercise. A "cult" fishing expedition will result either in a detailed, specific, and unconstitutional report or in a vague, ambiguous, and practicably unusable report. In either event, taxpayers' money and time is wasted. But more than this, the very existence of the Maryland report, for its relatively benign content, creates a dangerous precedent and justification for other states to engage in similar probes.

And perhaps even worse, the Maryland report comes at a time when a number of other countries, including some Western democracies, are engaged in their own "cult" and "sect" investigation programs. France, Germany, and Belgium all have ongoing government inquiries into new and minority religious movements. Eastern Europe and Russia are showing a renewed tendency to repress minority religions. China is involved in a notorious crackdown—with mass arrests, beatings, and imprisonment—against the nonviolent Falun Gong meditation movement. The Maryland incident makes it more difficult for the US government to bring moral pressure to bear on these countries to treat minority religions with respect and equality.

Cult committees and constitutional principles

The Maryland saga illustrates some themes that are often common to state-sponsored anticult efforts, wherever they may be found. Certainly, governments have a legitimate interest in investigating the activities of violent or criminal groups, religious or otherwise. A focused and discrete inquiry into particular alleged criminal acts, however, is amenable to constitutional guidelines of due process and evidentiary fairness. But if an inquiry committee reflects some combination of the following failings in due process, openness, and fairness, chances are that the effort is an unconstitutional and improper inquisition, rather than a legitimate government inquiry.

The prejudging of certain groups as abnormal or pathological

While the Maryland legislation identified no particular "cult," it named to the task force parents of cult members and charged the committee with interviewing cult-awareness experts. Thus, prior to the task force's reviewing one iota of evidence, the state was expected to identify certain groups as "cults" so the task force could be constituted.

Similarly, in France and Germany, only certain suspect religious groups appear before the inquiry committees. None of the state or mainstream churches are forced to appear or undergo review. Rather, these churches help identify the suspect groups. Thus the very fact that a group is reviewed by the committee requires an act of prejudging. Prejudging is, of course, where the word *prejudice* comes from—and it is no surprise that this is what minority religious groups experience before these committees.

Vague targets, standards, and mandates

The Maryland task force soon realized that the term *cult* was so amorphous and ill defined that they abandoned it as a guide to their efforts. Unfortunately, the replacement—*group*—was so broad as to be meaningless. Similarly, in Germany, the committee to review "sects and psycho groups" could not define *psycho group*, so put the label on the Church of Scientology just to fill the category.[8]

Further, as the initiative did not charge the task force with any concrete incidents to examine or review, there was no real guidance as to what evidence was material or relevant. This meant that the arbitrary biases of the committee members and the chair dictated what evidence would be accepted. "Anticultists" came and spoke disparagingly, and even slanderously, of groups from around the country, sharing incidents that allegedly occurred in other states or even overseas.

In at least one instance, testimony and documents proffered by a major academic sympathetic to religious freedom concerns of the target groups was rejected by the chairperson as irrelevant. The absence of clearly defined targets to investigate or incidents to review is an invitation to a due process–free fishing expedition, when guided only by the biases and whims of the committee members.

Witnesses and evidence from natural enemies

The Maryland legislation listed seven groups from which testimony should be taken, but did not include representatives of the "cults" under investigation. Rather, the groups consisted generally of the natural enemies of these groups, such as anticult groups, former cult members, families of cult members, and campus ministers. The latter persons represent groups who are usually active opponents of new religious groups.

In western Europe, where legal separation of church and state is nonexistent, the mainstream churches are often the driving force behind antisect activities and seek to use the state to inhibit the functions of those they view as competitors.

In Germany, church representatives will participate as experts in antisect inquiries and will work hand in hand with the state in educating the public about the dangers of "sects."[9] It is not surprising that the results of this unbalanced inquiry are unfavorable to the targeted groups.

An air of secrecy

The chair of the Maryland task force at one point ordered that no one was to communicate with any member of the task force except through his office. His command was not only rather arbitrary but probably unconstitutional, as several members of the committee were elected state officials, and anyone has a constitutional right to communicate with their representatives. But the unguided and divisive nature of the inquiry made some level of arbitrary control over information almost inevitable.

Other examples of the tendency toward secretiveness include a witness who refused to publicly release documents submitted to the committee and the choice by the chairperson not to include any substantive testimony in the report released to the public. Overseas, "sect" committees make direct use of covert surveillance and intelligence gathering—an example being the formal surveillance that Germany placed the Church of Scientology under in 1997.

Insider-versus-outsider, us-versus-them mentality

While academics sympathetic to the plight of new religious groups were called to testify before the Maryland task force, no members of the "cult" groups themselves were asked to testify. Rather, any "cult" member or leader who wished to address the task force was forced to speak during the open forum time at the end of each meeting, where, as previously mentioned, remarks were limited to five minutes. Apart from time limitations, these speakers were also accorded much less respect and deference than those formally invited. All this reinforced the "outsider" status that these groups had already been labeled with. If you were a member of a group under discussion, it was as though you were a wayward child, forced to listen to those in authority discuss what is in your best interests, with very little chance for you to speak for yourself.

The strengthening of this insider-versus-outsider mentality is one of the common results of antisect committee work. In Germany, the government's reports on "sects" have produced a wave of anticult media coverage that has prompted much private sector harassment, including widespread employment discrimination against suspected cultists. In 1996, after a French commission on sects released a report identifying 172 groups as sects, the French newspaper *Le Monde* called for something to be done about sects. Shortly after this, the Unification Church headquarters in Paris was firebombed. Ironically, much of the violence by the community was carried out against outsider groups.[10] The evidence shows that "overwhelmingly, nonconventional religious groups have been free of reported incidents [violence or coercion] atypical of their day-to-day life."[11]

One could conclude that the violation of due process, disregard of constitutional rights, and divisiveness of this type of inquiry is more of a threat to a community than any of the groups being investigated. Indeed, the Maryland task force perhaps tacitly admitted as much when, in its report, it acknowledged as the first fact that the "divergent views, [and] constitutional issues" may cause state "intervention . . . [to] exacerbate the problem." It then admitted, as fact number two, that the extent of the problem "is statistically very small considering the enormous number of students attending USM institutions."[12]

After-the-fact admissions, however, that discriminatory and divisive investigation may have been unnecessary is not much comfort to those "cults" caught in the sights of private interests and public scrutiny. While it is a relief to emerge relatively unscathed, the Constitution is meant to protect peaceful religious groups from having to undergo the gauntlet at all. In Maryland, while the original target may have been cults, it is the Constitution and religious freedom that really got caught in the crossfire.

1. David's exploits as an outlaw in the Judean wilderness are recorded in 1 Samuel 22–31 and 2 Samuel 1:2.

2. The story of Moses and the Exodus, including the drowning of the Egyptian army and the purging of the people after their worship of the golden calf, is found in Exodus 13–32.

3. *Webster's Encyclopedic Unabridged Dictionary of the English Language* (New York: Random House, 1966), s.v. "cult."

4. Academics are becoming aware that the popular usage of *cult* is overshadowing its technical meaning, and many of them are now referring to minority religious movements as new religious movements, or NRMs. W. Cole Durham Jr., "The United States' Experience With New Religious Movements," *European Journal for Church and State Research* 5 (1998): 213.

5. Task Force to Study the Effects of Cult Activities on Public Senior Higher Education Institutions, H.J.R. 22 (May 21, 1998).

6. The present author, in his capacity as a citizen and taxpayer in Maryland, is a plaintiff in the suit.

7. Task Force to Study the Effects of Cult Activities on Public Senior Higher Education Institutions, "Report of the Task Force to Study the Effects of Cult Activities on Public Senior Higher Education Institutions," Religious Freedom, accessed April 17, 2017, http://www.religiousfreedom .com/documents/tskfrce/MDrpt.htm.

8. Gabriele Yonan, "Religious Liberty in Germany Today: How the Public Debate on Sects Has Affected Religious Liberty in Germany" (paper in author's possession).

9. Ibid.

10. J. Gordon Melton, *Encyclopedic Handbook of Cults in America*, rev. and updated ed. (New York: Garland Publishing, 1992), 366–369.

11. Ibid., 362.

12. Task Force to Study the Effects of Cult Activities, "Report of the Task Force to Study the Effects of Cult Activities."

Chapter 16

Cults and Psycho Groups

Sometimes it has to happen to a celebrity before the world pays attention. In 1993, acclaimed American jazz pianist Chick Corea was disinvited from a concert in Stuttgart, Germany. The government of the German state of Baden-Württemberg canceled the concert because Mr. Corea is a Scientologist.

For many, this was the first indication that all was not well with religious minorities in Germany. Then, a year later, Germany's major political party attempted to generate a boycott of the movie *Phenomenon* because it starred well-known Scientologist John Travolta. Shortly afterward, a similar attempt was made against *Mission: Impossible* because its star was Scientologist Tom Cruise.

This discrimination against American celebrities evoked strong protest in international artistic and political communities. The response was heightened by a controversial series of full-page ads that the Church of Scientology ran in leading US newspapers, which compared the current treatment of Scientologists in Germany with the treatment of Jews by the National Socialists in the 1930s. Indeed, the reaction was such that Chick Corea has performed in Germany a number of times since his canceled concert (but not without controversy), and both Tom Cruise's and John Travolta's films have achieved some success in Germany as well. However, celebrity discrimination appears to be only the tip of an iceberg of harassment and unequal treatment, both official and otherwise, directed at Scientologists in Germany today.

This chapter originally appeared in *Liberty*, January/February 1998.

A pattern of harassment

Since about 1990, Church of Scientology members have been discriminated against and harassed in Germany by both public and private agencies. The discrimination began at the state and local levels, where Scientologists were banned from regional political parties, from civil service positions, and (for Scientologist businesses) from obtaining government contracts. The government also sponsored anti-Scientology literature for distribution to schoolchildren. More informal types of animus against Scientologists include denial of bank accounts and loans and refusal to admit their children to private schools. The church has cataloged a list of almost one hundred instances of threats of violence and of actual violence against Scientologists and vandalism on their properties since 1990.

More recently the German federal government has targeted Scientology. To become a member of Germany's ruling political party, the Christian Democratic Union (CDU), a candidate must sign the following statement: "I apply for enrollment in the CDU and state that I am not a member of another party and I am not a member of the Scientology sect."[1] The other major political parties in Germany have followed the CDU in either banning or expelling Scientologists from party membership. The Church of Scientology reports that in 1996 the CDU demanded that the federal minister of the Interior ban all Scientologists from public service jobs; and later that year Germany's federal and regional governments agreed to exclude them, as far as possible, from public contracts.

In a statement released by its US embassy, the German government defended its actions by asserting that Scientology uses "inhuman and totalitarian practices," including, it asserted, the use of "pseudo-scientific courses" that cause "serious harm to some individuals," affecting both their "mental and physical health." This makes persons "psychologically and financially" dependent on the church, which then allows it to "exercise undue influence in certain economic sectors." The German government alleges that it's not alone in refusing to recognize Scientology as a religion, but that other countries, including France, Belgium, Italy, and Spain, also do not accept Scientology as a bona fide religion.[2]

In October of 1996, the German government considered the request of the CDU to place the church under surveillance by the Federal Office for the Protection of the Constitution (OPC), an antiextremist government security agency. At about that same time, the United States was finalizing its Country Reports on Human Rights Practices, which included a section on Germany. The German government's treatment of the Scientologists had become a sore point in German-American relations, and the US State Department was looking closely at the issue. At that time, the German government released a report that concluded that "no concrete facts exist currently to substantiate the suspicion of criminal acts" by the Church of Scientology and rejected the CDU's call for surveillance of the church by the OPC.[3] But just a few months after the United States published its human rights report—which noted favorably the German government's decision to not place the Church of Scientology under surveillance—all sixteen German federal states and the federal government decided in June of 1997 to conduct the surveillance anyway, claiming that it will focus on the "structure" of the church and "not on individual members." Germany's federal Minister of the Interior has said that the "year's surveillance will establish whether the organization is simply an unpleasant group, a criminal organization, or an association with anti-constitutional aims."[4]

Though the government will not comment on what the surveillance entails, it typically involves wiretapping and mail interception of communications, as well as observation and possibly infiltration. Whatever the long-term consequences, Germany's maneuvering on the issue has paid off: the US State Department has recently backed away from the issue and, in an apparent attempt to foster more positive relations with the German government, has openly criticized the Church of Scientology for comparing current German government policies with those of the Nazis.

The Enquete Commission

Much of the discomfort felt by Scientologists seems to originate with the Enquete Commission (Commission of Inquiry), recently established by the Bundestag (the lower house of the German federal parliament) to investigate "cults and psycho groups." The committee is comprised of eleven voting members of the Bundestag, along with eleven selected experts; its purpose is to investigate groups that pose potential danger to the German people and to advise the Bundestag on the necessary political decisions that can be made to avert the danger.

The Enquete Commission began its work with almost six hundred different groups on its investigatory list. Its final report is not yet out. The process of the investigation left religious minorities feeling vulnerable, especially because of the requirement that they justify their beliefs before the commission, which was conspicuously heavy with "experts." The commission has members with ties to large Christian denominations that compete with small religions in the marketplace of faith, and many of its members are openly antagonistic to minority faiths such as Scientology. Also, the very request to testify before the commission insinuates that the religious group is suspected of being a dangerous cult. In addition, there is the question of why certain religions have been singled out to be brought up before the commission, while other larger denominations have not been required to testify and actually have representatives on the commission.

Gabriele Yonan, from the Free University of Berlin, has been active in supporting the rights of minority religions in Germany. She blames the recent focus on Scientology, which she likens to the 1950 McCarthy hearings in America, to two troubling trends: the present economic malaise and the reduction in membership of the official churches.

Germany's unemployment had been hovering at almost twice the US rate. In some areas of the former East Germany, it is more than 16 percent. It is not coincidental, Yonan believes, that one of those most vehement in his efforts to "expose the dangers" posed by small religious groups is the German federal minister for labor, Norbert Blüm. It seems that whenever economic pain meets a loss of confidence in traditional religious institutions, populist leaders are tempted to find scapegoats to blame. Religious minorities are often a convenient target. Such targeting and scapegoating should be resisted in the name of religious freedom and basic human dignity.

---

1. Translated from German.

2. Cong. Rec. H10509–H10524 (daily ed. November 9, 1997), https://www.gpo.gov/fdsys/pkg/CREC-1997-11-09/html/CREC-1997-11-09-pt2-PgH10509.htm.

3. Bureau of Democracy, Human Rights, and Labor, "Germany," in *Country Reports on Human Rights Practices for 1996* (Washington, DC: Government Printing Office, 1997), accessed April 17, 2017, https://www.state.gov/www/global/human_rights/1996_hrp_report/germany.html.

4. Cong. Rec. 510513 (daily ed. November 9, 1997).

Chapter 17

Freedom Under Fire:
The First Amendment in Times of Crisis

The flash point could come via civil unrest, a devastating terrorist act, or break-downs caused by the Y2K millennium bug. In response, the president uses a series of executive orders to invoke martial law and suspend our civil liberties. Or the United Nations activates foreign troops already stationed on American soil to enforce compliance with a globalist, secularist agenda that tramples on individual rights of conscience and freedom. Or the Trilateral Commission conspires with the Council on Foreign Relations to override democracy and—well, you get the picture. As we move into the new millennium, any number of "conspiracy watch" groups are painting what-if scenarios in which a conjectured time of crisis is used as a pretext by some powerful person or group to steal away our civil liberties, including religious freedom.

Most of the scenarios envisioned by these groups are, to most reasonable minds, far-fetched. But the concern they raise about the possible loss of liberties during times of crisis is legitimate. No less a personage than William Rehnquist, chief justice of the Supreme Court, recently wrote a book entitled *All the Laws but One: Civil Liberties in Wartime*, with the thesis that during times of war civil liberties are curtailed and limited. The book is mainly historical and does not make claims about the possible fate of freedom and speech in future crises. But the history Rehnquist lays out, combined with other legal and legislative decisions from the

---

This chapter originally appeared in *Liberty*, January/February 2000.

crises that he explores, can provide insights into the possible shape and effect of future threats to the closely related freedoms of speech and religion.

Three lessons emerge from the history of religious and expressive rights during times of crisis. The first is that rights are generally degraded by an anxious majority and not by a powerful individual or semisecret cabal. The second is that the respect for rights is eroded over a period of time in the hearts and minds of the public before they are infringed by an executive, judicial, or legislative act. The third, and most unexpected, is that after a crisis passes, infringed rights are often established on a firmer basis than prior to the crisis. It seems that times of crisis create moments of contrast and contradiction in which the true value of those rights is highlighted by their very violation.

Tyranny of the majority

One price of democracy is an inefficient bureaucracy and a cumbersome separation of powers, which makes it supremely difficult for any single person or agency to wield plenary powers. This means that if a single person, even a president, wishes openly and notoriously to violate or degrade civil rights, he or she must gain the acquiescence of a vast number of other persons. Even a Supreme Court justice has to convince four other justices to agree with him or her in modifying constitutional rights. And the Supreme Court cannot make such a modification of its own accord, but may only respond to the action of a separate branch of government.

Those who speculate that a president can suspend the Constitution via executive order miss the fundamental point that executive orders are subject to the Constitution. While President Clinton promulgated a number of executive orders relating to the conduct of executive agencies during times of crisis, none of these orders could lawfully supersede, violate, or suspend the Constitution. We have been blessed with a system of government in which the only "emergency power" given to the president by the Constitution is the right to suspend the writ of habeas corpus during war.[1]

As Lincoln argued, the ability of the president to authorize detention of suspected enemies during times of invasion or rebellion can be necessary to the preservation of the government itself.[2] (Curiously, his application of the principle put him in direct conflict with Supreme Court chief justice Roger Taney, who declared the action unconstitutional and was then threatened with arrest by Lincoln.) The government may, during times of war, assert the twin needs of order and security to justify a more narrow application of citizens' rights to free speech, movement, and due process. But even then, those state claims are subject to constitutional review by the courts. Of course, judges are human as well and may not uphold the Constitution as they should, but the system of checks and balances in place means that any major disruption in civil rights will be the work of the many and not of the few.

The most widely cited example of a president's executive order infringing upon personal rights—the internment of US citizens of Japanese ancestry during World War II—is an apt illustration of this point. It is often overlooked that on the heels of President Roosevelt's executive order requiring the internment, Congress imposed criminal penalties for violation of the order or its implementing regulations. Thus, while the initial internment order was the act of one man, it was the affirmative power of Congress that gave the order its life and teeth.[3]

But even the support of Congress was not the final say in the matter. The constitutionality of President Roosevelt's internment order was challenged all the way to the Supreme Court. While the court largely upheld the president's use of wartime power, they did so because they believed the exercise was consistent with the Constitution and not because the Constitution was suspended. Indeed, in one instance during World War II, the court invalidated the government's continued detention of a Japanese American.

Thus, even given the exigencies of a wartime crisis, neither the president nor Congress can unilaterally "suspend" or "annul" the US Constitution. As a practical matter, they each have to gain the acquiescence of the other, as well as the agreement of the US Supreme Court. And, despite the infamous example of the wartime internment of the Japanese, such acquiescence is by no means a meaningless rubber stamp.

This truth was illustrated in the 1950s when, during the Korean War, President Truman issued an executive order authorizing the federal seizure of US steel mills to prevent a threatened labor strike. The president claimed a national emergency, as a steel strike would interfere with the war effort. The mill owners then went to federal court and argued that this act was beyond the president's power. The court agreed and reversed the president's order. The court noted that the president's role was to execute the laws—not to make the laws. On a number of occasions since then, federal courts have struck down executive orders on the basis that they exceeded the power given to the president by the Constitution or delegated to him by Congress.[4]

Obviously, then, the shrill claims that the president will unilaterally suspend our civil liberties ignore basic legal principles of our constitutional system. Neither could the real threat to civil liberties come from a "scheming" United Nations. While a force for humanitarian good, the UN's ponderous procedures and conflicted leadership make it a highly unlikely candidate to operate a conspiracy to infiltrate or subvert the US government. Frankly, most people who have worked for a government bureaucracy find it entirely unbelievable. No, the real threat to civil liberties is not from the executive order of a despotic president, the insidious infiltration of the Trilateral Commission, or the black helicopters of the United Nations. Rather, history shows that the threat to civil liberties, if it is to come, will arise from the acts or acquiescence of the majority of Americans as expressed through the representatives.

Inattention and apathy

It follows, then, that the greatest threat to civil liberties is not from a single, dramatic event, such as a terrorist attack or computer blackout. Rather, the true danger lies in a popular loss of esteem for the civil and religious rights of minorities. Our constitutional order is endangered most by the inattention and apathy that allow the spirit of its liberties to fade away from the consciousness of the people, and then, by natural progression, from our civil institutions and courts of justice.

Whether it is the rise of Fascism in the Europe of the 1930s or the shift of ancient Rome from republic to imperium, history shows that the loss of personal liberties occurs over a period of some time. When chronically indulgent, apathetic, and spiritually careless people are plunged into economic, social, or military distress, they will often allow their freedoms to be exchanged for a stronger economy and greater security. But the willingness to make this trade-off cannot happen overnight, especially in a democracy—it takes years of civic inattention. The irony is that those predicting a sudden, spectacular loss of liberty may well be distracted from the day-to-day work of preventing the slower degradation of those same liberties.

And this is the critical point. Those who paint grim scenarios of an apocalyptic loss of liberty in the new millennium often overlook the subtle but insidious degradation to religious liberty that occurred during the 1990s. During that decade, the Supreme Court's decisions in *Employment Division v. Smith* and *City of Boerne v. Flores* rolled religious liberty protection in America back at least fifty to one hundred years. This reality birthed a nationwide movement to pass religious-freedom acts at the state level in hopes of restoring this protection state by state. More than twenty such bills were introduced into state legislatures in 1998 and a roughly equal number in 1999. That there is no major, headline-making "crisis" to highlight the state religious-freedom-act movement should not detract from its urgency. During the past year, the difficulties faced by minority religions in their use of worship sites, their operation of welfare missions, and their ministries to prisoners have been documented. Those awaiting a great crisis before responding to lost religious freedoms will have missed the real crisis unfolding more subtly around them.

The accelerating drift toward intolerance of minority faiths and nonfaiths was illustrated by an incident last year at a high school graduation ceremony in Maryland.[5] The school allowed for a moment of silence at graduation, but not for public prayer, as school officials agreed that the latter was unconstitutional. But those attending the graduation took matters into their own hands and disrupted the moment of silence by reciting the Lord's Prayer. Beginning with a few persons, the prayer of protest swelled to a chorus of thousands, including public officials on the platform. One student, who had appealed for the moment of silence rather than prayer, walked out in protest. He tried to return to claim his diploma when the ceremony resumed, but he was arrested by state police and forced to miss the rest of the ceremony. He was also prevented from attending his class's post-graduation boat trip, for which he had already paid.

One suspects that He who gave us the Lord's Prayer intended it for nobler purposes than division, suppression, and making nonbelievers unwelcome at their own high school graduations. The increasing willingness of the majority to insist on the acceptance and practice of its religious traditions in the public sphere does not bode well for the fate of First Amendment freedoms in whatever crisis we first encounter in the new millennium.

Freedom in the furnace

It is true that the crisis and conflict can produce a rollback of freedoms of conscience. To the examples above can be added other wartime stories of dissidents arrested and suppressed in violation of rights of speech and religion. However, this is not the full story. The big picture shows that from the furnace of oppression, rights often emerge with greater force and vigor. This story can be seen vividly in the three great crises of our country: the Civil War and the two world wars.

Chief Justice Rehnquist begins his book on the suppression of civil liberties during wartime with the story of Abraham Lincoln suspending the writ of habeas corpus during the Civil War. This act allowed persons suspected of aiding or abetting the enemy to be arrested and held without the civil safeguards and court review usually available when a citizen is arrested. The Constitution allows the writ of habeas corpus to be suspended during times of war, although it is not clear whether the president can do this himself or if it is an action to be taken by Congress. In any event, Rehnquist makes a good case that the civil rights of expression and movement were, to varying degrees in varying places, among the casualties of the Civil War.

But what is not noted is that the Civil War laid the groundwork for the single greatest flowering of rights in America since the Bill of Rights was drafted. Prior to the Civil War, the Bill of Rights protected citizens only against actions of the federal government. Early in the 1800s, the Supreme Court had ruled that state governments were not bound by the restrictions of the federal Bill of Rights.[6] As state guarantees of civil liberties varied in degree and breadth of protection, freedom in this country was an uneven patchwork of protection. In many places, protections were extended only to whites and, in some instances, only to males.

The Civil War gave vigor to the previously uncertain idea that America was a single, unified nation; not only North and South, but black and white. Blacks as well as whites had fought and died in defense of the Union. Furthermore, the sacrifice of thousands had been given not merely to save the Union but to end an institution that was the obverse of human rights. The war crystallized the truth, as incisively expressed by Lincoln at Gettysburg, that America was defined less by its diverse geography and more by its unity of ideas about equality and freedom. Flowing from this experience was the idea that all Americans, of whatever race and in whatever state, deserved the legal protections that came with being an American citizen.

To make this truth a legal reality, the postwar Congress passed the Reconstruction amendments, known as the Thirteenth, Fourteenth, and Fifteenth Amendments to the Constitution. These were intended to outlaw slavery and to apply the federal Bill of Rights to the states, thus protecting the basic rights of all citizens. Although it took many years for the Supreme Court to give these amendments their full-intended effect, the application of the First Amendment freedoms to the states during the past century can be directly traced to the foundation laid by these amendments.

But it seems that each new generation must rediscover the value of rights. By the time of World War I, government leaders were once again ready to suppress and persecute speech and dissent in the name of the war effort. Some progress had been made in that these suppressive acts were more frequently reviewed by courts than in the Civil War era. But in most instances the courts rejected the free-speech claims of opponents of the war. The one bright moment came in an opinion by Justice Oliver Wendell Holmes, in which he objected to state persecution of speech and famously argued that "the best test of truth is the power of the thought to get itself accepted in the competition of the market."[7]

Holmes's opinion was in dissent and did not prevent several war activists from going to jail for twenty years for publishing two leaflets against the war. The severity of the sentence, however, seemed to impact Holmes's thinking on the matter, as in earlier cases he had sided with the government and against free speech claims of war opponents. Over the next several years, the ideas expressed in Holmes's dissent took root in legal and popular thought. Before long, his "marketplace of ideas" model became an integral part of a greatly stronger protection for speech under the Constitution.

Thus the very denial of speech rights during World War I highlighted the unfairness of such suppression. Out of this denial emerged the constitutional test that guaranteed future generations the right to a robust exchange of ideas. By the time of the Vietnam War, it was unthinkable that someone would be arrested for merely speaking or writing against the war effort.

World War II provides perhaps the starkest example of a right suppressed that was transformed into a right vindicated. In 1940, the country was caught up in a fervor of nationalism inspired by the menace of the expanding Nazi regime. Some public schools insisted that children salute the flag at the beginning of the class day. This practice conflicted with the religious scruples of the Jehovah's Witnesses, whose religion forbids them from taking oaths. A local school district in Pennsylvania expelled two Witness children because of their refusal to take the flag oath. On appeal, the Supreme Court sided with the state, holding that "national cohesion" was an "interest inferior to none in the hierarchy of legal values." "National unity," the majority wrote, "is the basis of national security."[8]

Following this decision, hundreds of physical attacks upon Jehovah's Witnesses' meetings were broken up, and individual Witnesses were beaten by mobs. "Almost without exception, the flag and flag salute were the causes."[9] And the flag-salute requirement continued to spread.

In West Virginia, a resolution was passed requiring all public schools in the state to regularly administer the flag oath to students. The language of the resolution drew on the Supreme Court's opinion and justifications in the 1940 Pennsylvania case. Jehovah's Witnesses in West Virginia challenged the resolution; and in 1943, the flag-salute issue was again before the Supreme Court. But this time the court sided with the Witnesses.

In striking down the flag-salute resolution, the court penned one of the most memorable lines on the topic of civil and religious freedom. It wrote: "If there is any fixed star in our constitutional constellation, it is that no official, high or petty, can prescribe what shall be orthodox in politics, nationalism, religion, or other matters of opinion or force citizens to confess by word or act their faith therein."[10] Critical to the changed result were two justices who had supported the flag-oath requirement in the first case, but who opposed it in the second. In explaining their switch, they wrote that "long reflection" convinced them that the case had been wrongly decided and that "words uttered under coercion are proof of loyalty to nothing but self-interest. Love of country must spring from willing hearts and free minds."[11]

The instances of harassment and persecution experienced by the Jehovah's Witnesses no doubt informed the "long reflection" of the justices who changed sides. The ordeal of the Jehovah's Witnesses during the period between the cases was harrowing. And yet the ordeal itself was the catalyst that redounded not only to the vindication of the Witnesses' rights but also to greater freedom for all religious minorities. It seems to be a law of sorts: the tree of freedom must be watered by the rain of oppression before real growth takes place. But suppression alone is not the mechanism of growth; it only offers the opportunity. There must be onlooking minds sensitive to the unfairness and injustice inherent in the mistreatment of minorities and willing to speak and act in their defense. A crisis does not "produce" rights, but gives those who value rights the raw materials to advance them.

History tells us that further crises await us in the new millennium. How these times of trial will affect our freedoms depends on our values as a people. *Crisis* is from a Greek word meaning "judgment." The Bible uses it to describe a time when destinies hang in the balance and truths about people are revealed. Future crises will reveal our true values as a people; whether we love freedom and fairness or hold as the higher values self-interest and a majority-pleasing "national unity." In such a revelation of character and values hangs the destiny of both individuals and nations, as earthly crises are merely a shadow of and preparation for the great crisis, or final judgment. There, all will be called to account for their use, or misuse, of power in relation to others' freedom.

---

1. See Article I, Section 9 of the Constitution.

2. William H. Rehnquist, *All the Laws but One* (New York: Knopf, 1998), 192. President Lincoln, in a message to a special session of Congress on July 4, 1861, justified his suspension of habeas corpus by arguing, "Are all the law, but one, to go unexecuted, and the government itself to go to pieces, lest that one be violated?" Quoted in ibid., vii.

3. Ibid., 201.

4. Youngstown Sheet and Tube Co. v. Sawyer, 343 US 579 (1952).

5. Lyndsey Layton, "Prayer and Punishment," *Washington Post*, May 28, 1999.

6. Barron v. Mayor and City Council of Baltimore, 7 Pet. 243, 8 L.Ed. 672 (1833).

7. Abrams v. United States, 250 US 616, 64 (1919) (Holmes dissenting).

8. Minersville School District v. Gobitis, 310 US 586, 595 (1940).

9. Leo Pfeffer, *God, Caesar, and the Constitution: The Court as Referee of Church-State Confrontation* (Boston: Beacon Press, 1974), 144, quoted in Nat Hentoff, *The First Freedom: The Tumultuous History of Free Speech in America* (New York: Delacorte, 1988), 177.

10. West Virginia State Board of Education v. Barnette, 319 US 624, 642 (1943).

11. Ibid.

PART IV

Other Modern Legal Issues in Church and State

The twenty-first century dawned with a greater uncertainty regarding the status of religious freedom in the United States than probably any decade since the Civil War. And some of the issues were quite similar, including whether the interest and beliefs of a local majority should be able to override federal constitutional rights of minorities—particularly, in the modern case, religious minorities. Despite eight years of Democratic governance under Bill Clinton, the court was relatively evenly balanced, with perhaps a slight leftward lean. The election of Republican George Bush in the 2000 presidential election was suggestive that the leftward lean was probably going to be short lived, and the court would moderate, or even turn, in a somewhat conservative direction.

Bush did not appoint his first Supreme Court justice, however, until his second term, when he was able to appoint first John Roberts in 2005 and Samuel Alito a year later. But the hoped for conservative majority did not fully materialize. Justice Anthony Kennedy, an ostensibly conservative Catholic appointed by Reagan, began to vote more and more often with the left wing of the court on issues connected with culture conflicts. Early indicators of this were his joining with O'Connor in 1992 in a decision that reaffirmed the abortion framework in *Roe v. Wade*, even while allowing for some restrictions on abortion.

In the mid-1990s, he authored the opinion for *Romer v. Evans* that invalidated a law in Colorado seeking to ban LGBT discrimination laws. This was the beginning of a series of pro-LGBT decisions: continuing in *Lawrence v. Texas*, which invalidated criminal laws against sodomy, and reaching an apex in the decisions of *United States v. Windsor*, which invalidated the federal Defense of Marriage Act, and *Obergefell v. Hodges*, which ruled that same-sex marriage was a right protected by the Constitution.

As important as these sexual freedom cases are to the story of religious freedom and civil rights in the twenty-first century, they do not represent the full story. A number of other legal developments and cases provided greater breathing room for religious freedom than the single narrative of the rise of LGBT rights may indicate. First of all, at the state level, the country became more accepting of homeschooling as a parental right. From fewer than two states in the 1970s to more than thirty in the 1990s, all states had some formal arrangement to allow for homeschooling by the late 2000s. This was largely the result of a strong Christian homeschooling movement. My personal experience with that movement and an overview of the applicable law, updated to the present, is found in the chapter "Homeschooling and the Law." This is followed by a discussion of who should pay the price for someone's rights of conscience. "The Price of Faith"—focusing on the case of a Jehovah's Witness involved in an accident who refused a blood transfusion—asks the practical question of who should pay for the resulting damages. The answer might surprise you.

Of course, the matter of funding and religion always provides fireworks and disagreement. The court has decided that in most instances the indirect flow of money, in the form of grants or vouchers, to adults, which are then applied to religious institutions, is acceptable under the Constitution. But just because it is constitutionally acceptable does not mean that the receipt of voucher money is always a good idea for schools. I gave some remarks at the National Press Club in Washington, DC, after the voucher decision was handed down in *Zelman v. Simmons-Harris*, where I shared the potential pitfalls that vouchers could create for religious schools. The principle of the acceptability of indirect state aid was put to the test when some recipients of government largess wanted to use the funds to study theology and become ministers and theologians. The court's wrestling with this issue is discussed in "Tax-Tutored Theologians."

Then there are questions about the state's own involvement in religious practices. State and legislative chaplains and clergy invited to give prayers became an issue that the court visited in *Town of Greece v. Galloway*. Another challenge was found in the question of whether commercial enterprises deserved religious-liberty protections. This has become a hot topic in this era of Christian florists, photographers, and bakers who do not wish to participate in same-sex weddings. The principle found in these cases was explored at the Supreme Court level in the case involving the religious convictions of the owners of Hobby Lobby. I explore this important case in both "Is Religion a Hobby?" and "Religion Is Not a Hobby!"

Finally, I address the contest between religious freedom and LGBT rights in a pair of chapters: "Religious Freedom: The New Bigotry?" and "Gay Marriage and the Supreme Court: What's at Stake for Religious Freedom?" I think that the main problem in the contest is the absolutist approach that both sides want to take to it. Religious conservatives were perhaps first guilty of this, wanting to make no accommodation for LGBT concerns in the 1980s and 1990s. When the political tides shifted the other way, left-wing activists became guilty of the same overreach. Any conflict between religious freedom and LGBT rights, they insist, must be resolved by protecting LGBT rights.

But we have never treated conflicts of rights in this way before. Courts have used a balancing test to assess the degree of hardship and inconvenience experienced by both sides and sensitively handled these conflicts on a case-by-case basis. There is every reason that this latest conflict can be handled in the same way. The state of Utah passed legislation working out evenhanded compromises on these matters. They protected persons of the LGBT community from discrimination in housing and employment, but also guarded the religious freedom of individuals, institutions, and Christian business owners. Insisting on an absolutist approach is dangerous, as once the political tides shift again, it can be one's own boat that is left high, dry, and defenseless. The 2016 federal election should give progressives pause and cause them to consider the possibilities of a national bill based on the Utah compromise.

Chapter 18

Homeschooling and the Law

Somehow a reporter from a local paper found out about my mother's decision. And that was when I found out the terrible truth—I was living with a criminal. There it was in black and white in our local newspaper: "Vera Miller is in violation of the law, as she refuses to send her son to school in defiance of state compulsory attendance regulations." (The irony, however, was that, unlike many school-attending first-graders, I could actually read the article.)

Despite the publicity, my parents never received a visit from school-board officials. And the following year they also held my younger sister out in continuing violation of the law. Enrolled in school at the age of seven-plus, both my sister and I skipped grades and went on to successful scholastic careers, pursuing terminal degrees in our respective fields. (And that may be one of the points of the story, that the success of homeschoolers has paved the way for widespread legal protection for homeschooling.) But it is only since my family's early 1970s brush with a life of crime that laws have been passed in most states protecting the kind of educational choices my parents made.

Many people are surprised to learn that homeschooling is not explicitly protected by the federal Constitution. In the 1925 case of *Pierce v. Society of Sisters*, the Supreme Court did affirm the right of parents to direct their children's education by sending them to private religious schools.[1] This case, often referred to as the "Magna Carta" of parochial schools, means that the state cannot force its

---

This chapter originally appeared in *Liberty*, November/December 1999.

citizens to attend public schools. Parents have the right to send their children to qualified private schools.

The Supreme Court said nothing, however, about homeschooling and stated that the regulation and oversight of education was still within the province of the state. In *Wisconsin v. Yoder*, the court upheld the right of the Amish to withdraw their children from formal schooling after the eighth grade.[2] But this decision relates only to compulsory secondary school attendance, and much homeschooling takes place at the elementary, or primary, level. The *Yoder* case is also probably limited to its facts: a unique Amish community and way of life was being threatened by having their teenage children kept in the classroom rather than helping in the fields and workshops of their farms. The typical homeschooling family does not resemble this picture.

So while the federal Constitution protects generally the right of parents to provide a religious education for their children, it is left to the states to protect the particular form that education can take—such as homeschooling. My family's violation of the law in the seventies may have been the norm for homeschooling families overall. Very few states formally protected homeschooling before the 1980s. In 1999, when this piece was originally published, thirty-eight states had homeschool statutes, but thirty-five of those statutes were passed after 1980. Only Utah and Nevada had such statutes before the 1970s.[3]

As of 2017, all states have some sort of regulatory provision to allow for homeschooling. The Home School Legal Defense Association has graded state regulations at four levels:[4]

1. States requiring no notice. This means that parents can begin homeschooling their children with no notification to the state. These states are Alaska, Connecticut, Idaho, Illinois, Indiana, Iowa, Michigan, Missouri, New Jersey, Oklahoma, and Texas.

2. States with low regulation. These states require parents to notify officials about homeschooling, but requires little else. These states are Alabama, Arizona, Arkansas, California, Delaware, Georgia, Kansas, Kentucky, Mississippi, Montana, Nebraska, Nevada, New Mexico, Utah, Wisconsin, and Wyoming.

3. States with moderate regulation. These states require not only notification of homeschooling intent but also the submission of test scores and/or other professional evaluations of student progress. These states are Colorado, District of Columbia, Florida, Hawaii, Louisiana, Maine, Maryland, Minnesota, New Hampshire, North Carolina, North Dakota, Ohio, Oregon, South Carolina, South Dakota, Tennessee, Virginia, Washington, and West Virginia.

4. States with high regulation. These states are the most intrusive and require all the above, plus some sort of curriculum approval by the state, teacher qualification of parents, or home visits by government workers. These states are Massachusetts, New York, Pennsylvania, Rhode Island, and Vermont.

With so many different laws and statutory schemes regulating homeschools, any prospective homeschooler must become familiar with his or her state's requirements.

To those who value the God-given duty of parents to shape their children's education, it is gratifying to know that every state presently offers some opportunity for homeschooling. It is troubling, however, that the basis of this important right may rest on the precarious whim of the state legislature, the state court, or even a single state official. One would hope that the Supreme Court would extend the reasoning of its decisions in *Pierce* and *Yoder* to constitutionally protect the practice of responsible homeschooling. Unfortunately, recent Supreme Court decisions have contracted rather than expanded civil and religious rights. The trend is toward allowing the states to protect, or infringe, individual rights as the state legislature sees fit.

Some hope is offered by State Religious Freedom Restoration Acts, which were passed in many states in the late 1990s and early 2000s. State courts could choose to protect homeschooling under these Acts, as they would restore the test that produced *Pierce* and *Yoder*. But nationwide protection could only come from a federal law protective of homeschooling parents. Until then, homeschooling families are only a small step removed from the notorious homeschooling crime families of the seventies!

---

1. Pierce v. Society of Sisters of the Holy Names of Jesus and Mary, 268 US 510 (1925).

2. Wisconsin v. Yoder, 406 US 205 (1972).

3. According to a 1999 report by the Home School Legal Defense Association, states with statutes protecting homeschooling were the following: Alaska, Arizona, Arkansas, Colorado, Connecticut, Delaware, Florida, Georgia, Hawaii, Idaho, Iowa, Louisiana, Maine, Maryland, Michigan, Minnesota, Mississippi, Missouri, Montana, Nevada, New Hampshire, New Mexico, New York, North Carolina, North Dakota, Ohio, Oregon, Pennsylvania, Rhode Island, South Carolina, Tennessee, Utah, Vermont, Virginia, Washington, West Virginia, Wisconsin, and Wyoming.

4. "Homeschool Laws in Your State," Home School Legal Defense Association, accessed April 19, 2017, https://www.hslda.org/laws/default.asp.

Chapter 19

The Price of Faith

I n May 1991, a rental car that Gwendolyn Robbins's father was driving in up-state New York skidded, plunged down an embankment, and overturned. Both her parents were killed, and Robbins, fifty-five, was severely injured. She was rushed to nearby Glens Falls Hospital, where her condition was so critical—chest injuries, a fractured right femur, a fractured ankle, and a fractured hip—that upon admission, last rites were administered. The doctors stabilized her and prepared for surgery to reset displaced bones and ligaments. The surgery was important for her recovery and critical for any opportunity that she might have to walk again.

But Robbins refused the surgery. A devout Jehovah's Witness, she believed—based on the tenets of her faith—that she could undergo no blood transfusions, even if that refusal led to life-threatening progressive anemia.

Fortunately, she did survive the immediate threat of infection and was transferred to a hospital in New York City. There she was placed in traction for several weeks, where she continued to refuse any treatment that required blood transfusions. Her orthopedic surgeon stated that without joint replacement surgery she would become wheelchair bound or bedridden for the rest of her life. Robbins's decision to forego surgery would thus greatly increase her need of medical services and home care.

The story might have ended there, except that Robbins then sued her insurance company, a suit that raised difficult moral and legal questions. Though it was Robbins's First Amendment right to refuse surgery, should the insurance company

This article originally appeared in *Liberty*, July/August 1997.

have to pay for the ongoing disability suffered by Robbins directly because of that refusal?

The insurance company, Meritor Capital Resources, argued that Robbins had a duty to mitigate, or lessen, her injuries when she could reasonably do so. But because she refused an opportunity to reasonably lessen the damage from her injuries, the company argued that it should not have to pay for the results of that choice.

Meritor had good legal precedent. The law requires that a person injured by the acts of another take reasonable steps to mitigate, or prevent a worsening of, those injuries. If such steps are not taken, the person causing the injury can be held responsible only for the initial injury and not for any damage caused by the injured person's failure to act reasonably in a way that would prevent the worsening of the situation. Often a jury is called on to decide whether an injured person has done all he or she reasonably should have done to treat his or her injuries.

But here's where the insurance company ran into a church-state problem. Because Robbins's decision had been based on her *religious* convictions, the jury would be asked to decide if Robbins's religious convictions and beliefs were reasonable.

Yet the trial judge was troubled by the idea of a jury passing judgment on the reasonableness of someone's religious beliefs. The Supreme Court had prohibited juries from passing judgment on the "plausibility of a religious claim." The trial judge ruled that the insurance company could not argue against the reasonableness of Robbins's choice because it was based on religion. The company would have to take Robbins and her belief system as it found them, those of a devout Jehovah's Witness. The court thus ordered that the insurance company would have to pay for all Robbins's damages, despite her refusal of surgery.

This decision showed a great deal of sensitivity to the protected status granted religious beliefs in the American constitutional system. The picture of a jury deciding the reasonableness or unreasonableness of anyone's religious convictions is, indeed, troubling. Under this scenario, the moderate Protestant and Catholic would do well, but the Hare Krishna, the Christian Scientist, or the Hindu would likely be denied justice—not an acceptable outcome in our society of equality under the law.

But did the judge, in arriving at the balance of rights and responsibilities, overlook a necessary corollary of personal freedom: the responsibility to live with the consequences of one's choices? This principle is also found in the American legal system under the name "assumption of risk," which states that a person cannot recover from another when he or she knowingly "assumes the risk" that the other person may present to him or her. This principle prevents you from suing if you sprain or fracture your ankle while playing basketball, even if the injury is caused by the negligence of another player. Before entering the court, you knew that basketball was a lively game with a fair amount of incidental contact. By playing, you accepted the risk that you might sprain your ankle or worse. The logic is that as you voluntarily and knowingly placed yourself in the way of the possible negligence of others, you cannot sue even if they negligently injure you.

An application of this doctrine may have been appropriate in Robbins's case. To decide whether Robbins had assumed the risk of her choices, the jury would not have had to assess the reasonableness of her beliefs. Rather, they would merely have had to decide if Robbins knew that foregoing surgery could lead to further suffering and disability and that she knowingly and voluntarily chose to accept this possibility. If they had seen the matter this way, they could have made Robbins accept the consequences of her religious choices rather than place those consequences on her insurance company. This approach would have satisfied the protections of the free exercise clause while avoiding the apparent unfairness of imposing the consequences of one person's religious choices on a third party.

All major Western religions teach that what a man sows that shall he also reap. They teach personal accountability and responsibility and that the moral choices that people make will impact both their earthly lives and their eternal destinies. If those religious decisions have toxic results, the decision maker will live with the consequences, at least partially in this life and fully in the next, according to his or her various beliefs. Meanwhile, in this life, the insurance company had to pay Robbins $7,732,900—quite a handsome sum for the religious choices of another.

Chapter 20

Comments on Tuition Vouchers:
Zelman v. Simmons-Harris

*T*he following is the text of remarks made at a panel discussion, sponsored by the Pew Forum on Religion and Public Life, held at the National Press Club in Washington, DC, the day after the Supreme Court's decision in the school voucher case of Zelman v. Simmons-Harris.* In that case, a majority of the court upheld the constitutionality of a voucher system offered in the city of Cleveland, Ohio. The decision deeply divided the court, with five justices broadly upholding the program as constitutional because the government aid was neutral toward religion and passed through the hands of parents who themselves made the final decision of where to send the aid, whether secular or religious schools. Four justices strongly dissented. They questioned the neutrality of a program in which 96 percent of the students using vouchers attended religious schools and argued that the decision was a dramatic departure from the long-standing constitutional principle that taxpayers should not be compelled to support religious views in which they do not believe.

I should say at the outset that I am sympathetic to school choice and religious schools. I'm the grateful product of sixteen years of Christian education, and I have sent my own children to church schools. I belong to a church, the Seventh-day

---

* The full discussion entitled "Judgment Day for School Vouchers" can be viewed at the Pew Research Center's website, http://www.pewforum.org/2002/06/28/judgment-day-for-school-vouchers/.

This chapter is from a panel discussion at the National Press Club on June 28, 2002.

Adventist Church, that has the second-largest parochial school system in the world, behind the Catholic Church. Therefore, I hope that this decision is good for religious schools, but I fear it is not. I think *Zelman* may be bad for religious freedom generally, and bad for religious schools in particular. I will explain why, but first let me put this decision in a larger context.

Return of majoritarianism

Twelve years ago in the *Smith* decision, the Supreme Court, in the words of the *Harvard Law Review*, "eviscerated" the free exercise clause. Yesterday, in *Zelman*, the court appears to have basically abandoned the long-standing establishment clause principles that prohibit tax support of religion.

Many observers view these two decisions as being in tension or in downright conflict. The *Smith* decision is viewed as being hostile to religion, cutting back on religion's constitutional protections and rights, whereas yesterday's decision is, I believe, viewed as supportive and favorable toward religion, allowing it to use tax monies for religious teaching and mission. But I think there is an underlying theme or principle that unifies these decisions, and it is not support or hostility or even neutrality toward religion; rather, the unifying principle of these cases can be expressed in one word—*majoritarianism*—giving power to the majority in religious matters.

The *Smith* decision left the protection of religion to the majority controlled legislatures; now *Zelman* has given power over the funding of religion to those same legislatures, meaning inevitably that state funds will find their way, disproportionately, into the coffers of large and/or popular religious groups.

Both decisions, I believe, misconceive the role of the courts in our constitutional scheme, which is to protect religious minorities under the Bill of Rights against the insensitivity or hostility of majorities or from having to support popular religious views with their tax dollars. For this reason, both decisions, I believe, represent tremendous setbacks for religious freedom in America, although for different reasons.

Now, it will be argued that *Zelman* does not allow the legislature to support any particular religion, whether it is popular or unpopular, large or small, as the money is guided by private, individual choice and not by the government.

First, the assumption that truly neutral voucher schemes can be created is unsafe; to begin with, such schemes will only benefit religions that actually have educational systems presently—Catholic and Adventist theologies will receive far more state support than other religious views. And I believe that very quickly we will see unfavorable treatment of less popular groups.

I question whether Muslim schools or those sponsored by Louis Farrakhan will get funds. This is one of Justice Breyer's main points in his dissent. But even more profound, the public- and private-choice distinction, at least as embraced in this case, assumes that society can do directly what it cannot do indirectly through the legislature. That is, use taxpayer money to fund systems of religious teaching.

The Founding Fathers directly considered this distinction between the legislature and society carrying out religious programs with taxpayer funds, and they rejected it. In the closest analog to vouchers we have in the eighteenth century, Patrick Henry and James Madison debated over Henry's bill in Virginia to establish teachers of the Christian religion. This was a bill that was as neutral as one could get in the 1700s. It levied a tax that was distributed to the religious organization of the taxpayer's choice. There was an exemption for Quakers, who did not have a professional clergy; and for those with no religious preference, there was a general legislative fund for education. But Madison memorably rejected this scheme in his "Memorial and Remonstrance." His first point was that society had no business forcing people to support religion, and his second was that the legislature, deriving its authority from society, certainly had no authority to do so.

Now, the Supreme Court has stood Madison's point on its head and ruled that what the legislature may not do, the people, or society, may do—use tax monies to fund religious schools. This means that where a particular religious group predominates—the Mormons in Utah, Southern Baptists in the South, or even on the county or city level—they will, through neutral legislation, be able to use public funds to create religious school systems that will rival public school systems in quality and resources and educational opportunities, thereby producing distinct pressures for nonmembers to attend these religious schools, creating a de facto establishment that is contrary to constitutional principles.

I think this will be bad for our constitutional system of religious freedom, causing, as Justice Breyer so eloquently points out, political fissures along religious lines, which drives the conflicts in so many of our world's troubled spots.

Bad for religious schools

But it will also be bad for the religious schools themselves, as it will attract students for academic rather than primarily religious reasons, thereby watering down the religious commitment of the student body. This is no speculation; but rather, it is illustrated in Cleveland, where two-thirds of the voucher users attended schools sponsored by religions of which they were not members. The schools will become more responsive to government goals and concerns and correspondingly less responsive to the religious goals of their churches, and they will be constrained by government regulation in student admissions and faculty hiring and employment decisions.

This is also no speculation but is part of this very case, as Justice Souter points out. The voucher law at issue in *Zelman* forbade discrimination on the basis of religion; the language of the statute encompasses both student admissions and faculty hiring, and this, at least for religious schools, is the real reason to be concerned about this decision. Now that vouchers are going to be instituted, religious schools may well have to accept them to survive in a competitive educational market, but to accept the vouchers means that they will likely have to give up the main way in which they define and carry out their religious mission—the ability to choose students and staff that have commitments to the schools' religious ideals. The cost of the voucher system to the state legislature and even the public school system may be miniscule compared to the cost of the voucher system to the mission and identity of religious schools.

I may be wrong. I hope that I am wrong. But I fear that this will happen, and it will serve as another indicator of the practical, moral, and legal bankruptcy of the majoritarian view of the Bill of Rights now espoused by a majority of the court.

Chapter 21

Tax-Tutored Theologians

What is the cost of discipleship? It cost Joshua Davey twenty-five hundred dollars when he decided to declare a major in pastoral studies.

Joshua won a Washington State scholarship based on academic achievement and financial need to pursue almost any field of study—including religion if he studied it from a dispassionate academic view at a place such as the University of Washington. But he would lose the scholarship if he chose to major in religion at a college that taught religion from a viewpoint of faith—such as the Assemblies of God–affiliated Northwest College (now Northwest University), where Joshua was enrolled.

The question is, in taking Joshua's scholarship away, was Washington State merely avoiding state sponsorship of religion, or was it guilty of invidious religious discrimination?

In answering this, a federal appeals court ruled that the state was guilty of religious discrimination and struck down the exclusion of theology students from the program. This decision was at odds with a decision of the Washington Supreme Court. Thus, the US Supreme Court agreed to hear the case.

The Supreme Court's ruling could create a sea change in the area of voucher law, not only making religious institutions eligible for vouchers but *requiring* states to give vouchers to religious institutions if they provide them to secular organizations. For this reason, the case has attracted more than a dozen friend of

---

This chapter originally appeared in *Liberty*, March/April 2004.

the court briefs, representing scores of religious and civil rights groups across the country. Despite the strong feelings on both sides of the dispute, Joshua's case seems a particularly difficult one for people to decide which side they are on. The right result seems to change depending on how the case is framed.

Thought of in terms of improper state support of religion, it seems to be a case at the center of the Constitution's prohibition against state funding of the church. What is more of a religious calling than that of the ministry? And how can one more directly support organized religion than to financially support those who preach and teach it or are training to do so?

The founders strongly opposed tax funds going to ministers or teachers of religion. James Madison wrote his famed "Memorial and Remonstrance" as a challenge to a bill to provide funds to all teachers of religion. Madison's arguments were so well received that not only was the bill defeated but impetus was also created to pass an opposing bill by Thomas Jefferson that explicitly prohibited tax funds from going to ministers.

Jefferson's bill, which became the Virginia Statute for Establishing Religious Freedom, stated, "To compel a man to furnish contributions of money for the propagation of opinions which he disbelieves . . . is sinful and tyrannical; that even the forcing him to support this or that teacher of his own religious persuasion, is depriving him of . . . liberty."[1]

The special role of clergy in relation to their churches and temples is embedded in our law today. Courts recognize that the close-knit relationship calls for special legal protection and have described ministers, priests, rabbis, and similar church leaders as the "lifeblood" of the church. They are thus exempt from certain oversights by the state.

Known as the "ministerial exemption," this constitutionally based protection exempts religious leaders from the coverage of employment discrimination statutes such as Title VII. The courts are loath to involve themselves in the close and special relationship between religious leaders and their congregations or religious hierarchy.

So how can the state now fund the education of the very persons that it has termed to be so religious as to be exempt from discrimination laws? Groups such as the ACLU, People for the American Way, the American Jewish Congress, and the Baptist Joint Committee for Religious Liberty say that it cannot and that the Supreme Court should reverse the decision.

But other groups, even some traditionally supportive of church-state separation, believe there is another way to look at the case. And indeed, thought of in terms of discrimination, Joshua's case seems a straightforward instance of improper religious discrimination by the state.

To the onlooker, the Washington State program seems to target those of religious belief for second-class treatment. Anyone who is academically and financially qualified can get the scholarship to study any subject matter except religion and then only when taught from a faith perspective. Thus, the exclusion arguably penalizes persons of certain religious beliefs.

One may be a rabid Republican or Democrat or Marxist, major in government studies, be taught by teachers who may promote the views of Republicans or Democrats or Marxists, and still receive the state aid. One could be an avid atheist, major in philosophy or even religion, be taught by teachers who believe and promote atheism, and still receive the state aid. It is only those who believe in and study about religion, while being taught by teachers who believe it as well, who cannot receive the state aid.

Any notion that sending money to ministerial students causes the state to endorse religious views seems undercut by the indirect nature of the aid. The state does not determine on which schools and programs the money is spent. Rather, the aid money goes directly to the student, who, from a wide variety of largely nonreligious choices and options, chooses to spend the money on the program, religious or otherwise, that he or she desires.

To argue that the state is *endorsing* the views of the program at which the money ends up seems specious. The state would no more endorse the views of either Joshua or the religion professors at Northwest College than it would the views of the rabid Republican or Democratic or Marxist or atheist students and professors in the prior illustration.

Indeed, if any tax money that went to religious programs inherently involved government endorsement, then state employees could not pay tithes and offerings to their churches or temples. Neither could ordinary citizens use tax credit checks for religious purposes.

The Supreme Court has accepted this direct-indirect aid distinction. Thus, one thing that both sides in the dispute agree on is that Joshua's case will not be decided by the federal Constitution's establishment clause. Some years ago the US Supreme Court ruled in *Witters v. Comm'n for the Blind*, virtually an identical case to Joshua's, that the federal Constitution provided no barrier to the use of the Washington State scholarship funds by ministerial students.

The *Witters* court noted the indirect nature of the aid and that it was a private choice that sent the aid to the religious school. It commented on the large number of choices a student had in using the aid—the majority of which were secular. It concluded that there was no danger that the state could be viewed as endorsing the religious program to which the funds were put.

But when *Witters* was sent back to the Washington court for a final decision, the state court decided that even though the federal Constitution was no barrier to the funds, the state constitution barred the religious use of the funds. It ruled that the Washington Constitution called for a wider separation of church and state than that mandated by the federal Constitution.

So the question at the heart of Joshua's case is whether a state may have a greater separation of church and state than that required by the federal Constitution.

Those who say No argue that any discrimination against religion not absolutely required by the establishment clause is prohibited as unlawful by the free exercise clause. This might be described as the yin-yang view of the religion clauses. Where one ends in requiring separation and exclusion, the other begins by mandating equality of treatment.

But there is another view of the clauses, one that has been termed "play in the joints." This view holds that there is a gray area between the two clauses. States can experiment with church-state relations, either protecting religion more strongly than mandated by the federal Constitution or separating church from state more widely than required by the same.

Once again, both sides agree on something: there is some sort of "play in the joints." Both sides have worked on projects to provide religious freedom at the state level that is more protective of religion than that required by the federal Constitution.

Such an effort is based on "play in the joints." Otherwise, protecting religion beyond that required by the free exercise clause would run smack into the law against the establishment clause's prohibition against giving religion special benefits.

So is there only a one-way "play in the joints"? A flexibility only to benefit religion but not to hamper it? Well, that remains to be seen. In Joshua Davey's case, the oral arguments before the Supreme Court revealed a deeply divided court. There seems to be four votes for and four votes against overruling the lower court decision.

The deciding vote, as happens frequently, will likely be cast by Justice O'Connor, whose questioning revealed concerns on both sides of the issue. While sensitive to issues of religious discrimination, she was also very troubled about the decision's impact on voucher programs across the country. At one point, Justice O'Connor asked Joshua's attorney, "Suppose a state has a school voucher program. . . . Now, if the state decides not to give school vouchers for use in religious or parochial schools, do you take the position it must, that it has to do one or the other? It can have a voucher program, but if it does, it has to fund all private and religious schools?"

"Yes," answered Joshua's lawyer.

"So what you're saying here," O'Connor responded with concern, "would have a major impact, then, would it not, on . . . voucher programs?"[2]

Clearly, O'Connor is very nervous about putting state and local governments in a position of being forced to fund religious groups whenever a voucher program is created.

One way out of the dilemma would be to keep open the possibility for states to have a broader separation of church and state than that compelled by the federal Constitution, but to rule that, the justification given by Washington State in Joshua's case is inadequate.

An earlier case, raised in oral argument, dealing with state laws against clergy serving in the legislature, could serve as a good road map for such a result. In *McDaniel v. Paty*, the court ruled that while such clergy-exclusion laws had a long historical pedigree, the state had not provided the factual basis to show how clergy serving in the legislature would presently threaten religious freedom.

Similarly, in Joshua's case, Washington State has shown a long historical practice of not funding ministers or ministerial students. But the record is quite silent as to modern-day facts that show how such indirect funding would threaten the peace and stability of church-state relations. Without such findings, the exclusion of ministerial students becomes justified on grounds of tradition and antiquity alone—hardly a reliable basis for laws targeting religion for unfavorable treatment.

Such a result would seem to be supported by the rest of Joshua's story. His experience with law inspired him to refocus his career. He is presently a law student at Harvard Law School. Joshua would not be the first to discover that training in theology can serve as an excellent basis for fulfilling one's calling in a pathway outside the conventional ministerial path. The author of this article also studied theology as an undergraduate before attending law school, as have many others.

Denying scholarship aid to theology students penalizes not only future ministers but all that view the path of discipleship as broader than the traditional ministerial path. It also weakens society by depriving it of professionals schooled in the ethics and morality offered by traditional religious studies.

That would be a shame in this day and age of Enron, Arthur Andersen, and celebrity inside trading. And it would hardly seem to be a necessary cost of discipleship or of the separation of church and state.

Update: My predictions in this article turned out to be a bit off. Rather than a divided Court with a deciding vote by O'Conner, the Court ruled by a 7 to 2 margin that the Washington limit on educational funds was constitutional. The majority opinion was written by Chief Justice Rehnquist, and only Justices Antonin Scalia and Clarence Thomas dissented. Funding theologians, even if just indirectly, was too much state support for religion, even for most of the conservatives on the Court.

---

1. Va. Code Ann. § 57-1 (passed January 16, 1786).

2. Sandra Day O'Connor and Jay Sekulow, "Locke v. Davey," December 2, 2003, Oral Argument transcript and audio recording, 29:08–30:40, Oyez, https://www.oyez.org/cases/2003/02-1315.

Chapter 22

Town of Greece v. Galloway—
the "Christianization" of Local Government?

I n May 2014, the Supreme Court ruled that prayers given by clergypersons at a
monthly town board meeting were acceptable under the establishment clause of
the US Constitution. This ruling came despite the fact that the vast majority of
the prayers were given by Christian ministers, invoking the name of Christ and a
general Christian perspective. Indeed, in the first eight years of the prayer program,
only Christian ministers prayed.

This Christian monopoly was due in part to the fact that clergy were drawn exclusively from congregations within the town limits—the vast majority of which were
Christian. After the program was criticized for its lack of diversity, the town council
invited leaders from other faith traditions, such as Judaism, Bahaism, and Wicca,
to pray. But the large majority of the prayers continued to be offered by Christian
ministers. What follows are reflections on the decision based on postruling responses.

In his opinion for the majority, Justice Kennedy wrote, "Ceremonial prayer is
but a recognition that, since this Nation was founded and until the present day,
many Americans deem that their own existence must be understood by precepts
far beyond the authority of government to alter or define."[1]

I basically agree with this idea. But I am concerned that the case itself will

---

This chapter originally appeared as blog entry on *Freedom Law* (blog),
May 8, 2014, http://www.freedom-law.com/town-of-greece-v-galloway/.

serve as precedent to move beyond a mere recognition of a power higher than the government and serve as an excuse for "Christianizing" local governments.

Some people say that they do not worry too much about "Christianizing" local government since the ACLU, Americans United (AU), and other left-wing groups will continue their hypervigilance in trying to remove religious references from public life. Others suggest that the recognition of the Creator in public goes back to our founders, who saw the necessity of maintaining a certain reverence in our public consciousness, which is something we have lost sight of today.

But I am concerned that Kennedy's ruling will go beyond the mere recognition of a power higher than the state. Rather, it will allow whatever position is dominant in a local community to "color" or even dictate the religious atmosphere that will pervade in a particular community. This result flows, I believe, from Kennedy's "coercion" establishment clause test. This standard says that the Constitution is only violated if someone is coerced in his or her religious beliefs or actions.

Kennedy overlooks, in my view, the power of state endorsement to marginalize outsider religions and to turn those with minority religious beliefs into second-class citizens. The endorsement test was the standard of O'Connor, who said that the government should not put the weight of its approval or endorsement behind a particular religion. I believe that this standard expressed a very appropriate constitutional concern. O'Connor is gone, however, and I think we have just seen the first move toward the victory of the coercion test.

For many of us, this is a troubling day for establishment clause jurisprudence. One must consider the impact of allowing overtly sectarian and denominational prayer to have pride of place and official state endorsement in our public square. The result will go far beyond acknowledging a Creator to which the state is subject and will quickly turn into defining the "right" kind of religion in a community. When the founders spoke of God and the Creator in our public documents, they spoke of Him in His publicly accessible, natural-law sense, not in the biblical, divinely revealed sense that most modern Christian prayers assume.

If one could construct a truly open public space and moment, where all religions could truly and freely express their public faith, that might be one thing. But the situation in *Greece* did not, in my opinion, meet that standard. Indeed, given demographics and the unequal distributions of religions in various parts of the country, in most places such a forum would be impractical, if not impossible.

The decision is perceived differently, of course, by those who are in favor of some kind of Christian-America model. They view this result as a great day for establishment clause jurisprudence, as they see the court returning to how religion was treated by the founders. As Kennedy himself put it: "The Congress that drafted the First Amendment would have been accustomed to invocations containing explicitly religious themes of the sort respondents find objectionable. One of the Senate's first chaplains, the Rev. William White, gave prayers in a series that included the Lord's Prayer, the Collect for Ash Wednesday, prayers for peace and grace, a general thanksgiving, St. Chrysostom's Prayer, and a prayer seeking 'the grace of our Lord Jesus Christ.' "[2]

But the founders also owned slaves, and I would not view a return to that as an advance. Neither would my Kennedy-supporting friends, to be sure. But the point is that it is the founding principles that matter, not the applications of the founders, which were sometimes very cramped and inconsistent. Let us be guided by the founders' principles, not by their blind spots.

The prayers allowed by the founders in legislative session were essentially non-sectarian, given the almost entirely Christian—indeed, nearly all Protestant—makeup of America of that day. Furthermore, Madison himself recognized them as a departure from a strict separation but, given the "de minimis" impact, tolerated them, as long as they were not used as precedent for further infringement. And this is precisely the problem with citing them as precedent for today's decision.

We are doing just what Madison feared, using the de minimis violations of his day to justify and excuse more egregious violations in our much more pluralistic society. Kennedy's claim notwithstanding, it is *not* just the general acknowledgment of the Divine that has been approved. Rather, the court has authorized the very specific acknowledgment of a biblical, Trinitarian, orthodox Christian view of the Divine to be given advantageous pride of place in our public institutions—at least where Christianity is in the majority, which is to say, in much of America.

Surely the impact of this will be to tell Hindus, Jews, and Muslims—not to mention agnostics and atheists—that they are essentially political outsiders in much of our Christian American republic. There is the principle of the golden rule at stake here. I am not referring to the version that says she who has the gold makes the rules, though that may be applicable here as well. It is the other, less popular version given by the Savior. It is a rule of which even we Christians need constantly to be reminded. As I would not have imams regularly invoking Allah and Muhammed or Wiccans the triple goddess of nature at my government's meetings, so I should not impose on them my religious worship, correct though I may believe it to be.

---

1. Town of Greece v. Galloway, 572 US 17 (2014).
2. *Town of Greece*, 572 US at 10.

Chapter 23

Is Religion a Hobby?

Two views of the role of religion in American public life clashed in the spring of 2014 in oral arguments before the US Supreme Court. On one side, attorneys for the government argued that religious conviction is really a private, personal matter that should be kept at home or within the confines of the church and its closely connected ministries. On the other side, attorneys for Hobby Lobby Stores and Conestoga Wood Specialties, both family owned, corporate businesses, argued that businesspersons cannot be expected to leave their private moral and religious convictions at home when they enter the business world.

At issue in this case were provisions of the Patient Protection and Affordable Care Act (PPACA, popularly known as "Obamacare") that require private employers who provide medical insurance to make available a wide range of contraceptive options to their employees. On the government's required list are some contraceptives that operate after conception and implantation of the fertilized egg. Some medical experts use the term *abortifacients* for these drugs that induce abortions.

The owners of Hobby Lobby, the Green family, who run their large chain of hobby stores, have strong religious convictions against abortion. The PPACA has exemptions from these provisions for churches and their closely affiliated ministries. But there is no exemption for businesses and private companies, no matter how large or small or how strong their owners' religious beliefs.

This chapter originally appeared in *Liberty*, July/August 2014.

Hobby Lobby is, by any measure, a large company. It has more than five hundred stores and thousands of employees. But the depth and sincerity of the Green family's religious convictions is also unquestioned. David Green, who founded the company in his garage, is the son of a preacher and says that he built the business on biblical principles. The company plays Christian music in their stores, pays their employees at least double the minimum wage, and closes on Sundays, which are busy retail days.

But the family's commitment to religious values goes even beyond these apparent business sacrifices. David Green, according to *Forbes*, donates one-half of the company's pretax earnings to Christian causes. Over the years, he has funded Christian colleges and universities, Christian missions, and the distribution of nearly 1.4 billion pieces of gospel literature. These gifts through the years have totaled nearly five hundred million dollars.[1]

Despite this impressive evidence of deep religious conviction and commitment, David Green and his family are faced with a skepticism that their religion should be taken seriously by the government and the business world. The fundamental question faced by the Supreme Court is whether religion is a hobby that the owners of Hobby Lobby and similar businesses must leave at home.

The oral arguments revolved around three subquestions, the answers to which will shape the future of religious freedom in the business world, and hence in many of our lives, for years to come. These questions and their possible answers are the following:

1. Can corporate owners bring their moral and religious convictions into the commercial marketplace and use them to shape their business decisions and actions?

From the arguments, it would seem that a clear majority of the justices believe that corporations, at least privately held ones with a small ownership group, should at minimum have the right to raise claims of religious freedom and conscience on behalf of their companies. From left-leaning justices, such as Stephen Breyer and Elena Kagan, to those on the right, such as Antonin Scalia and Chief Justice John Roberts, the message was sent that it would be going too far to say that incorporating as a business prevented the raising of a religious-freedom claim. Can for-profit businesses, as opposed to churches or not-for-profit religious institutions, assert religious rights at all? In short, can a corporation have a conscience? This is not such a strange idea, as the court has previously ruled that corporations are persons under the Constitution and that as such they have free-speech rights that protect them in their expression of political advocacy.

Should the majority decide that indeed businesses do have basic religious freedoms, this will help provide clarity to a range of disputes in society, including the balance between religious freedom and gay rights. Shortly after the *Hobby*

Lobby argument, the court declined to hear a case from New Mexico in which a photographer was successfully sued for refusing, on religious grounds, to take pictures at a lesbian commitment ceremony. Should the Supreme Court in *Hobby Lobby* make clear that businesses have religious-freedom rights, it will provide greater protections for a variety of Christian businesses, including florists, bakers, photographers, and wedding caterers, to service clients consistently with their religious convictions.

But beyond the wedding industry, the principle that business owners can, and even should, consult moral and religious teachings in operating their businesses should be good for business and the country, generally. The financial meltdown of 2007 happened in good part because business leaders consulted only their short-term financial interests and not larger moral or religious principles. To paraphrase Thomas More in *A Man for All Seasons*, when executives forsake their own private consciences for the sake of their business duties, they lead their business, and their country, by a short route to chaos. Hopefully, the Catholic majority on the court can make room for principles of morality and conscience in America's marketplace.

2. Can the religious convictions of corporate leaders be allowed to inconvenience others or the government?

Again, a majority of the court suggested that the right to religious freedom itself only made sense in the context of some amount of inconvenience to the government and others. Exempting conscientious objectors from the army, allowing employees their holy days off, and providing kosher foods in jail—all these require some extra effort or expense on the part of the government, or even private citizens. The question related to the first is, even if businesses can invoke religious freedom, should they be able to do so if it inconveniences other citizens or the government? The discussion of this point before the court revolved around the question of whether the government could find some alternate way of meeting its interest of providing family planning health care to employees. Could the government, asked some justices, be required to directly supply the disputed contraceptive services to employees should their employers have conscientious objections to it?

Minority rights of any kind only become an issue when they annoy, intrude, or otherwise inconvenience some other party. Still, as a country, we think rights are sufficiently important to accept at least some level of inconvenience in their vindication. Why should this calculus be any different for businesspeople than for employees or other persons in society? Do we sign away our religious rights when we obtain business licenses?

The government's attorney made a great deal of the fact that no business or company had prevailed on a First Amendment religious-freedom exercise claim in the history of the Supreme Court. The plaintiff's attorney pointed out, however, that the court had considered a number of free-exercise cases involving businesses, and although the businesses had lost, the court had never ruled that they did not actually have the rights to religious freedom because they were businesses.

The court's answer to this question may seem to be less clear than the first one. But a majority of the justices do seem to be leaning toward giving businesses, at least closely held ones, the benefit of meaningful religious-freedom protection, even if it causes some inconvenience to others. Again, this seems the right result for a country that is committed to the religious freedom of all, and it was based on the belief that a republic and its marketplaces could only flourish as morality and virtue were seen in its citizens, including its merchants.

3. Can corporate morality or religious belief be used to trump the individual morality and freedom of employees?

The most difficult question the court faces is this final one: should the religious convictions of business owners be allowed to significantly infringe on the moral views, rights, and freedoms of its employees? At one level, it is fine to say that the state must endure some inconvenience to accommodate the religious convictions of business executives. But when should those convictions be allowed to impact the hundreds, and even thousands, of employees of companies, when those employees do not share those values and convictions?

A case in point is that of the employees of Hobby Lobby. Many of them probably have no moral objection to abortifacients and would like to use these forms of birth control. If Hobby Lobby refuses to provide them, does this become an infringement of their right to make private moral choices about family planning? In this case, the infringement will probably not be great, as it was pointed out that the employees would have alternate sources for these services, either through the government or by purchasing the relatively low-cost products directly themselves.

But other cases may not be so easy. The liberal justices asked what would happen with a company that does not believe in contraceptives at all or business owners that have religious objections to vaccines, antibiotics, or blood transfusions. Such convictions could keep very important, even life-sustaining, medical care from employees who would otherwise be unable to purchase or obtain these services. And what about business owners that might have religious convictions against the mixing of the races or women in the workplace? How far are we willing to bend or break our other discrimination laws to accommodate these more extreme convictions?

The court seemed to be searching for some guidance to these questions. One principle that a majority proposed was that religious convictions will probably be limited to privately, versus publicly, held corporations. Companies owned by a large number of shareholders will have a great deal of difficulty in showing a shared, common religious conviction. So the protection will likely be limited to closely held companies run by individuals or families with a shared sense of religious identity. This will often limit the size of the company, though as Hobby

Lobby itself shows, there can be very large privately held companies.

The court also acknowledged that religious freedom is not an absolute right; it must be balanced against the compelling interest of the state in protecting the life, liberty, health, and property of all its citizens. Religious convictions that could threaten the basic health and life of others will not, as case law has already shown, be given legal protection. As far as other socially offensive views relating to race or gender or, increasingly these days, sexual orientation, the court will probably have to take these on a case-by-case basis. The result in any given case will depend on the size and nature of the business, the magnitude of the impact on the protected class, and the nature of the burden on the religious practice.

Too often these days rights groups want to make their right absolute, whether it is race, religion, gender, or sexual orientation. But the reality is that all rights exist in a balance and tension with other rights. Religious freedom could actually be injured if the court extends too absolute a right of freedom to businesses, as corporate employees could see a corresponding loss of their own rights and freedoms in the workplace. While the court should not treat religious liberty as a hobby, neither should it give business owners so much freedom that their employees are required to leave their own moral and religious freedoms at home.

There is some danger of this result, as the court has shown a willingness to extend freedoms to corporations at the expense of the individual. We saw this in the case of *Hosanna Tabor v. EEOC*, where the court ruled that an elementary-school teacher at a parochial school had no civil rights protections in the workplace because her church had designated her as a minister, despite the fact that she spent most of her time teaching secular subjects. We do not want religion sidelined as a hobby; but neither do we want it elevated as a right primarily for the powerful, whether measured by majoritarian support or financial resource and power.

Ultimately, we can hope for, and the justices seemed open to, a decision that would grant business owners meaningful religious freedom, but in a manner that preserves and safeguards the civil and religious freedoms of their own employees. Anything less would be to replace state infringement of religious freedom with private business intrusions into personal freedoms. Hobby Lobby and its co-plaintiffs should certainly understand the problem of forcing employees to leave their basic freedoms at home when they come to work.

---

1. Brian Solomon, "Meet David Green: Hobby Lobby's Biblical Billionaire," *Forbes*, September 18, 2012, https://www.forbes.com/sites/briansolomon/2012/09/18/david-green-the-biblical-billionaire-backing-the-evangelical-movement/#4c369aec5807.

Chapter 24

Religion Is Not a Hobby!

On the last day of June 2014, the Supreme Court handed down one of the most anticipated results of this year, affirming that business and corporate owners do possess rights of religious freedom under federal law. Running a business or filing as a corporation does not mean that one must set aside one's basic religious convictions. The religious beliefs of businesses, at least those that are closely held by persons or families with strong religious identities, will receive protection from federal legislation.

Much was at stake in this case, as there have been growing conflicts between various businesses operated by people of faith and the increasingly secular legislation of modern America. The court's ruling is being generally criticized in popular media. But much of the criticism is based, I believe, on either misunderstandings of the decision or an underlying ideology that is opposed to religion. Consider the following points:

First, the basic principle the court has vindicated is straightforward, untroubling, and indeed important: persons of faith do not leave their beliefs behind when they enter the business world, either in unincorporated or incorporated form. The whole argument over corporations as persons is really irrelevant, despite all the attention it is getting. Religious not-for-profit institutions are also corporations, and nobody suggests that they should not receive religious freedom.

The critical distinction is whether the entity is organized for profit or not.

This chapter originally appeared in *Liberty*, September/October 2014.

While the dissent spends a long time mulling over the corporate status, ultimately, if you look at the justices' concluding paragraph, they are concerned about the profit purpose for the enterprise. But this is a very strange distinction. On this basis, we would not protect the religious freedom of employees, because they are working for money, not for a religious purpose. Why is it that employees have their religious convictions protected, but employers—those who own the corporation—do not? To install a rule as proposed by the dissent would be to prevent Christians and other persons of faith from meaningful presence as owners and leaders in the business world as our regulatory environment becomes increasingly secularized.

Second, the court's decision is limited in a way that just does not make the parade of horribles proposed by the dissent meaningfully realistic. The dissent appears to be provoked in part by their ideological commitments to feminist views regarding reproductive rights and birth-control choice. The fact is that the majority opinion assumed that access to this kind of medical care is in fact an important state interest. What they found, however, was that there were "less restrictive means" of achieving it.[1] Nobody would be denied access to these health benefits; the issue is who would pay for them: the company, the government, or third-party insurers. Nobody proposed that the women themselves would need to pay.

The majority suggested that the government might pay or third-party insurers cover the expense, which is what is already being done for not-for-profit religious corporations. The existing exemptions, in my opinion, should caution anyone from viewing this case as troubling. It merely extends an existing exemption, which does not deny anyone coverage, to a somewhat broader group of entities. The court majority carefully distinguished this decision from people who would deny vaccination coverage, which, like blood transfusions, would implicate important health concerns for many people and for which no existing exemption exists.

Third, the majority simply did not say that the religious convictions of employers might trump the rights of employees or other individuals. Indeed, they assert that third-party rights are very much a concern in these situations and that statutes regarding racial, ethnic, and other types of discrimination would continue to provide a compelling interest. It is unlikely, the court said, that there would be other "less restrictive means" of enforcing these statutes than actually requiring employers to follow them. Thus any speculation that the religious rights of employees, such as rights to Sabbath observance or other religious accommodations are not taken into consideration, is simply unfounded.

Finally, I think the unspoken agenda of much of the media and elite opinion on this case is driven in part by concerns over the gay-rights agenda. This case will bring a greater balance to the contest between religious rights and gay rights. That will be, in my opinion, a good thing. I think this is what is most important about the *Hobby Lobby* case: it has given much greater protection to Christian businesses in dealing with gay-rights issues. It does not mean that religion will always trump gay rights, but it will mean that gay rights will not always trump religion, which is what has basically been happening.

The *Hobby Lobby* majority relied entirely on the Religious Freedom Restoration Act, which applies only to the federal government, and not the First Amendment, which applies also to state governments. Thus, this decision does not create a general protection from state regulations for private businesses and their religious convictions. It should be a very persuasive precedent, however, for interpreting any state religious-freedom acts. There are quite a number of these acts, and a lot of the florist/photographer/bakery versus gay marriage cases that have appeared in the news during the past year will now come out in a way that protects the rights of religious business owners. In all these instances, there have been other vendors who could supply the desired services, and thus there was no "less restrictive means" requirement to insist that the Christian vendor provide the service.

Indeed, the court may well have not taken *certiorari* earlier this year on the photography versus gay marriage case out of New Mexico because *Hobby Lobby* essentially decides that case, and in the right direction for people of faith. Some will not like this outcome, but it is one of the few legal breaks for people of faith in the recent past in a legal and political environment that has become increasingly and aggressively secular.

Could this ruling have some unintended consequences? Could it lead to the assertion of corporate religious interests over the consciences of employees? One suspects that business and corporate interests will try at times to push it in this direction. Perhaps they may find a judge or two sympathetic to their goals. But there is no reasonable basis in the decision to justify such outcomes, and no real threat of them gaining any real traction. On the contrary, Justice Kennedy's concurrence makes it clear that he sides with the dissent in ruling that the health-care services involved do represent a compelling interest and the rights of women to these services must be protected.

That Justice Kennedy is the swing vote should remind people that the court is not poised to engage in a radical shift of religious rights from individuals to corporations. His concurrence signals that he will join the dissent if such an attempt is made. In the meantime, the faith community owes the Green family and their legal allies a debt of gratitude. Because of their commitment, faithfulness, and perseverance in standing for their religious beliefs, religion will not be just a hobby that must be left in the lobby whenever one enters the business world.

---

1. Burwell v. Hobby Lobby, 573 US 59 (2014).

Chapter 25

Religious Freedom: The New Bigotry?

I s supporting religious freedom an act of bigotry? This question is seriously being asked in the wake of the recent media eruptions surrounding the Religious Freedom Restoration Act (RFRA) bills passed in Indiana and Arkansas. The firestorm surrounding these bills has brought the tension between religious freedom and gay rights to a new level of public scrutiny and focus.

The discussion about the balance between religious liberty and sexual freedom is not new. It has been happening for about two decades now. But there has been a recent and significant change in its tenor and tone. The underlying assumption of the discussion has become that if protection of religious freedom has any chance of even remotely impacting gay rights, it is indefensible bigotry that must be boycotted, shamed, vilified, and hounded beyond the bounds of polite, commercial, and even civil society.

The problem with this new assumption is that it upends two centuries of how a system of rights works under our Constitution and law. Previously, the classic liberal view envisioned a sort of multipeaked landscape of rights, where rights to speech, assembly, privacy, religion, and the rest were balanced with each other and with societal concerns in a careful and judicious manner.

But in the last decade, this mountainous landscape, which harbored and protected a wide array of religions, ideologies, and outlooks, has been flattened into a featureless plain, scoured and ruled by the powerful, inescapable winds of a new secular, sexual

This chapter originally appeared in *Compass Magazine*, April 3, 2015.

egalitarian ideology. Anything that has the temerity to stand in its way must be pulled down—or so the media, celebrities, and business elites have declared.

This change in approach to rights is underscored by the reaction to the recent state RFRAs in Indiana and Arkansas. Indiana's was initially signed into law by Governor Pence. But under a barrage of media, celebrity, and business criticism and boycotting, Pence ordered the Indiana legislature to change it, which they have done. The governor of Arkansas preempted such criticism by asking for changes before he signed it. Yet these laws were essentially identical in substance to RFRA laws that have existed in about twenty other states for more than a decade and to a federal RFRA that has existed for more than twenty years.

The Indiana and Arkansas laws: Are they really that different?

Some claim that these RFRA bills contain important differences from the earlier RFRAs. It is said that the new RFRAs specifically include businesses and for-profit enterprises in their protections and that they also can be applied against private parties and not just governments. But this is to overlook the fact that both of these elements were part of how RFRAs were understood to operate, even if they did not contain this language. The "sin" of the more recent RFRAs was making explicit what was already implicit in the previous RFRAs, as acknowledged by the US Supreme Court itself.[1]

This is something I know about personally, as in the late 1990s, I was involved in the framing of the Religious Land Use and Institutionalized Persons Act of 2000 (RLUIPA), as well as in coalitions to support the passage of state RFRAs. At the center of our efforts was an attempt to understand and apply the "compelling interest" standard, which is the heart of all RFRAs. There was a clear sense among the drafters and promoters of these laws that they were to protect business owners with religious convictions.

In the RLUIPA and state RFRA coalitions of the time, there was a great deal of attention paid to the "Mrs. Smith" case out of California. This case involved an elderly religious lady who refused to rent an apartment to a couple living out of wedlock. Should her concerns be protected by RFRA? The California Supreme Court had denied her right to make rental selections based on her religion, as renting apartments was not an activity "central" to her system of religious belief.[2]

The religious-freedom community opposed this centrality argument, and RLUIPA and state RFRAs almost all have language about religious behavior being protected even if it is not "central" to one's system of belief. For our purposes, the important point is that the drafters of these acts viewed them very much as applying to both private individuals and businesses. This view was subsequently vindicated by the Supreme Court's decision in *Hobby Lobby*, which made clear that the law applied not only to small businesses but also to large family run or closely held corporations.

So, in stating that businesses were covered by RFRA, the Indiana legislature was merely making explicit what had been assumed about earlier RFRAs and had indeed been confirmed by the Supreme Court. The issue of application of RFRA to private parties is perhaps only slightly more contentious. Again, this was not mentioned in the original RFRA, as it was assumed that RFRA would be a shield primarily against laws, and the concern about parties was secondary. Whether you were sued by the state or by a private party, you could challenge the validity of that law under RFRA.

While the *Hobby Lobby* case was brought by private parties against the government, it could have been brought as a defense to lawsuits by female employees seeking to obtain abortifacient coverage. There is some difference on this question between some of the federal circuits, and it has not been ruled on by the Supreme Court. But it seems again the obvious implication of RFRA logic and, indeed, has been accepted and promoted by the Obama administration's Justice Department itself.

Rights in the balance

The important thing about RFRA is that it did not envision religious freedom prevailing at the expense of all other rights. Rather, it proposed a continuation of our classical constitutional system of rights where various rights were weighed and measured, and the result differed depending on the magnitude of interference with various rights and interests.

To give you a sense of the way this was thought of, let me quote from a booklet I was the main author of, titled, *Questions and Answers About State Religious Freedom Restoration Acts*. This was published in the late 1990s and was circulated widely in the civil rights community in Washington, DC, as well as to legislatures where state RFRAs were being considered. It is, in a sense, legislative history of the early RFRAs and is quite illuminating on this point.

After acknowledging that the Supreme Court had already ruled that eradicating racial discrimination was generally a compelling interest, the booklet addressed other interests, including gender and sexual orientation:

These interests [gender, sexual orientation, marital status] have been found by some courts to override religiously based housing and employment decisions. In other cases the free exercise right has prevailed, protecting the freedom of choice of the landlord or employer with religious scruples.

The lesson is that each instance of alleged discrimination will likely require its own weighing of the facts and circumstances. A devout widow who rents the apartment over her garage or who is a live-in landlord at a four-unit complex may be protected in her conviction that she does not want to facilitate and live with what she views as immoral conduct. However, the claim of an absentee religious landlord who owns a forty-unit facility will come out differently, with the balance likely tipping in favor of the associational rights of the renters.[3]

The careful balancing of rights envisioned by the framers and promoters of RFRA was based on a history of cases worked out by federal courts for judging among competing rights claims. The truly alarming thing for all rights claims is that the latest media "discussions," if they can be called that, are demanding a very different approach to rights. Now it seems we have been given a hierarchical set of rights, with historic rights to freedom of religion, speech, and association set down beneath the all-important and central rights of a secular, sexual ideology.

To illustrate this point, consider these hypotheticals: Should a gay baker be legally required to bake a cake for the Westboro Baptist Church that says on it "God Hates Gays"? Or should a black baker be forced to bake a cake that says "We Love the KKK"? Nobody I know on the liberal or the conservative side would say that they should. Why do we have a different outcome when it comes to the Christian and gay-marriage cases?

I would suggest that it is because underneath the new secular, sexual ideology, gays are now a politically correct, popular minority. But these societal facts do not change the basic legal principle involved: the freedom of religious and ideological expression, as well as freedom of association, should cause the gay baker, the black baker, *and* the Christian baker to be protected. But in our new regime, it is equality that is paramount; and that is to be an equality based on a view of humanity, sexuality, and society that is modern, secular, and hostile to almost all traditional religious outlooks. The logic of rejecting a balancing of rights—a balance which state RFRAs aim to protect—has fearful implications.

"Equal rights" at any cost?

Serious questions are now being raised in the mainstream media: Will religious colleges and schools be able to teach and implement their beliefs regarding sexual behavior and domestic relationships? Can Christians, Jews, and Muslims who hold to traditional sexual ethics serve as public employees? Can they hold positions of responsibility at important private institutions? Should churches that hold these traditional beliefs lose their tax-exempt status? Should officials of these religious organizations be allowed to marry anyone? Should private religious schools even be allowed at all?[4]

Some of these questions seem extreme. But ten years ago, even five, it would have seemed extreme to say that nearly two-thirds of the states would have legalized gay marriage and the Supreme Court would be on the verge of making it a federal right. In less than a decade, the unthinkable has become the inevitable—and even the morally necessary, according to our social elites.

Those crying discrimination in Indiana and Arkansas need to look closely at the real issues at stake here. We need to consider the new regime of rights we are embracing as a society and stop and ask if the cost is not too great—that of insisting on erasing, publicly at least, many of the core values and teachings of the world's great historic religions. The result would be the ghettoizing of traditional religious peoples into secluded communities that have minimal contact with the outside world.

We see this pattern developing in Europe already, and it has not made for a peaceful or positive coexistence. Rather, it has tended toward the breeding of radicalization, extremism, and violence. Indeed, the European experience is part of what provoked the American experiment with religious freedom: a robust separation of church and state but a charitable, benevolent, and protective attitude toward the free exercise of religion by the great diversity of individuals that came to our shores.

Milton Friedman once said, "The society that puts equality before freedom will end up with neither. The society that puts freedom before equality will end up with a great measure of both."[5] Perhaps it is not necessary to put freedom "before" equality, but history and our founding values suggest a mutual balancing of the two. To renege on our founding promise of religious freedom, and to try to fight "religious bigotry" with the new regime of a secular egalitarianism, will lead to a new and more intensive kind of bigotry—one toward religion and religious people. *That* is the true new bigotry.

---

1. "In response, the United States has formally taken the position that religious organizations can assert RFRA as a defense in lawsuits brought by private parties: '[I]f plaintiff were sued by a plan participant or beneficiary in the future, plaintiff, in its defense of such an action, would have an opportunity to raise its contention that the contraceptive coverage requirement violates the Religious Freedom Restoration Act ('RFRA').' Reply in Support of Motion to Dismiss at 3-4, Wheaton Coll. v. Sebelius, No. 12-01169 (D.D.C. Aug. 20, 2012)." Brief for the Becket Fund for Religious Liberty as Amicus Curiae, at 13, Elane Photography, LLC v. Willock, 309 P.3d 53 (N.M. 2013), quoted in Josh Blackman, "Comparing the Federal RFRA and the Indiana RFRA," *Josh Blackman's Blog*, March 26, 2015, http://joshblackman.com/blog/2015/03/26/comparing-the-federal-rfra-and-the-indiana-rfra/.

2. Smith v. Fair Employment and Housing Commission, 12 Cal.4th 1143, 913 P.2d 909 (1996).

3. Sidley, Austin, Brown, and Wood, *Questions and Answers About State Religious Freedom Restoration Acts*, 2nd ed. (Washington, DC: Sidley, Austin, Brown, and Wood, 2000), 10.

4. Ross Douthat, "Questions for Indiana's Critics," *Evaluations* (blog), *New York Times*, March 30, 2015, http://douthat.blogs.nytimes.com/2015/03/30/questions-for-indianas-critics/?smid=fb-share&_r=0.

5. Milton Friedman, quoted in "Free to Choose 1990–Vol. 5 Created Equal–Full Video," YouTube video 27:35–27:47, from "Created Equal," *Free to Choose*, vol. 5, 1990, posted by "Free to Choose Network," December 30, 2015, https://www.youtube.com/watch?v=Fr5cDWBgibU.

Chapter 26

Gay Marriage and the Supreme Court: What's at Stake for Religious Freedom?

f I were a Supreme Court justice who had to decide on gay marriage, and all I could rely on were the oral arguments made to the court last week, I would almost certainly vote in favor. This is bad news for supporters of traditional marriage.

I have been a vocal supporter and advocate for the traditional position over the last decade. But the arguments made this week for traditional marriage seemed self-defeating and contradictory.

Before I detail the shortcomings of these arguments, let me mention a couple of glimmers of hope for traditional marriage. First, the court is not limited to the facts and arguments made at oral argument. The main parties filed hundreds of pages of briefs. In addition, various outside parties have filed a record 148 friend-of-the-court briefs, with 58 supporting the traditional position. Surely amid this pile of paper are some careful, thoughtful, and evidence-based arguments about the importance of a mother and a father to the nurture and development of children, as well as the importance of state policies in encouraging and protecting those relationships.

Second, a couple of the swing-vote justices revealed that they still have questions on gay marriage. Justice Kennedy is generally understood to be the main swing vote on the issue. He has voted for gay rights in the past, but his reasoning has suggested that his support might not extend to marriage.

This chapter originally appeared in *Compass Magazine*, May 8, 2015.

His questions revealed some of this uncertainty. He pointed to the short period of time gay marriage has been seriously considered:

Ten years is—I don't even know how to count the decimals when we talk about millennia.

This [traditional] definition has been with us for millennia.

And it—it's very difficult for the Court to say, oh, well, we—we know better.[1]

More surprisingly, Justice Breyer—generally considered a firm pro-gay vote—voiced a similar question: "[Traditional marriage] has been the law everywhere for thousands of years among people who were not discriminating even against gay people, and suddenly you want nine people outside the ballot box to require States that don't want to do it to change . . . what marriage is to include gay people. Why cannot those States at least wait and see whether in fact doing so in the other States is or is not harmful to marriage?"[2]

Now, both of these justices also asked hard and pointed questions of the traditional side, so these questions do not tip their hands as to the direction they are leaning. But they do suggest that one or two centrist minds on the court are not entirely made up and that the result is not a foregone conclusion.

A weak argument for traditional marriage

But I am quite pessimistic about that eventual result. And it has to do in good part with the weak showing in the oral argument. The counsel for the state of Michigan, who was defending the state's traditional marriage statute, rested his entire argument on the view that gay marriage is bad for children.

Now this is not a poor argument in itself, as many studies show that, for optimum development, children do better with the influence of both a mother and a father. But he did not cite these studies or even really make this argument. Rather, he argued that the acceptance of gay marriage will, in the popular mind, disconnect marriage from procreation and child-rearing, thus leading to the birth and raising of more children outside of marriage.

This claim may or may not be true. There is insufficient data in the United States, as gay marriage is so new, to prove it one way or the other. But the simple fact is that this philosophical shift from family-centered to adult-centered marriage had already largely occurred before gay marriage became a popular social cause. This adult-satisfaction-centered marriage is a result and a symptom of the social and cultural revolution of the sixties and seventies. At that time, the rise of birth control and the spread of a self-centered hedonism took the public's focus off the health of the family unit and transferred it to the satisfaction and actualization of adults.

To blame the gay community for this fundamental shift in outlook is myopic and ahistorical; it is a symptom rather than a cause of this change. Indeed, the gay community's attempt to enter into long-term marriage relationships could be seen as mitigating against this self-focused, individualistic construct. (Indeed, that is why marriage itself is controversial within the gay community. Some vocal factions oppose it, and many gay people do not marry for these reasons.)

But those gay persons who do want to enter into marriage can plausibly argue that such a step strengthens the bonds and duration of their relationships and that this is actually good for kids. The fact is, as the court noted, there are hundreds of thousands of children being raised by gay couples. Their family bonds would be reinforced and made more enduring by gay marriage, and this would actually achieve the goals that Michigan is concerned about in regard to strengthening families for children.

The argument that this practical support of children is outweighed by a purported, but yet unseen, "philosophical shift" in the public mind regarding marriage and procreation seems a thin reed indeed for the court to rest on in denying gays the right to marry.

A better argument for traditional marriage

So why do I think that the court should protect and preserve the traditional definition of marriage? Well, I, too, agree that it is about the children and preserving an optimum environment for their upbringing. There is extensive support for the notion that children do much, much better with the care and attention of both a mother and a father.

A number of very recent studies, as well as older studies, have shown the importance of both genders to child-rearing.[3] Yes, of course, we have many single-parent homes, but in these instances society generally recognizes that there is a gap that needs to be filled. Big Brother programs, men at Boy Scouts and at church, uncles and grandfathers—all are enlisted to play the role of the missing father (and 80 percent of the time, it is the father that is missing).[4]

But once gay marriage is recognized, there will be a legal presumption, and increasingly a popular assumption, that these are fully adequate child-rearing environments. Society will assume that little boys can grow into well-rounded men without the benefit of masculine influence; that little girls can become mature women without feminine nurture and guidance.

This is an unsafe and even foolish assumption that goes against the common experiences of those raised by a mother and a father, most who cannot imagine choosing between them. It also goes against the experience of those raised by single parents and who feel very deeply the lack of the "other" parent in their lives. Increasingly, children raised by gay parents are expressing their unhappiness at the lack of, usually, a father figure. Amicus briefs were filed at the Supreme Court by such persons.

There is a reason that the fifth commandment not only calls for honor from child to parents, but also specifies mother and father. In a patriarchal age, where fathers had supreme command, it is remarkable—and a point for Christian feminism—that the commandment includes the mother as deserving equal honor.

But there is also a significant point for heterosexual marriage here. The duty of the child to honor assumes a corresponding right of the child to have the nurture and protection of the complementary duo of mother and father. That right cannot always be realized in a fallen and sinful world, and one must fill the gaps as best as one can; but neither should that right be extinguished or disregarded as a matter of policy simply because of the subjective desires of those who cannot biologically produce children.

Now I do not cite the fifth commandment as authority for the proposition that gay marriage should be rejected. That would be an inappropriate biblical argument for a matter of public policy. But I am noting that our most ancient religious wisdom supports our historical, commonsense, intuitive, and empirical observations that men and women are both crucial to the development and well-being of children.

The deeper issue at stake: Religious liberty

I'll conclude with one thought about the risks and dangers faced by the church should gay marriage be declared a national right. Justice Alito raised with the lawyer for the Justice Department the *Bob Jones* case, in which the Supreme Court had stripped the tax-exempt status of a religious college. "So would the same apply," Alito asked, "to a university or college if it opposed same-sex marriage?"

The response by Donald Verrilli, solicitor general for the United States, was telling:

It's certainly going to be an issue. I—I don't deny that. . . .
   It is—it is going to be an issue.[5]

An issue, indeed. The religious community has been alerted: religious institutions, at least colleges and universities, and quite possibly hospitals and healthcare institutions, will be very much on the government's radar in enforcing this newly found right, should the court grant it. Standards relating to sexual behavior in hiring, employment, admissions, student and faculty conduct, and even classroom teaching would all come under close scrutiny and, very likely, eventual challenge. Institutions that stand firm would risk losing their tax-exempt status. In many instances, this would simply close their doors.

In sixteenth-century England, the Protestant Reformation was announced and implemented by a "stripping of the altars," a practice whereby state churches had Catholic vestments and icons removed from their altars. We are coming to the point where a new, secular "stripping of the altars" is being threatened: one that does not remove vestments and icons, but strips institutions of either their core Christian identity or their tax-exempt status.

This Hobson's choice should be a sobering thought, even for those who support gay marriage. Rather than "pluralism" and "tolerance"—which is what we were told the gay-rights movement is about—there is much more "uniformity" and "intolerance" than in the system it seeks to replace. No responsible Christian thinker or organization that I know of has called for a loss of tax-exempt status for gay-friendly churches, schools, or organizations. The Christian community has expressed a general sense of moral disagreement with gay groups and institutions. But that community has also largely understood that in a pluralistic country people have the right to hold and express those morally contrary views. Apparently, in our larger society, that principled tolerance is no longer seen as important or true.

What is at stake in this decision is more than gay marriage in particular, or gay rights generally; rather, it is the fundamental right of moral disagreement with whatever conventional wisdom or wave of political correctness holds the political high ground. Today that ground is held by gay rights and, apparently, gay marriage. But tomorrow, who knows? Before we discard a system of principled, pluralistic tolerance, we should consider carefully what beasts and dragons might lie around the next corner, waiting to enforce their own intolerance.

---

1. Anthony Kennedy, "Obergefell v. Hodges," April 28, 2015, Oral Argument (Part 1) transcript and recording, 3:40–3:55, Oyez, https://www.oyez.org/cases/2014/14-556.

2. Stephen Breyer, "Obergefell v. Hodges," April 28, 2015, Oral Argument (Part 1) transcript and recording, 13:51–14:30, Oyez, https://www.oyez.org/cases/2014/14-556.

3. To see a list of these studies, visit " 'No Differences?' (2014): Contents," Witherspoon Institute, http://winst.org/publications/no-differences-2014-contents/.

4. Joseph Chamie, "320 Million Children in Single-Parent Families," Inter Press Service, October 15, 2016, http://www.ipsnews.net/2016/10/320-million-children-in-single-parent-families/.

5. Samuel Alito and Donald Verrilli, "Obergefell v. Hodges," April 28, 2015, Oral Argument (Part 1) transcript and recording, 38:17–38:29, https://www.oyez.org/cases/2014/14-556.

Conclusion:

From Martin Luther to Donald Trump?
Protestantism, Twenty-First-Century Populism,
and the Future of Religious Liberty

So what is it that makes America truly great? This is not just a central question in recent political discussions in the United States, but a continuing part of America's quest to understand itself. The 2016 American presidential campaign featuring the promise by then-candidate Donald Trump to "make America great again" is just part of a history of budding political leaders who call on a nation's past to exhort it to new heights. But this slogan, promise, or quest always raises the question of what it is that makes America, or any country for that matter, truly great.

For many historians, the rise of democracy, along with civil and religious liberty, during the last two or three hundred years, is the great achievement of the nations of the West. They point to the combination of liberal democracy, free enterprise, and human rights that have widely prevailed in significant parts of the globe. Arguably, this potent combination reached its zenith in the American republic, and the nations of the world aspire to it.

There are, of course, regimes that resist this trend toward democratization and human rights. Significant ones include China, North Korea, various Southern Hemisphere dictatorships, and many Islamic countries. But these nations keep democratic impulses at bay largely by suppressing information or people—and usually both.

Thus, both kinds of nations, democratic and authoritarian, pay homage to the idea of liberal democracy: one by implementation and emulation, and the other by admitting that censorship and force must be used to suppress its natural growth among the people. Such was the completeness of this picture that near the end of the twentieth century, one well-known philosopher of history famously wondered if all true historical questions had ended: the end of history, as Francis Fukuyama declared it—at least in the title of his book, if not so emphatically in his actual argument.[1]

Now, in the early part of the twenty-first century, this comfortable and self-satisfying (at least for Westerners) thesis is being challenged by a number of events. One is the publication of a number of books by Western scholars questioning whether the rise of civil rights in the modern world has anything meaningful to do with the truly universal values of either the Reformation or the Enlightenment. In their revisionist view, the modern rise of rights is a largely post–World War II phenomenon, where a weakened West sought to continue to impose its Western, individualistic, materialistic, and institutionally conservative principles on an increasingly independent, postcolonial world.[2]

Another development is the so-called Arab Spring. Many hoped that this wave of popular uprisings in North Africa and the Middle East portended an outbreak of freedom and democracy in the Muslim world; perhaps it would be the belated wish fulfillment of the American neo-conservatives' hopes about the impact of the invasion of Iraq under George W. Bush. But rather than leading to liberal democracies and rule by the people, these movements have degenerated into various versions of strongman—or at least elite "strongmen"—rule. This has had particularly violent results in places such as Egypt, Libya, and most disturbingly, Syria.

Another challenge to Fukuyama's thesis about the inevitability of the supremacy of liberal democracy and freedom has been the resurgence of a xenophobic populism in the very heart of the West. This populism appears very receptive to nonliberal ideas of governance, including an acceptance, and even a desire, for a strongman rule that will cut through the inefficiencies of a bureaucratic democracy. One must only mention the words *Brexit* and *Trump* to know that America and Britain—once the heart of the democratic, Protestant West—have become attracted to this latest and very alarming trend.

This nationalistic populism manifests itself in a variety of forms in a number of European countries and claims to be, at least in part, a defense of the West's Christian heritage. In his presidential campaign, Donald Trump purported to speak for mainstream Christianity and promised to return it to a position of influence and power. President Trump and various European nationalist factions play their Christian identity against the non-Christian roots of many immigrant groups—especially those from Muslim countries. But this populist Christianity seems to have much more to do with medieval versions that supported centralized power structures in both church and state, and viewed unbelievers as social and civil enemies to be dealt with by force and crusade.

This renewed Christendom stands in contrast with the more recent Protestant heritage of these countries, especially those with a dissenting, free-church Protestant influence, such as England and America, which we have explored in some depth in the previous chapters. Until recently, these countries held deeply philosophical, principled commitments to both open and free government, as well as religious pluralism and freedom.

The question is, what version of the "great" America is it that Donald Trump desires to return? He obviously rejects the "great" societies of the progressives, whether of the 1920s or the 1960s and 1970s, which aimed to achieve efficiency, fairness, and equality through government intervention. But he seems to be jumping over the greatness of our constitutional founding, with its values of republicanism (representative, divided, and accountable government) and Protestantism (protection of conscience and religious freedom of minorities).

Rather, President Trump now appears to promote the values of the colonial period: he embodies a mixture of the royal prerogative of the proprietors and governors of the middle and southern colonies, such as Pennsylvania and Virginia, and the religious intolerance and exclusiveness of early New England (minus Roger Williams's Rhode Island, of course). The American constitutional founders drew on the opposite values from these regions: they incorporated in the Constitution the principles of the representative governments of New England and implemented the religious and civil freedoms of the middle colonies, especially Pennsylvania, Delaware, and Maryland. To put it mildly, they would be surprised at the reverse values to which President Trump has attached national greatness.

So our political leaders are calling us to revive the "great" values of the past. Meanwhile, scholars question whether such values even exist, except as excuses for imperialism. And yet foreign countries are increasingly anxious to find a solution to the cycle of democratic excess and strongman intervention. At such a time, surely it is important to decide what values have given America a meaningfully great run. It has been a relative historic greatness—and with all the important caveats about slavery, Native American oppression, militarism, and chauvinism—based on freedom, stability, and prosperity. The caveats are significant. But they have not stopped the United States from becoming a desired destination for those of every nationality, color, and creed on earth. This envy factor is telling. It should cause us to appreciate the relative greatness that has been, and continues to be, America, even if that term has been abused by demagogues for their own political ends.

To truly understand the basis of America's greatness requires us to revisit America's Protestant heritage and the connection of that heritage with the growth of freedom and liberty. While certainly not a complete or exhaustive effort, the previous chapters have done this in some detail. I would contend that these chapters show there have forever been at least two competing strands of Protestant thought in American history. Ever since the constitutional founding, the major Protestant influence on law, public policy, and culture has been the dissenting, free-church Protestant outlook. But not far beneath the surface has been the magisterial, state-church-oriented Protestantism with roots in Puritan New England and Calvin's Geneva.

What President Trump appears to be promoting is a version of this latter brand of Protestantism, combined with a healthy dose of unfettered capitalism, a hawkish American militarism, and a nationalistic, xenophobic populism. This rather unique amalgam of ideas may draw on Protestant rhetoric and symbolism, but it is far from the true spirit of even the Magisterial Reformers, whether it be Luther's priesthood of all believers or Calvin's representative church ethos. It certainly runs strongly counter to the dissenting Protestant ethos of groups such as the Anabaptists, Moravians, Quakers, and Baptists, whose ideas did the most to shape the kind of Protestant nation America became by the late eighteenth century.

Rather than a logical result of Protestant ideas and ideals, the nationalist populism that seeks to exalt America at the expense of religious and ethnic minorities is, I believe, an imposition, or counterfeit. It has been generated by an inherent weakness in another strand of America's other founding philosophy—that of democracy itself.

As far back as democracy has been discussed, it has been acknowledged as possessing an inherent weakness that could easily turn into its fatal flaw: its susceptibility to the rise of demagogues—unprincipled and charismatic leaders who play on the passions and fears of the people. Plato himself was acutely aware of this problem with democracy and discussed it in his *Republic*. The longer a democracy lasted, Plato believed, the more "equal" it would become, to the point of overlooking natural differences in fathers and children, men and women, and masters and servants.

As one conservative intellectual summarizes it, Plato believed that in the final stages, "its freedoms would multiply; its equality spread. Deference to any sort of authority would wither; tolerance of any kind of inequality would come under intense threat; and multiculturalism and sexual freedom would create a city or a country like 'a many-colored cloak decorated in all hues.' " Once democracy enters this rainbow-flag stage, "all the barriers to equality, formal and informal, have been removed; when everyone is equal; when elites are despised and full license is established to do 'whatever one wants,' you arrive at what might be called late-stage democracy. There is no kowtowing to authority here, let alone to political experience or expertise."[3]

It is when an unmoored democracy has ripened into this egalitarian, genderless, and sexually free and promiscuous state of enervation, free of traditional boundaries, but hemmed in by a new hierarchy of political correctness that the next phase emerges—descent into tyranny. Plato has a very specific description of the kind of man, because it almost always is a man, who seizes power then.

Again, as summarized by Sullivan, the would-be tyrant "is usually of the elite but has a nature in tune with the time—given over to random pleasures and whims, feasting on plenty of food and sex, and reveling in the nonjudgment that is democracy's civil religion. He makes his move by 'taking over a particularly obedient mob' and attacking his wealthy peers as corrupt. If not stopped quickly, his appetite for attacking the rich on behalf of the people swells further."[4]

If a majority of the citizens cannot act to head off the danger, "eventually, he stands alone, promising to cut through the paralysis of democratic incoherence. It's as if he were offering the addled, distracted, and self-indulgent citizens a kind of relief from democracy's endless choices and insecurities." The extremes of democracy provide a ready target for him. "He rides a backlash to excess—'too much freedom seems to change into nothing but too much slavery'—and offers himself as the personified answer to the internal conflicts of the democratic mess." He offers himself as the champion of the common people. "He pledges, above all, to take on the increasingly despised elites. And as the people thrill to him as a kind of solution, a democracy willingly, even impetuously, repeals itself."[5]

Our own founders were well aware of the dangers of demagoguery within a democracy. In the very first *Federalist* paper, Alexander Hamilton remarked on the tendency of those that wear a "specious mask of zeal for the rights of the people" to walk a "much more certain road to the introduction of despotism." History shows that "of those men who have overturned the liberties of republics, the greatest number have begun their career, by paying an obsequious court to the people . . . commencing demagogues, and ending tyrants."[6]

For the same reason, James Madison opposed a pure democracy and favored a representative republic shielded from the excesses of popular control. But even a republic may be subject to the demagogue, if not carefully guarded. In the tenth *Federalist* paper, Madison wrote that "men of factious tempers, of local prejudices, or of sinister designs, may by intrigue, by corruption, or by other means, first obtain the suffrages, and then betray the interests of the people."[7]

George Washington himself warned in his Farewell Address of the likelihood of such a betrayal in a democratic republic caught in partisan politics. He thought that party politics itself was a kind of despotism. "The alternate domination of one faction over another, sharpened by the spirit of revenge natural to party dissention, which in different ages & countries has perpetrated the most horrid enormities, is itself a frightful despotism."

But partisanship itself led to something else—a strongman who can transcend party bickering and gridlock. "The disorders & miseries, which result, gradually incline the minds of men to seek security & repose in the absolute power of an Individual: and sooner or later the chief of some prevailing faction more able or more fortunate than his competitors, turns this disposition to the purposes of his own elevation, on the ruins of Public Liberty."[8]

So if the rise of a demagogic populist is the result of a flaw in republican democracy rather than Protestant principles, why did more than 80 percent of white American Protestant evangelicals cast a vote for a secular populist who appears to have an equal disdain for traditional morality, our system of constitutional checks and balances, and the freedom of the press?[9] One clear answer, of course, is that the alternative advanced by the Democrats hailed from Plato's other extreme, the multihued, egalitarian, licentious democracy that was itself threatening traditional values and morality. Many evangelicals could not, with clear conscience, vote for that alternative either.

So why vote at all? Some would say that not choosing between two competing evils is to choose. But Christ Himself acknowledged situations where some evil was inevitable, but that one should still not choose to aid or abet it. "It is impossible but that offences will come: but woe unto him, through whom they come!" (Luke 17:1).

We must acknowledge that most Christians who voted for President Trump did so *in spite of* his encouragement of racist outlooks, his misogyny, and sexually impure comments and behavior. Their votes cannot be seen as an endorsement of that behavior. But credible observers from within evangelicalism have noted that in order to vote for Trump, most evangelicals had to shift or change their view of morality and politics. When Democrats controlled the White House, only 30 percent of evangelicals felt that an "elected official can behave ethically even if they have committed transgressions in their personal life" and fulfill public duties. But in 2016, as Trump was running his campaign, evangelicals switched on that question. Now 72 percent[10] thought that private immoral behavior was not relevant to a public official's fitness for office. It is hard to see this switch in any other light than changing fundamental moral positions for political advantage and gain.

The Bible predicts that there will come a time when religious men and women will sacrifice fundamental principles of right and wrong, of correctness in worship, in order to further their political and economic aspirations. The prophet John talks about this in the book of Revelation, foreseeing a time when economic and political power is put on the side of false, state-coerced worship that is embraced by the majority (Revelation 13:14–17).

Such a time of coercion in matters of worship has not yet come. But to get there, a majority of Christians will have to take steps down the road of putting political and economic goals ahead of moral principles in respecting the image of God in other humans. This is precisely the bargain that Martin Luther himself protested against in his day; that dissenting Protestants worked against in theirs; and that our country itself, with its separation of powers, checks and balances, Bill of Rights, and rule of law, was designed to prevent.

What can prevent Americans of all faiths, Protestant and otherwise, from falling into this abyss? A clearer conception of where America's true greatness lies is needed. Its greatness is not in its economic might, its military power, or its intellectual and technological accomplishments, as marvelous as these are. Rather, that greatness lies in its civil and religious freedoms, extending to all men and women the dignity that comes with being made in God's image, and being endowed by that Creator with inalienable rights to life and liberty. To deny or trample these things is to assure, not America's greatness, but its inevitable decline and ruin.

One of the best places to look for America's foundational principles of greatness is in the frame of government designed by William Penn for the colony of Pennsylvania. Penn believed that the principles of Pennsylvania's Great Law of 1682 were foundational, not only in Pennsylvania, but that they would serve as "the seed of a nation" and, indeed, as an example for many nations. What were the principles that Penn found so important for the greatness of a state? The charter and Great Law make provisions for judicial fairness, rule of law, and due process; a representative, accountable legislature; and an executive committed to the civil rights and liberties of the people. Penn placed a special emphasis on the equal treatment of people of all religious beliefs; this was a conviction rooted in his dissenting Protestant biblical and philosophical conceptions of the rights of individual conscience given by a Divine Creator.

These commitments to open, accountable government, the rule of law, and religious freedom and ethnic diversity, led to Pennsylvania becoming a magnet for immigrants from many nations of the world. English Quakers, German Moravians, French Huguenots, British Baptists, Dutch Anabaptists and Mennonites, European Jews, and Catholics—all outcasts somewhere—soon streamed into Philadelphia and its environs. There they found a new home of almost unparalleled inclusion and equality. (Rhode Island offered similar legal standards but was far removed from the center of the colonies, geographically, in commercial success, and in popular awareness.)

The results of this influx were startling. While Boston and New York had been founded decades earlier, Philadelphia soon passed them in population. It rapidly became the largest and most commercially successful city in the American colonies. By the 1720s, Philadelphia was considered the "Athens of North America" and the most cosmopolitan city on the continent.

What Penn had dreamed indeed came to pass: his commonwealth did become the model, "the seed," for the new American nation and eventually for many nations around the world. Some point to Roger Williams's Rhode Island as the precursor to American pluralism, and others to the Virginia of Thomas Jefferson and James Madison. These, no doubt, played a role. But the founders themselves, including Jefferson and Madison, more often pointed to Pennsylvania as the model for the new national American government.

The success and prosperity of Pennsylvania, located in the heart of the American colonies, showed that religious and ethnic diversity was not an obstacle to governmental and commercial success. Rather, it was seen that these qualities could be part of the engine to achieve such successes. This example was not lost on the founders. Certainly not on Jefferson, who called Penn "the greatest lawgiver the world has produced."[11]

I think it is no coincidence that our national Constitution was written in Philadelphia, surrounded by the diversity and prosperity of Penn's experiment in government. But the critical point is that Pennsylvania's success, its greatness, was not *based* on business acumen or industrial might. Rather, the commercial skill and prosperity were the *result* of a commitment to underlying principles of open, accountable government; an evenhanded, independent judiciary; and a principled embrace of religious and ethnic diversity. In seeking a return to American greatness, we would do well to keep these foundational values in mind.

Five hundred years after Martin Luther wrote and acted, American Protestants, Christians, and people of faith and nonfaith, are called to act with similar courage and conviction. They are called by the God who created all in His image to uphold the fundamental rights of humanity against united economic, political, social, and religious, even ostensibly Christian, interests and groups that would trample these rights. May the protests of Martin Luther, Martin Luther King Jr., and all those who joined similar protests in between, continue on into Protestantism's next five hundred years!

---

1. Francis Fukuyama, *The End of History and the Last Man* (New York: Free Press, 1992).

2. Samuel Moyn of Harvard University has developed a virtual cottage industry in deploying this argument in a number of books, including *The Last Utopia: Human Rights in History* (Cambridge, MA: Harvard University Press, 2010); *Human Rights and the Uses of History* (Brooklyn: Verso, 2014); and *Christian Human Rights* (Philadelphia: University of Pennsylvania Press, 2015). He is by no means alone, however, and similar arguments have been made by Eric Posner in *The Twilight of Human Rights Law* (New York: Oxford University Press, 2014).

3. Andrew Sullivan, "Democracies End When They Are Too Democratic," *New York*, May 1, 2016, http://nymag.com/daily/intelligencer/2016/04/america-tyranny-donald-trump.html.

4. Ibid.

5. Ibid.

6. Alexander Hamilton, *The Federalist*, no. 1, in Alexander Hamilton, John Jay, and James Madison, *The Federalist*, eds. George W. Carey and James McClellan, Gideon ed. (Indianapolis: Liberty Fund, 2001), accessed April 24, 2017, http://oll.libertyfund.org/titles/788#Hamilton_0084_184.

7. James Madison, *The Federalist*, no. 10, in Hamilton, Jay, and Madison, *The Federalist*, accessed April 24, 2017, http://oll.libertyfund.org/titles/788#Hamilton_0084_328

8. George Washington, "Farewell Address—Transcription," Papers of George Washington, University of Virginia, accessed April 24, 2017, http://gwpapers.virginia.edu/documents_gw/farewell/transcript.html#p17.

9. Sarah Pulliam Bailey, "White Evangelicals Voted Overwhelmingly for Donald Trump, Exit Polls Show," *Washington Post*, November 9, 2016, https://www.washingtonpost.com/news/acts-of-faith/wp/2016/11/09/exit-polls-show-white-evangelicals-voted-overwhelmingly-for-donald-trump/?utm_term=.ddf9a2adf618.

10. Ed Stetzer, "Evangelicals: This Is What It Looks Like When You Sell Your Soul for a Bowl of

Trump," *Christianity Today*, November 2, 2016, http://www.christianitytoday.com/edstetzer/2016/november/this-is-what-it-looks-like.html.

11. Thomas Jefferson to Peter S. Duponceau, Monticello, November 16, 1825, Thomas Jefferson Papers, 1606–1827, Manuscripts Division, Library of Congress, accessed April 24, 2017, https://www.loc.gov/resource/mtj1.055_0652_0654/?sp=3.